STU   **OK**

HUGH DELLA   Y

ELEMENTARY

OUTCOMES

HEINLE
CENGAGE Learning

Australia • Brazil • Japan • Korea • Mexico • Singapore • Spain • United Kingdom • United States

WELCOME TO *OUTCOMES*

Outcomes helps you learn the English you need and want. Each of the 16 units has three double-pages connected by a common theme. Each double page is a complete lesson – and each teaches you some vocabulary or grammar and focuses on a different skill. The first lesson in each unit looks at conversation, the next two at reading or listening.

WRITING UNITS

There are eight writing lessons in the **Outcomes Student's Book**, which teach different styles of writing. Each one has a model text as well as speaking tasks to do in pairs or groups. There are also extra vocabulary or grammar exercises to help you write each kind of text. In addition, there is a lot of writing practice in the **Outcomes Workbook**.

REVIEW UNITS

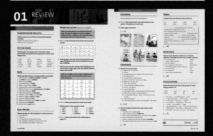

There are eight review Units in this book. Here you practise the grammar and vocabulary of the previous two units. The first page of each unit features revision games, a quiz and work on pronunciation (especially individual sounds). The second page features a test of listening, grammar and vocabulary. This is marked out of 50 ... so you can see how you are progressing.

Clear communicative goals in the unit menu, supported by grammar and vocabulary.

Listening exercises give examples of the conversations you try in *Conversation practice*.

Grammar taught in context, with natural examples and clear practice tasks.

Pictures to help with new vocabulary.

Interesting listening and reading texts. Very varied contexts .

A translation exercise helps you think about how sentences work in your own language compared to English.

---

01 PEOPLE AND PLACES

In this unit, you learn how to:
- introduce yourself
- say where you are from
- ask common questions
- describe your hometown
- talk about jobs and where you work

Grammar
- The verb *be*
- *there is / there are*
- Present simple questions and negatives

Vocabulary
- Countries
- Describing places
- Jobs

Reading
- My hometown
- Good job or bad job?

Listening
- An interview at a language school
- *What do you do?*

SPEAKING

A 1.1 Look at the photo. Listen to the conversation. Then repeat in pairs.

Hello. I'm Miguel. What's your name?

Dasha. Hi. Nice to meet you.

B Have similar conversations with students in your class. Use your names.

C Work in pairs. Try to say the names of everyone in your class. For example:

That's Yuki.

That's Carla.

What's his name?

Marco.

What's her name?

I don't know.

LISTENING

A student has an interview at an English-language school.

A 1.2 Listen. Tick ✓ the sentences that are true.
1 The student's name is Miguel.
2 His family name is Fernando.
3 He's from Spain.
4 He lives in Chihuahua.
5 Chihuahua is in the east.

B Listen again and correct the sentences in exercise A that aren't true.

GRAMMAR The verb *be*

A Write the full forms.

I'm	=	I am
You're	=	
He's	=	
She's	=	
That's	=	
We're	=	
They're	=	

▶ Need help? Read the grammar reference on page 146.

B Complete the conversation with the correct short forms of the verb *be*.
I: Hi. Come in. Sit down. My name ......¹ Ivy. I ......² a teacher here. What ......³ your name?
M: Miguel.
I: Right. Hi. Nice to meet you. And what ......⁴ your surname, Miguel?
M: Sorry?
I: Your surname. Your family name.
M: Oh, sorry. It ......⁵ Hernandez. That ......⁶ H–E–R–N–A–N–D–E–Z.
I: OK. And where ......⁷ you from, Miguel? Spain?
M: No, I ......⁸ not. I ......⁹ from Mexico.
I: Oh, OK. Which part?
M: Chihuahua. It ......¹⁰ in the north.

16 OUTCOMES

VOCABULARY Jobs

A How many jobs can you write in English in one minute?

B Find out what jobs people in your class do. Ask *What do you do?*

C Match the jobs 1–8 to the places people work a–h.

1 receptionist

2 teacher

3 shop assistant

4 nurse

5 police officer

6 designer

7 civil servant

8 waiter

a in a clothes shop / in a department store
b in a clinic / in a hospital
c in a tax office / in a local government office
d at home / in a studio
e in a big hotel / in a small company
f in a school / in a university
g at a local police station / in the traffic department
h in a café / in a restaurant

D Work in pairs. Which place is bigger / more important in a–h in exercise C?

E Work in pairs. Have three conversations like this:
A: What do you do?
B: I'm a waiter.
A: Oh, yes? Where do you work?
B: In a café in town. What do you do?
A: I'm a designer.
B: Where do you work?
A: In a studio in Berlin.

LISTENING

A 1.5 Listen to four conversations. Circle the correct words.
1 Jan is a *doctor / nurse* in a *clinic / hospital* in Warsaw.
2 Lara is a *designer / teacher* in a *school / an office* in Bristol. She *enjoys / doesn't enjoy* it.
3 Marta is a *civil servant / receptionist*. She works in *an office / a company* in the north of Brazil. Her job is *great / OK*.
4 Filippo is a *waiter / shop assistant* in a *department store / café* in the centre of town. He doesn't like it. He wants to become a *police officer / nurse*.

B Read the audioscript on page 170 and listen again.

C Choose one of the conversations and read it in pairs.

LANGUAGE PATTERNS

Write the sentences in your language. Translate them back into English. Compare your English to the original.
What do you want to do?
Where do you want to go?
He wants to become a policeman.
I want to study Arabic.
She wants to be a designer.

20 OUTCOMES

DEVELOPING CONVERSATIONS
Which part?

> We ask *which part* (of a place) someone is from to find out the town, city or region. To answer, say the town, city or region – and then add information.
>
> M: I'm from Mexico.
> I: Oh, OK. *Which part?*
> M: Chihuahua. It's in the north.

A Complete the sentences which the places on the map.

1 I'm from .... – the capital.
2 I'm from .... – in the north.
3 They're from .... – in the south.
4 I'm from .... – in the east.
5 My mum's from .... – in the west.
6 My dad's from .... – in the middle.

B Have conversations. Use countries from *Vocabulary*, or cities / areas in your country. For example:
A: I'm from *Argentina*.
B: Which part?
A: *Rosario*.

C: I'm from *Rome*.
D: Which part?
C: *Morena – in the south.*

C Where are your parents / grandparents from? Tell a partner.

CONVERSATION PRACTICE

A Have conversations with other students, using these questions:
• What's your name?
• And where are you from?
• Oh, OK. Which part?

Lots of expressions and grammatical patterns in spoken English are similar to other languages. These exercises help you notice them.

Information on interesting language common to native speakers of English.

Pronunciation activities integrated with the communicative goals.

The Conversation practice section allows you to put together what you learn.

C Listen again and read the audioscript on page 170 to check your ideas.

D In pairs, practise reading the conversation.

NATIVE SPEAKER ENGLISH
surname
We often say *surname* instead of *family name*.

What's your surname, Miguel?
My first name's Lisa and my surname is Sjukur.
His surname's Lansbury.

VOCABULARY Countries

A Work in pairs. Match the countries to the parts of the world.

Brazil
Panama
Japan
Thailand
Poland
Mexico
China
Argentina
Jordan
Morocco
Oman
Germany
Italy
Kenya

Africa
Asia
Europe
the Middle East
Central America
South America

B 1.3 Listen and say the countries.

01 PEOPLE AND PLACES 17

READING

A Read the three texts. Decide who is:
1 a journalist.
2 a designer.
3 an engineer.

B Which is the best job? Why?

1

I'm ....
I work at home and I **do** jobs for different companies and magazines. I don't get much money **because** I don't have much work, but I enjoy it because it's **interesting**.

I'm ....
I work for a local newspaper. I work strange hours – sometimes I **get up** really early, sometimes I work all night. Sometimes it's **boring** because I have nothing to do. I meet lots of interesting people, but sometimes people get **angry** and shout at me.

I'm ....
I work for a construction company. I'm a **manager** now, so it's a very important job. I like my job, but I work very long hours. I **start** work at eight in the morning and finish at eight or nine at night. I often work at the weekends and I don't see my wife or **kids** very much.

C Translate the words in **bold** in the text. Then complete the sentences with the words.
1 I .... work at nine and finish at six.
2 My boss isn't very nice. He sometimes gets really .... with us. I don't know why.
3 I don't like my job .... it's boring.
4 My .... is good. She helps me and she doesn't shout at me.
5 My town is .... because there isn't much to do.
6 I usually .... at six and leave the house at seven.
7 I have three .... – two girls and a boy.
8 I .... an important job in the company.
9 I love my job. It's really ....

D Choose one of the three people in the texts. Work in pairs. Have conversations using these questions:
• What do you do?
• Where do you work?
• Do you enjoy it?

GRAMMAR
Present simple questions and negatives

> To make questions, use *do / does*.
> *do* + I / you / we / they + verb?
> *does* + he / she / it + verb?
>
> To make negatives, use *don't / doesn't*.
> I / you / we / they + *don't* + verb.
> he / she / it + *doesn't* + verb.

A Complete the sentences with *do*, *does*, *don't* or *doesn't*.
1 A: What .... you do?
   B: I'm a cleaner.
2 A: What .... he do?
   B: I .... know.
3 A: Where .... your mother work?
   B: She .... have a job at the moment.
4 A: Where .... your parents live?
   B: Halifax.
5 A: .... you enjoy working there?
   B: No, not really.
6 A: We .... live near my office, so I take the train to work.
   B: So what time .... you leave home?
7 A: .... they have any kids?
   B: No, they ....

▶ Need help? Read the grammar reference on page 147.

B Put the words into the correct order to make questions.
1 you get time do what up?
2 travel do here how you?
3 bed you go do to when?
4 live do you where?
5 with you do who live?
6 your what free do time do in you?
7 how languages you speak many do?

C Match the answers a-g to the questions above.
a I go swimming, I play football, I read.
b In Belváros, near the river.
c I live on my own.
d At about 12 o'clock most days.
e I take the bus.
f Two – French and Spanish.
g At half past seven.

SPEAKING

A Choose five questions from these pages to ask another student. Write one more question. Remember your questions – then ask them.

More grammar and vocabulary points presented and developed through the unit.

Tasks to practise different skills.

More grammar explanations, examples and exercises are in the reference section at the back of the book.

Speaking activities allow you to exchange information and ideas. A longer speaking task ends every unit.

01 PEOPLE AND PLACES 21

LEARNING

Research shows words need lots of revision in context if you want to be able to use them properly. The authors of *Outcomes* try to make sure words reappear many different times in the course. Here are **twelve** ways to learn the word *interesting*.
• see it twice in **Reading** p. 21
• look it up in the *Outcomes* **Vocabulary Builder** p. 4
• practise it in **Reading** p. 21
• use it in **Vocabulary** p. 22
• revise it in **Review** p. 29
• use it again in **Developing conversations** p.51
• use it in **Writing** p. 139
• find an example in the **Grammar reference** p.155
• check it in the *Outcomes* **Vocabulary Builder** exercises p.
• write, read and listen to it in *Outcomes* **Workbook** Unit 1
• use it on **MyOutcomes** Online insert above
• test it with *Outcomes* **ExamView**

OUTCOMES VOCABULARY BUILDER

The *Outcomes* Vocabulary Builder provides lists of key vocabulary with space for translation, clear explanations, examples of common collocations and exercises focusing on the grammar of the words.

MyOutcomes ONLINE

The pin code at the front of the Student's Book gives you access to lots of interactive, online exercises. We have created extra exercises to go with each unit from the book, so you can continue developing your English. Visit **elt.heinle.com**

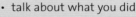

Grammar	Vocabulary	Reading	Listening	Developing conversations
• Present perfect 1 • Present perfect 2	• Good and bad experiences • Describing experiences	• Put it down to experience	• On holiday in Turkey • Different kinds of experiences	• *Me too / Me neither*
• *too, too much, too many* • Superlatives	• Trains and stations • Transport	• *Taxi!*	• Buying a train ticket • Asking for recommendations in a hotel	• Telling the time
• *a lot of, some, any, much, many* and *a bit of* • Invitations and offers	• Restaurants • Food • Cooking	• Vegetarians live longer	• A restaurant in France • Dinner with friends	• Checking
• *should / shouldn't* • Present perfect 3	• Health problems • Feelings	• Economics and happiness • Three newspaper articles	• *Are you OK?* • A mixed day	• Rejecting advice and offers
• *might* and *be going to* • Passives	• Weather • Country and city • Animals	• Six reasons not to ...	• *What's the forecast?* • National symbols	• Short questions
• *will / won't* for predictions • Verb patterns with adjectives	• Describing films, plays and musicals • Society	• A new life	• Opinions about films and musicals • A news report	• *What's it like?*
• *be thinking of* + *-ing* • Adverbs	• Machines and technology • Computers and the Internet	• A questionnaire about computers and technology • Going viral!	• *I'm thinking of buying ...* • A questionnaire about computers and technology	• *Do you know much about ...?*
• The past continuous • *will / won't* for promises	• Love and marriage	• Poems about promises	• News about relationships • Love at first sight	• *How long ... ?*

01 STARTER UNIT

Basic conversations:
· Hello
· Family and age
· Ordering in a café

Basic vocabulary:
· Numbers 1
· Food and drink
· Times and days of the week
· Verbs

Basic grammar:
· Plurals
· a / an / some
· Subject pronouns
· Grammar words

HELLO

Hello. I'm Andrew.

Hi. Rebecca.

A Say hello to other students.

VOCABULARY Numbers 1

A Write the numbers in the correct order.

~~two~~	0	zero
~~zero~~	1	one
ten	2	two
seven	3	....
~~one~~	4	....
five	5	....
eleven	6	....
twelve	7	....
fifty	8	....
thirty	9	....
three	10	....
six	11	....
four	12	....
twenty	20	....
eight	30	....
a hundred	50	....
nine	100	....

B 🔊 S1.1 **Listen and say the numbers.**

NATIVE SPEAKER ENGLISH

Zero

We say 0 in different ways:
zero /ˈzɪərəʊ/, *o* /əʊ/ and *nought* /nɔːt/.

READING Family

A **Look at the picture. Complete the text with numbers.**
This is the Burnham family. They are from Manchester in England. Mr and Mrs Burnham have .... children – .... boys and .... girls. Mr Burnham is a lawyer. Mrs Burnham works in the home.

father

brothers and sisters

mother

baby girl

B **Read out the text in pairs.**

C Complete 1–6 with words from the picture and text.

 Hi. I'm Matt. I'm 18.

1 I have .... brothers and .... sisters.
2 This is my ...., Jenny. She's 12.
3 This is my ...., Pete. He's six years old.
4 This is my .... He's 43.
5 This is my .... She's 42.
6 This is my .... sister. She's seven months old.

GRAMMAR Plurals

Regular

brother /ˈbrʌðə/	→	brothers /ˈbrʌðəz/
sister /ˈsɪstə/	→	sisters /ˈsɪstəz/
girl /ɡɜːl/	→	girls /ɡɜːlz/
baby /ˈbeɪbɪ/	→	babies /ˈbeɪbɪz/

Irregular

child	→	children
person	→	people
man	→	men
woman	→	women

LISTENING

A 🔊 **S1.2 Read the conversation. Then listen and write the numbers you hear.**
A: Do you have any brothers and sisters?
B: Yes. One brother and .... sisters.
A: How old is your brother?
B: ....
A: Are you married?
B: Yes.
A: Do you have any children?
B: Yes. One boy and .... girl.
A: How old are they?
B: The boy's .... and the girl is ....
   Do you have any brothers and sisters?
A: No.
B: How old are you?
A: ....

B Work in pairs. Read out the conversation.

C Ask the same questions to different students.

VOCABULARY Food and drink

A Match the words to the pictures.

a coffee   a green salad
a tea   a cheese sandwich
an orange juice   a chicken sandwich
a cola   a hamburger
a bottle of water an ice cream
a portion of chips an apple

B Find out the price of the things in exercise A.
Student A: look at File 1 on page 166.
Student B: look at File 10 on page 169.

C 🔊 **S1.3 Listen to Mr Burnham ordering things for his family. Tick ✓ the things in exercise A that he wants.**

D Work in pairs. You are in the same café as the Burnhams. Say what your family wants.

GRAMMAR *a / an / some*

a bottle of water	a sandwich	a man
an ice cream	*an* orange juice	*an* apple
some chips	some boys	some men

VOCABULARY Common verbs

A Match the verbs in the box to the pictures.

work	open	start	read	look	go	eat	listen
think	play	finish	write	say	put	close	talk

B 🔊 **S1.4** Listen to ten sentences and tick ✓ the words from exercise A you hear.

C Close your books.
Student A: act some words from exercise A.
Student B: say the words.

SPEAKING

A Work in groups. Do you prefer ...
- going to the park or going to the cinema?
- working or playing?
- talking or listening?
- reading or writing?
- tea or coffee?
- cheese sandwiches or chicken sandwiches?
- cola or orange juice?
- an ice cream or an apple?
- small portions or big portions?

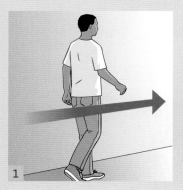
1

2

3

4

5

6

7

8

9

10

11

12

13

14

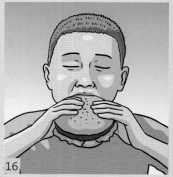
15

16

GRAMMAR Subject pronouns

A Complete the table.

singular	plural
....	we
....	you
he (*man / boy*)	
....	
(*woman / girl*)	....
.... (*thing*)	

B Replace the words in *italics* with a pronoun.
1 *My mum and dad* work.
  They work.
2 *My sister* is three and *my brother* is two.
3 *My children* aren't at school.
4 *My brother and I* play football a lot.
5 *The class* starts at nine.
6 *My sister* reads a lot.
7 *You and your friend* are late.

VOCABULARY Time and days of the week

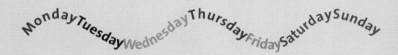

A Complete with a day or a time.
1 **Today** is ....
2 **Tomorrow** is ....
3 The **day after tomorrow** is ....
4 **Yesterday** was ....
5 The **day before yesterday** was ....
6 The **weekend** is ....
7 The **morning** is between .... o'clock and
   ....
8 The **afternoon** is between .... o'clock and
   ....
9 **Night** is between .... o'clock and
   ....

B Work in groups. Discuss these questions.
• Which day do you start work / school every week?
• Which day do you finish?
• What time do you start work / school each day?
• What time do you finish?
• Is today a good or bad day for you?
• Is tomorrow a good day or a bad day? Why?
• Was yesterday a good or bad day? Why?

DEVELOPING CONVERSATIONS
Everyday expressions

It's good to learn new expressions. Translate them into your language. Don't worry about the new grammar in them.

A Translate these sentences into your language.
1 Are you OK?
2 Do you have any brothers and sisters?
3 What time is it?
4 Do you like football?
5 What do you want?
6 What does he do?
7 How old are you?
8 Can you help me?
9 Sorry, what did you say?
10 Have you been to Britain?
11 I don't know.
12 I'm fine.

B Work in pairs. Ask each other the questions in exercise A. Give answers using language from this unit – or just say *yes* or *no*.

GRAMMAR Grammar words

Here are some useful grammar words.
Verb: I *want* an ice cream.
Noun: My *brother* wants a *coffee*.
Adjective: A *small* coffee, please.

Sentences are usually subject–verb–object.
Subject: *He* plays football.
Object: He plays *football*.

A Work in groups. Think of answers to these questions. Don't look at your book or at a dictionary. You have five minutes.
1 What verbs do you know in English?
2 What nouns do you know? For example, kinds of drink, food, family, jobs, animals.
3 What adjectives do you know in English? For example, for size, colour, cost.

B Which group has the most verbs, nouns or adjectives?

02 STARTER UNIT

Basic conversations:
· Questions
· Personal information
· *Me too*

Basic vocabulary:
· Numbers 2
· Everyday things
· Adjectives
· The *Vocabulary Builder*

Basic grammar:
· Pronouns
· *don't / do you …?*
· *be*
· The *Grammar reference*

VOCABULARY Numbers 2

A Play bingo. Choose six numbers. Circle them.

13	17	21	50	97	1,000
14	18	22	65	100	1,300
15	19	33	78	109	5,260
16	20	44	86	211	12,000

B 🔊 **S2.1 Listen to the numbers. Who hears their six numbers first?**

C Answer the questions.
1. How many weeks in a month?
2. How many days in a week?
3. How many months in a year?
4. How many hours in a day?
5. How many days in December?
6. How many minutes in an hour?
7. How many seconds in an hour?
8. How many days in a year?

D Change the numbers and / or the words in *italics* so the sentences are true for you.
1. My English class is *90 minutes*.
2. I have *three* English classes a *week*.
3. *Two hundred thousand* people live in my city.
4. I work *six* days a week.
5. I go on holiday for *two weeks* every year.
6. I read for *two hours* a day.
7. I go to the cinema every *month*.
8. It takes *45 minutes* to get to *work*.

E Compare your answers with a partner.

DEVELOPING CONVERSATIONS
Questions

A Match the question words 1–5 to the answers a–e. Then match 6–10 to f–j.

1. Who?   a By bus.
2. When?   b A coffee, please.
3. Where?   c Yesterday.
4. What?   d Poland.
5. How?   e My mum.

6. How much?   f Nineteen.
7. How old?   g 9.35.
8. What time?   h That big one.
9. How long?   i Two minutes.
10. Which one?   j £13.50.

B 🔊 **S2.2 Listen to the conversation with a teacher. Which seven question words in exercise A do you hear?**

C Listen again and look at the audioscript on page 170 to check.

D Read out the conversation in pairs.

VOCABULARY Everyday things

A Match the words in the box to the pictures.

| ticket | pen | chocolate | TV | camera | money | paper | phone | beer | book |

B Cover the words. What do you remember?

C Complete the sentences with words from exercise A.
1 Does the .... on your phone take good photos?
2 Do you have .... to buy the ticket?
3 If you don't have your book, write on some ....
4 I don't watch .... much.
5 I don't drink .... I don't like it.
6 Do you eat .... ?
7 Open the .... and look at page six.
8 I need a .... to write the address.
9 Take your .... so we can talk later.
10 I have a .... to see Real Madrid.

D Tell a partner which things from exercise A you have now.
I have ....
I don't have ....

GRAMMAR Pronouns

> **It is a pronoun. It can be a subject or an object.**
> The class starts at six. It finishes at nine. [subject]
> I don't drink beer. I don't like it. [object]
>
> **Most other subject and object pronouns are different.**
> I – me   she – her
> you – you   we – us
> he – him   they – them

GRAMMAR don't / do you ...?

> **Make negatives with don't (= do not) + verb.**
> I don't watch it.
> I don't drink it.
>
> **Make questions with do you + verb.**
> Do you like it?
> Where do you work?

A Write the sentences as negatives and questions.
1 I have a brother.
2 I like football.
3 I drink beer.
4 I speak French.
5 I play tennis.

B Work in pairs. Ask and answer the questions.

C Complete the sentences so they are true for you. Then tell a partner.
1 I don't like ....
2 I don't drink ....
3 I don't eat ....

D Complete the questions. Then ask a partner.
1 Do you like .... ?
2 Do you have .... ?
3 Do you want .... ?
4 Do you .... ?

VOCABULARY Adjectives

A Say the sentences.

1 It's cheap.

2 I'm hungry.

3 She's old.

4 He's busy.

5 We're cold.

6 They're late.

B Cover exercise A and write the sentences.

C Look at exercise A again and check your sentences.

D Work in pairs. Ask and answer the questions.
1 Are you hungry?
2 Are you cold?
3 Are you busy?
4 Are you sometimes late for class?
5 Is your house old?
6 Is food cheap in your country?

Adjectives go before nouns:
~~a car big~~ a big car

. . . .

Adjectives go after *be*:
My car is old.

. . . .

Adjectives don't change when we use them with plural nouns.
They are ~~goods~~ good parents.

E Put the words into the correct order to make sentences.
1 tired I am .
2 have I a car new .
3 My good is teacher .
4 This book is an easy .
5 small flat is My .
6 an mobile phone have expensive I .

F Tell a partner which sentences in exercise E are true for you.

GRAMMAR *be*

The verb *be* is special. Look how it changes.
It also has short forms. The word order changes in questions.

I am	I'm	Am I late?
you are	you're	Are you OK?
he is	he's	Is he here?
she is	she's	Is she English?
it is	it's	How old is it?
we are	we're	Where are we?
they are	they're	Who are they?

To make negatives, add *not* after the verb *be*.
I'm not late

A 🔊 **S2.3** Listen and say the short forms.

B Look at how we use the verb *be*. Add one more thing to the sentences.
1 I'm a student / a teacher / ....
2 I'm 16 / 25 / ....
3 I'm hungry / tired / ....
4 I'm from Spain / China / ....
5 It's Monday / Saturday / .... today.
6 It's six o'clock / eight thirty / ....

C Say your new sentences to a partner.

D Write four questions to ask other students.

DEVELOPING CONVERSATIONS *Me too*

I'm tired.   Me too.

If a person says something that is also true for you, you can show this by saying *Me too*.

A **Student A:** say sentences 1–6.
Student B: say *Me too, I'm not* or *I don't*.
1 I'm 25.
2 I'm married.
3 I'm from Poland.
4 I live in London.
5 I like coffee.
6 I have a car.

B Write five sentences with *I'm, I like, I have*, etc.

C Take turns to say your sentences. Your partner says *Me too, I'm not* or *I don't*.

VOCABULARY The *Vocabulary Builder*

The *Outcomes Vocabulary Builder* is the small book at the back of your coursebook. It helps you learn the words you meet in class. When a new word appears in the book, find the word in the same unit of your *Vocabulary Builder*.

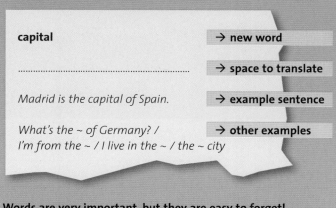

capital	→ new word
....	→ space to translate
Madrid is the capital of Spain.	→ example sentence
What's the ~ of Germany? / *I'm from the ~ / I live in the ~ / the ~ city*	→ other examples

Words are very important, but they are easy to forget!
Look at the *Vocabulary Builder* before and after class.
Use it to test each other.
Do the exercises at the end of each unit.

HEINLE CENGAGE Learning

VOCABULARY BUILDER
SHEILA DIGNEN and GUY DE VILLIERS

ELEMENTARY

OUTCOMES

A Look at the first two pages of the *Vocabulary Builder* for Unit 1, and do 1–3.
1 Tick ✔ all the words you know.
2 Translate the words you don't know. Use a dictionary or ask your teacher if you need help.
3 Is your translation good for the examples?

B Work in groups. Close your *Vocabulary Builder*. In three minutes, write all the words you remember. Which group has the most words?

GRAMMAR
The Grammar reference

The Grammar reference is on pages 144–165 of this book. It has explanations with examples. Sometimes it has extra information. It also has more exercises.

In the Grammar sections you do in class, you see this:

▶ Need help? Read the grammar reference on page 146.

You can read the Grammar reference and / or do the exercises in class or at home.

A Find out what grammar is on:
1 page 146.
2 page 152.
3 page 157.
4 page 158.

B Read the Grammar reference for the Starter units on pages 144–145 and find three pieces of new information.

C In class, choose one exercise and do it.

D Do the others after class.

SPEAKING

A Read these ideas for learning English with *Outcomes*.
- Relax.
- Speak English in class.
- Don't worry if you are wrong.
- Laugh.
- Say the words you learn.
- Study the *Vocabulary Builder*.
- Use the Grammar reference.
- Talk some English outside class.
- Do ten minutes every day in the Workbook or on *MyOutcomes*.
- Think in English every day.

B Work in pairs. For each sentence above, say one of a–e below.
a I do it.
b I don't do it, but it's a good idea.
c I don't do it, but it's not important.
d I can't do it.
e I don't understand this.

01 PEOPLE AND PLACES

In this unit, you learn how to:
- introduce yourself
- say where you are from
- ask common questions
- describe your hometown
- talk about jobs and where you work

Grammar
- The verb *be*
- *there is / there are*
- Present simple questions and negatives

Vocabulary
- Countries
- Describing places
- Jobs

Reading
- My hometown
- Good job or bad job?

Listening
- An interview at a language school
- *What do you do?*

SPEAKING

A 🔊 **1.1 Look at the photo. Listen to the conversation. Then repeat it in pairs.**

> Hello. I'm Miguel. What's your name?

> Dasha. Hi. Nice to meet you.

B **Have similar conversations with students in your class. Use your names.**

C **Work in pairs. Try to say the names of everyone in your class. For example:**

> That's Yuki.

> That's Carla.

> What's his name?

> Marco.

> What's her name?

> I don't know.

LISTENING

A student has an interview at an English-language school.

A 🔊 **1.2 Listen. Tick ✓ the sentences that are true.**
1 The student's name is Miguel.
2 His family name is Fernando.
3 He's from Spain.
4 He lives in Chihuahua.
5 Chihuahua is in the east.

B **Listen again and correct the sentences in exercise A that aren't true.**

GRAMMAR The verb *be*

A **Write the full forms.**

I'm	=	*I am*
You're	=	....
He's	=	....
She's	=	....
That's	=	....
We're	=	....
They're	=	....

▶ **Need help? Read the grammar reference on page 146.**

B **Complete the conversation with the correct short forms of the verb *be*.**
I: Hi. Come in. Sit down. My name ......[1] Ivy. I ......[2] a teacher here. What ......[3] your name?
M: Miguel.
I: Right. Hi. Nice to meet you. And what ......[4] your surname, Miguel?
M: Sorry?
I: Your surname. Your family name.
M: Oh, sorry. It ......[5] Hernandez. That ......[6] H–E–R–N–A–N–D–E–Z.
I: OK. And where ......[7] you from, Miguel? Spain?
M: No, I ......[8] not. I ......[9] from Mexico.
I: Oh, OK. Which part?
M: Chihuahua. It ......[10] in the north.

C Listen again and read the audioscript on page 170 to check your ideas.

D In pairs, practise reading the conversation.

VOCABULARY Countries

A **Work in pairs. Match the countries to the parts of the world.**

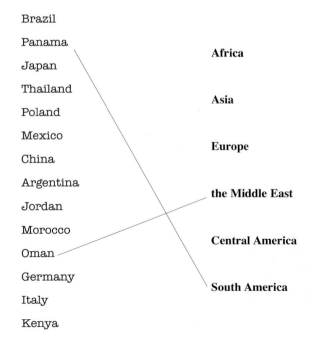

Brazil

Panama

Japan   **Africa**

Thailand

Poland   **Asia**

Mexico

China   **Europe**

Argentina

Jordan   **the Middle East**

Morocco

Oman   **Central America**

Germany

Italy   **South America**

Kenya

B 🔊 **1.3 Listen and say the countries.**

DEVELOPING CONVERSATIONS
Which part?

We ask *which part* (of a place) someone is from to find out the town, city or region. To answer, say the town, city or region – and then add information.

M: I'm from Mexico.
I: Oh, OK. *Which part?*
M: Chihuahua. It's in the north.

A **Complete the sentences which the places on the map.**

1 I'm from .... – the capital.
2 I'm from .... – in the north.
3 They're from .... – in the south.
4 I'm from .... – in the east.
5 My mum's from .... – in the west.
6 My dad's from .... – in the middle.

B **Have conversations. Use countries from *Vocabulary*, or cities / areas in your country. For example:**
A: I'm from *Argentina*.
B: Which part?
A: *Rosario*.

C: I'm from *Rome*.
D: Which part?
C: *Morena – in the south*.

C **Where are your parents / grandparents from? Tell a partner.**

CONVERSATION PRACTICE

A **Have conversations with other students, using these questions:**
· What's your name?
· And where are you from?
· Oh, OK. Which part?

VOCABULARY Describing places

A **Match the words in the box to the pictures.**

| a church | a palace | a cathedral | traffic | a park | a beach | a restaurant | an art gallery | a factory | a river |

The *Vocabulary Builder* has more information about the words in each unit. Read it after each class.

B Say the plurals of the ten words. For example:
a church → churches.
Which word has no plural?

C Say the names of three other things in your town. For example:
a hotel.

READING

A Read the four texts. Answer these questions.
1. Where is each person from?
2. Is the place nice? Why? / Why not?

Jeff: 'I'm from New Romney, in the south of England. It's near the sea, so there's a nice beach, and there's some lovely countryside near there, but there's not much to do. There aren't any cinemas or art galleries or museums. It's a small town.'

Nancy: 'I'm from Pinedale, in the middle of California. It's not very nice. There's a lot of crime. It's not very safe – and there aren't many jobs now, but it is cheap.'

Rolando: 'I'm from Seville, in the south-west of Spain. It's a great place to live. There are lots of nice cafés and restaurants and there's a great cathedral as well. There's a river in the city and there are lots of beautiful parks as well.'

Yu Tsan: 'I'm from Shenyang. It's in the north-east of China. It's not a bad place to live. There are lots of factories and lots of people, and there's a lot of traffic too. But there are also lots of places to go shopping as well, so that's nice – and there are some great old buildings as well. There's a palace called Mukden Palace. It's very famous.'

B Which of the four places is best / worst for you? Why? Compare your ideas with a partner.

GRAMMAR *there is / there are*

> Use *there is / there's* with singular nouns.
> Use *there are* with plural nouns.
>
> *There's a nice beach and there's some lovely countryside near there.*
>
> *There are lots of nice cafés and restaurants. There are some great old buildings.*

A Translate the examples in the explanation box into your language. Is the grammar the same or different?

B Complete the sentences with *there's* or *there are*.
1. .... a cinema in the town.
2. It's nice. .... lots of trees and parks.
3. .... lots of hotels near the station.
4. It's not very safe. .... a lot of crime.
5. It's not a bad place, but .... too many people!
6. It's a nice city, but .... a lot of traffic!
7. .... some nice shops and restaurants near here.
8. It's OK. .... a nice beach and .... a few cafés.

> We usually say *there's* and *there are* as /ðeəz/ and /ðeərə/.

C 🔊 1.4 Listen and check your answers to 1–8. Then practise saying the sentences.

D Which sentences describe the place that you are from?

▶ Need help? Read the grammar reference on page 146.

SPEAKING

A Work in pairs. Tell your partner about three places you know well. Use *There's ...* and *There are ...* .

B Where's the best / worst place in your country to live? Why?

VOCABULARY Jobs

A How many jobs can you write in English in one minute?

B Find out what jobs people in your class do. Ask *What do you do?*

C Match the jobs 1–8 to the places people work a–h.

1 receptionist

2 teacher

3 shop assistant

4 nurse

5 police officer

6 designer

7 civil servant

8 waiter

a   in a clothes shop / in a department store
b   in a clinic / in a hospital
c   in a tax office / in a local government office
d   at home / in a studio
e   in a big hotel / in a small company
f   in a school / in a university
g   at a local police station / in the traffic department
h   in a café / in a restaurant

D Work in pairs. Which place is bigger / more important in a–h in exercise C?

E Work in pairs. Have three conversations like this:
A: What do you do?
B: I'm a waiter.
A: Oh, yes? Where do you work?
B: In a café in town. What do you do?
A: I'm a designer.
B: Where do you work?
A: In a studio in Berlin.

LISTENING

A 🔊 1.5 Listen to four conversations. Circle the correct words.
1   Jan is a *doctor / nurse* in a *clinic / hospital* in Warsaw.
2   Lara is a *designer / teacher* in a *school / an office* in Bristol. She *enjoys / doesn't enjoy* it.
3   Marta is a *civil servant / receptionist*. She works in *an office / a company* in the north of Brazil. Her job is *great / OK*.
4   Filippo is a *waiter / shop assistant* in a *department store / café* in the centre of town. He doesn't like it. He wants to become a *police officer / nurse*.

B Read the audioscript on page 170 and listen again.

C Choose one of the conversations and read it in pairs.

LANGUAGE PATTERNS

Write the sentences in your language. Translate them back into English. Compare your English to the original.
What do you want to do?
Where do you want to go?
He wants to become a policeman.
I want to study Arabic.
She wants to be a designer.

READING

A Read the three texts. Decide who is:
1 a journalist.
2 a designer.
3 an engineer.

B Which is the best job? Why?

1

I'm ....

I work at home and I **do** jobs for different companies and magazines. I don't get much money **because** I don't have much work, but I enjoy it because it's **interesting**.

2 I'm ....

I work for a local newspaper. I work strange hours – sometimes I **get up** really early, sometimes I work all night. Sometimes it's **boring** because I have nothing to do. I meet lots of interesting people, but sometimes people get **angry** and shout at me.

3 I'm ....

I work for a construction company. I'm a **manager** now, so it's a very important job. I like my job, but I work very long hours. I **start** work at eight in the morning and finish at eight or nine at night. I often work at the weekends and I don't see my wife or **kids** very much.

C Translate the words in **bold** in the text. Then complete the sentences with the words.
1 I .... work at nine and finish at six.
2 My boss isn't very nice. He sometimes gets really .... with us. I don't know why.
3 I don't like my job .... it's boring.
4 My .... is good. She helps me and she doesn't shout at me.
5 My town is .... because there isn't much to do.
6 I usually .... at six and leave the house at seven.
7 I have three .... – two girls and a boy.
8 I .... an important job in the company.
9 I love my job. It's really ....

D Choose one of the three people in the texts. Work in pairs. Have conversations using these questions:
* What do you do?
* Where do you work?
* Do you enjoy it?

GRAMMAR
Present simple questions and negatives

To make questions, use *do / does*.
do + I / you / we / they + verb?
does + he / she / it + verb?
....
To make negatives, use *don't / doesn't*.
I / you / we / they + *don't* + verb
he / she / it + *doesn't* + verb

A Complete the sentences with *do, does, don't* or *doesn't*.
1 A: What .... you do?
   B: I'm a cleaner.
2 A: What .... he do?
   B: I .... know.
3 A: Where .... your mother work?
   B: She .... have a job at the moment.
4 A: Where .... your parents live?
   B: Halifax.
5 A: .... you enjoy working there?
   B: No, not really.
6 A: We .... live near my office, so I take the train to work.
   B: So what time .... you leave home?
7 A: .... they have any kids?
   B: No, they ....

▶ **Need help?** Read the grammar reference on page 147.

B Put the words into the correct order to make questions.
1 you get time do what up ?
2 travel do here how you ?
3 bed you go do to when ?
4 live do you where ?
5 with you do who live ?
6 your what free do time do in you ?
7 how languages you speak many do ?

C Match the answers a-g to the questions above.
a I go swimming, I play football, I read.
b In Belváros, near the river.
c I live on my own.
d At about 12 o'clock most days.
e I take the bus.
f Two – French and Spanish.
g At half past seven.

SPEAKING

A Choose five questions from these pages to ask another student. Write one more question. Remember your questions – then ask them.

02 FREE TIME

In this unit, you learn how to:
- ask what people like
- arrange to meet
- talk about your free time
- ask about common daily activities
- ask for things in the classroom

Grammar
- Verb forms
- Adverbs of frequency
- *a / any* and *one / some*

Vocabulary
- Free time activities
- Daily life
- Things in the classroom

Reading
- Do you have any free time?

Listening
- *Do you like ...?*
- A language class

VOCABULARY Free time activities

A Work in pairs.
Student A: act or draw activities from the box.
Student B: say the words or phrases.

shopping	watching TV
reading	going to the cinema
dancing	meeting new people
walking	listening to music
swimming	chatting on the Internet
studying	playing computer games
doing sport	going out for dinner

B Change.
Student B: act or draw activities from the box.
Student A: say the words or phrases.

C Complete the sentences with different activites from exercise A.
1 .... is boring.
2 .... is good fun.
3 .... is interesting.
4 .... is expensive.
5 .... is great.
6 I'm bad at ....
7 I'm good at ....

D Work in new pairs. Tell your partner your ideas. Does your partner agree?

LISTENING 1

A Look at the people in the picture. What do you think they like / don't like?

B ⏵ 2.1 Listen to the two people talking and complete the table with *doesn't like*, *OK* and *loves*.

	woman	man
sport		
walking		doesn't like
computer games		
cinema	loves	

C Listen again and then read the audioscript on page 171. Practise the conversation.

NATIVE SPEAKER ENGLISH

What about you?
We say *What about you?* to return a question someone asks.

A: *Do you like walking?*
B: *No. What about you?*
A: *It's OK.*

A: *How are you?*
B: *OK. What about you?*
A: *Fine.*

SPEAKING

A Work in pairs. Ask each other *Do you like ...?* Use the words in *Vocabulary*, exercise A or your own ideas. Reply with *I love it, It's OK* or *Not really*.

GRAMMAR Verb forms

> Look at the different verb forms after *like, love* and *want.*
>
> I *love playing* tennis and football.
> I *don't like going* to the cinema.
> Do you *want to see* 'Love Train'?

A Write full sentences from the notes.
1 I / like / meet / new people.
2 my daughter / want / get / a new phone.
3 my sister / love / play / tennis.
4 I / not / like / shop.
5 you / like / dance?
6 you / want / go out / this weekend?

B Write two different sentences about your free time for each of 1–3. Use a dictionary if you need to.
1 I love ....
2 I don't really like ....
3 Tomorrow, I want ....

C Tell a partner.

▶ Need help? Read the grammar reference on page 148.

DEVELOPING CONVERSATIONS
Arrangements

> You will learn more later in this book, but you can make simple arrangements using the present simple:
>
> A: *Do you want to go* shopping on Saturday?
> B: OK. Where *do you want to meet*?
> A: Outside Harrods – the big department store.
> B: OK. What time?
> A: *Is* ten OK?
> B: Yeah. Fine.

A Match the questions in the box to the pairs of answers in 1–5.

> Do you like going to the cinema?
> Do you want to see *Monsters 6* on Sunday?
> What time do you want to meet?
> Where?
> What time does the film finish?

1 a Is four good?
   b Is seven OK? The film starts at eight.
2 a I don't know. Around seven.
   b About 11.30. It's a long film.
3 a OK. That sounds nice.
   b Sorry, I'm busy then.
4 a Yes, it's OK.
   b Not really.
5 a Outside the train station.
   b Outside the cinema.

B In pairs, write three different short conversations using the questions and answers in exercise A. Then say them to another pair of students.

LISTENING 2

You are going to hear two conversations where people are making arrangements.

A 🔊 2.2 Listen and choose the correct words in the notes.

Saturday

Watch ¹*match / film* with Jack

Meet outside ²*café / Green Street station* at ³*four / five*

Sunday

Lunch with Tina
⁴*French / Italian* restaurant

Meet ⁵*one / two* o'clock outside the ⁶*cathedral / restaurant*

B Which do you think is better – to go with Tina or to go with Jack? Why?

CONVERSATION PRACTICE

A On your own, write notes about two things you want to do at the weekend (on Friday night, Saturday or Sunday). Decide where you want to meet and what time.

B Work in pairs. Have similar conversations to the ones in *Developing conversations* and *Listening 2*.

VOCABULARY Daily life

A Which activities in the box can you see in the pictures?

have a shower	get up
go out for dinner	sleep
get home from work	leave work
go out dancing	have breakfast
have a coffee	go to bed
go to a concert	have lunch
watch the news	drink whisky
do homework	finish school

a

b

c

d

e

f

g

h

B When do people normally do the activities in exercise A? Put the words in the three groups.

in the morning	in the afternoon	at night

C Compare your answers with a partner.

D Look at the words in exercise A for two minutes. Close your books. In pairs, how many can you remember?

GRAMMAR Adverbs of frequency

We use some adverbs to show how often we do something. Notice their position in the sentence.

I *always* have a shower in the morning.
I *usually* go to bed at midnight.

A Complete the line below with the adverbs in the box. Then translate all the adverbs into your language.

always	never	often	sometimes

100% | ....
      | usually
      | ....
      | ....
      | occasionally
      | hardly ever
0% | ....

B Tick ✓ the sentences which are true for you. Change the adverbs in the other sentences to make them true for you.

1 I always watch the news in the evening.
2 I usually have a coffee after my lunch.
3 I never drink beer or wine.
4 I hardly ever read novels.
5 I often listen to music when I go to sleep.
6 I occasionally go to rock concerts.
7 I always do my homework for my English class.
8 I sometimes go swimming at the weekend.

C Work in groups. Take turns saying your sentences. Who is most similar to you?

D Write four true sentences using the phrases in the box and an adverb. Then say them to a partner.

drink tea	go out for dinner
have a shower	read novels

▶ Need help? Read the grammar reference on page 148.

READING

You are going to read about how three people spend their free time.

A **Read the article on the right and decide:**
1 Who is most similar to you? Why?
2 Who do you think is the happiest person? Why?

B **Read again and decide which person:**
1 does sport or exercise.
2 spends a lot of money.
3 is tired at the weekend.
4 likes TV.
5 seems quiet.
6 has a busy social life.
7 goes to bed quite early.
8 works long hours.

C **Complete the sentences with the prepositions in bold in the article.**
1 I sometimes have a short sleep .... the afternoon.
2 I go .... a gym near my house to keep fit.
3 I often go .... a walk with my wife after dinner.
4 I'm always very busy .... Mondays.
5 We don't usually do very much .... the weekend – just relax.
6 I listen to English radio .... an hour or two every night.
7 Our school day finishes .... four.
8 .... the week, I stay at home in the evening.

LANGUAGE PATTERNS

Write the sentences in your language. Translate them back into English. Compare your English to the original.
Maybe once or twice a year,
I usually have a shower twice a day.
He works at the weekend once a month.
She goes running maybe four times a week.

SPEAKING

A **Work in groups. Ask each other these question.**
- What do you normally do on Friday nights?
- What do you normally do on Saturdays?
- What do you normally do on Sundays?
- Do you go out in the evening during the week? When? What do you do?

B **Who is the busiest person in the group?**

DO YOU HAVE ANY FREE TIME?

Birgit from Germany

I do something most nights. **On** Mondays and Wednesdays, I go to an English class, and on Tuesdays, I usually go to the cinema with friends, because the tickets are cheap then. On Thursdays, I always go **to** the gym. I usually go out dancing on Saturday nights. I often get home at four or five in the morning, so on Sundays, I sleep! I sometimes get up at three **in** the afternoon.

Frankie from the UK

Free time? I don't have any free time because I have my own business. I occasionally go to a rock concert – about once or twice a year – and I sometimes go shopping **at** the weekend. I like buying expensive things with the money I earn. I have a really big TV and I have a very nice car.

Svetlana from Russia

I don't go out much **during** the week. I usually study **for** two hours in the evening. I never watch TV, really. I usually play the piano every day. It helps me to relax. Then I go to bed **at** nine or ten and read. At the weekend, I go out with my family to a park or the countryside, and we go **for** a walk. I sometimes go to a shopping centre with friends, but I hardly ever buy anything!

SPEAKING 1

A **Work in pairs. Discuss these questions.**
- Do you like doing courses in your free time?
- Is this your first English course?
- Do you like learning English?
- Do you like ...
  ... doing homework?
  ... watching films or TV shows in English?
  ... listening to songs in English?
  ... reading in English?
  ... finding new words in a dictionary?
  ... practising your pronunciation?

> **Do you like doing homework?**

> **No, not really. What about you?**

> **It's OK.**

LISTENING

A **Who would usually say each sentence – a teacher, a student or both?**
1 Match the words to the pictures.
2 Can I go to the toilet?
3 Everyone, turn off your mobile phone, please.
4 Compare your answers with a partner.
5 I'm sorry I'm late.
6 For homework, do exercise 1 in your Workbooks.
7 How do you say this word?
8 Sorry, I don't understand.
9 OK. Let's check the answers.
10 What does 'turn off' mean?

B **Compare your ideas with a partner.**

C ● **2.3 Listen to a teacher checking the answers to exercise A with her class. Check your answers.**

D **Listen again. Which of the sentences in exercise A do you hear?**

VOCABULARY Things in the classroom

> **You might need to ask for something or ask to do something in class. Try to always do this in English. For example:**
>
> A: Do you have a *dictionary*?
> B: Yes. Here (you are). / No (I don't). Sorry.

A **Match the words to the pictures.**

a dictionary	a pen	a rubber	a tissue
paper	a pencil	a ruler	scissors
a board	a window	a seat	a blind

1

2

3

4

5

6

7

8

9

10

11

12

B **Remember the things in exercise A. Close your books. In pairs, say which things are in your classroom now.**

C **Do you know the English word for any other things you can see in your classroom?**

PRONUNCIATION
Syllables and word stress

> In English, the number of syllables a word has is not always clear from the spelling. For example, *dictionary* only has three syllables because we don't say the *a*.
>
> dic-tion-ary
> ······································
> In every word, one syllable has the main stress.
>
> ● ● ● ●
> dictionary

A 🔊 2.4 **Listen. Mark these words as in the second example above. Mark the number of syllables and the main stress.**

scissors   social

homework   cathedral

tissue   interesting

mobile   manager

pronunciation   strange

B **Compare your answers. Listen again and check.**

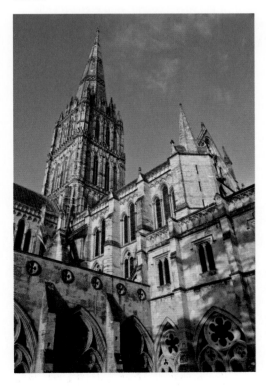

GRAMMAR *a(n) / any* and *one / some*

> **Look at these questions.**
> *a* goes with singular nouns, *any* with plurals.
> Do you have *a dictionary*?
> Do you have *any coloured pens*?
> ···
> *Any* also goes with some singular uncountable nouns: *paper, money, water, milk, sugar.*
> Have you got *any paper*?
> ···
> **Note: *have you got* means the same as *do you have*.**

A **Complete the questions with *a* or *any*.**
1 Do you have .... rubber?
2 Do you have .... scissors?
3 Do you have .... money?
4 Have you got .... tissue?
5 Do you have .... lined paper?
6 Have you got .... mobile phone?
7 Do you have .... water?
8 Have you got .... coloured pencils?

B **Ask each other the questions. Give true answers like this:**

Yes. Here.   No. Sorry.

> **In answers, you can replace singular nouns with *one*.**
> A: Do you have *a dictionary*?
> B: No, but Pepe has *one*.
> ···
> **You can replace plural / uncountable nouns with *some*.**
> A: Do you have *any scissors*?
> B: No, sorry. Ask Sam. I think she has *some*.

C **Ask each other the questions in exercise A again. This time reply using *No, but* .... *has* .... Add a name of someone in the class and *one* or *some*.**

▶ Need help? Read the grammar reference on page 149.

SPEAKING 2

A **Write five *Do you have ...?* questions to ask other students in the class.**

B **Ask your questions to different students. They must give true answers. See if you can find people who answer *Yes* to all your questions.**

CONVERSATION PRACTICE

Work in pairs. Do one of these *Conversation practice* activities.
People and places, Unit 1, page 17.
Free time, Unit 2, page 23.

ACT OR DRAW

Work in pairs. One person acts or draws the words.
***Don't* speak. Your partner tries to guess the words. Then change roles.**

dance	chat	boring	a train
walk	get up	a church	shower
study	angry	a factory	a window
a beach	a pen	swim	a waiter
a river	a tree	a board	turn off

QUIZ

Work in groups. Answer as many questions as possible.
1 When do you eat **dinner**, **breakfast** and **lunch**?
2 Are **kids** the same as **children**?
3 Where do you **sleep**?
4 Say two things you **watch**.
5 Where do you have a **coffee**?
6 Say two places where people **teach**.
7 What's the job in a local **government** or **tax office**?
8 Say three things you **drink**.
9 What's the opposite of **expensive**?
10 If there's a lot of **crime**, is a place **safe**?
11 Which is bigger: **a town** or **a city**?
12 Say two things you **read**.
13 What are the opposites of **south** and **west**?
14 How do people **keep fit**?
15 Where does a **nurse** work?

FAST WRITER

Work in groups. See who is quickest to write each of 1–5.
1 Five countries.
2 Five jobs.
3 Four questions in the present tense.
4 Four negative sentences in the present tense.
5 Four sentences with *there's / there are*.

PRONUNCIATION Sounds in English

There is pronunciation in each Review unit in this book. You learn the different sounds in English, understand how a dictionary shows pronunciation, and practise with words from the book.

A ✎ R 1.1 Listen and repeat the words and consonant sounds.

/θ/ south	/f/ free	/p/ pen	/t/ take	/tʃ/ chat	/s/ sit	/ʃ/ she	/k/ car
/ð/ the	/v/ live	/b/ big	/d/ bed	/dʒ/ job	/z/ trees	/ʒ/ Asia	/g/ go
/h/ he	/m/ man	/n/ nice	/l/ like	/ŋ/ long	/r/ read	/w/ walk	/j/ yes

B Work in pairs. Say each word and consonant sound again. Circle the sounds that you think you have in your language.

C Work in pairs. Say the sounds with a circle again. Do you use your tongue, lips or the top of your mouth to make each sound?

There are 12 single vowel sounds and eight vowels with two sounds. All are in the first units of this book, except one.

/iː/ eat	/ɪ/ fit	/ʊ/ good	/uː/ food
/e/ bed	/ə/ river	/ɜː/ work	/ɔː/ sport
/æ/ bad	/ʌ/ fun	/ɑː/ art	/ɒ/ boss
/eɪ/ great	/aɪ/ write	/ɪə/ here	/eə/ where
/aʊ/ town	/ɔɪ/ boy	/əʊ/ go	/ʊə/ pure

D ✎ R 1.2 Listen and repeat the words and sounds.

E Work in pairs. Try to say these words.
1 /pɑːk/
2 /ʃɒp/
3 /miːt/
4 /waɪf/
5 /bɔːd/
6 /lʌnʃ/
7 /njuːz/
8 /brekfəst/
9 /mʌðə/
10 /bɪzɪ/
11 /rɪlæks/
12 /steɪʃnz/

F ✎ R 1.3 Listen and check in the audioscript on page 171.

LISTENING

You are going to hear four conversations.

A ✎ R 1.4 **Listen and match each conversation to one picture. Two pictures are not used.**

B Listen again and check.

[... / 8]

a   b   c

d   e   f

GRAMMAR

A Choose the correct words.

1 A: Where *are / is* he from?
   B: France
2 A: Do you want *to go / going* to the cinema later?
   B: OK. What time?
3 A: Do you have *a / any* tissues?
   B: Yes. There are *one / some* in my bag.
4 A: What *are / do* you do?
   B: I *am / are* a teacher.
5 A: Do you like *play / playing* tennis?
   B: Yes, *it's / he's* great.
6 A: Is your town big?
   B: Not really. There *is / are* only about 10,000 people.
7 A: What do you do *at / in* the weekend?
   B: I usually stay at home. *I don't / I'm not* earn much money.
8 A: Do you like sport?
   B: I love watching, but I don't do it *very often / sometimes*.

[... / 12]

B Put the word(s) in **bold** in the correct place in the sentence.

1 I need do some shopping. **to**
2 I play computer games. **hardly ever**
3 Sorry, I understand. What does 'journalist' mean? **don't**
4 Do you have pencil and paper? **a**
5 There's a palace near the river. It's great. **beautiful**
6 She speaks English very well, but she's from the UK. **not**

[... / 6]

VERBS

Complete the text with the verbs in the box.

go	spend	work	keep
get	finish	listen	have

I ¹.......................... in a department store in town. I usually start at eight o'clock and ².......................... at four. I leave the house at seven and ³.......................... home at seven. I often ⁴.......................... to the gym after work. I usually ⁵.......................... about an hour there. I want to ⁶.......................... fit. In the evening I'm usually tired, so I just ⁷.......................... dinner with my wife and watch TV. We sometimes sit and ⁸.......................... to music.

[... / 8]

ADJECTIVES

Replace each adjective in *italics* in 1–8 with its opposite on the right. In three cases, change *a* and *an*!

1 It's a *boring* job.   cheap
2 I have a *busy* social life.   best
3 He has a *big* car.   quiet
4 It's an *expensive* restaurant.   interesting
5 It's the *worst* place to live in the UK.   west
6 It's in *east* Paris   old
7 It's a *long* film.   small
8 I have a *new* mobile phone.   short

[... / 8]

COLLOCATIONS

Match the verbs in the box to the groups of words they go with in 1–8.

check	open	get	play
watch	help	go	live

1 ~ the news / ~ a football game / ~ a film
2 ~ in the countryside / ~ in the capital / ~ on my own
3 ~ in the park / ~ the piano / ~ a game
4 ~ to a concert / ~ swimming / ~ for a walk
5 ~ a seat / ~ some tickets / ~ angry
6 ~ my grandparents / ~ me / ~ to do my homework
7 ~ the answers / ~ the word in a dictionary / ~ it's OK
8 ~ the blind / the shop ~s at nine / ~ the window

[... / 8]

      [Total ... /50]

03 HOME

In this unit, you learn how to:
- talk about the area you live in
- name things you often buy and do
- explain where things are
- explain what you need to do
- describe your house / flat
- ask people to do things

Grammar
- Prepositions of place
- Possessive adjectives and pronouns
- *can / can't*

Vocabulary
- Local facilities
- In the house
- Collocations

Reading
- Where I live

Listening
- *Is there one near here?*
- Problems at home

SPEAKING

A Think about the areas you live / work / study in. What shops, restaurants and other facilities are there in each area? Compare with a partner. Which area is best?

There's a really good supermarket near my home and there are lots of different restaurants.
There's only a small café and a bank near my home.

VOCABULARY Local facilities

A Which of the places in the box can you see in the pictures on this page?

a bank	a post office	a chemist's	a bookshop
a café	a shoe shop	a clothes shop	a restaurant

B Match these things that people do to the places in exercise A.
1 buy a novel / buy a dictionary
2 buy some toothpaste / buy some aspirins
3 have a sandwich / have a cup of tea
4 buy a shirt / buy a jacket
5 buy some boots / buy some shoes
6 have a steak / have some wine
7 buy some stamps / send a package
8 change money / get some money

C Work in groups. Discuss these questions.
- Which of the places in exercise A do you go to most?
- What do you usually buy – or do – in each one?

GRAMMAR Prepositions of place

When we explain where things are, we usually use prepositions – words like *next to, on, at, between* and *opposite* – to make it clear. These prepositions are often in expressions.

A Name the places A–H described in 1–8 on the map on the opposite page.
1 There's a post office *opposite* the church.
2 There's a bank *down this road – next to* the supermarket.
3 There's a great museum down here – *on the right*.
4 There's a hotel *in the next street – on the left*.
5 There's a café on Jones Street – *next to* the station.
6 There's a cinema *at the end of this road*.
7 There's a big department store *on the corner of* Church Street *and* Jackson Lane.
8 There's a clothes shop *between* the Internet café *and* the department store.

▶ Need help? Read the grammar reference on page 150.

B Work in pairs. Cover exercise A. Look at the map. Ask and answer questions like this:
A: Is there a post office near here?
B: Yes, there's one opposite the church.

LISTENING

Three people ask about local places.

A 🔊 3.1 Listen. What places do they ask about? Why?

B Listen again. Tick ✓ the sentences that are true.
1 a The chemist's is on New Street.
   b It's on the right.
   c It's next to a clothes shop.
2 a There are lots of good places to eat in the area.
   b The café is on Dixon Road.
   c It's next to a shoe shop.
3 a The bookshop is on the corner of Chester Street and Hale Road.
   b It's on the right.
   c It's opposite a supermarket.

DEVELOPING CONVERSATIONS
I need to …

When we ask people we know where places are, we often explain why we need to go there. For example:
I need to get some money. Is there a bank near here?

A Work in pairs. Think of two reasons to go to each of the places below.

I need to … . Is there	a post office a chemist's a clothes shop a computer shop a café a supermarket an Internet café	near here?

B Have conversations about where you are. Ask and answer the seven questions in exercise A.
A: I need to send a package. Is there a post office near here?
B: Yes, there's one on Junction Road – next to an Italian restaurant.

CONVERSATION PRACTICE

A Work in pairs.
Student A: look at the map in File 3 on page 166.
Student B: look at the map in File 9 on page 169.

B Ask each other *Is there a … near here?* to find the places you want. Explain why you need to go to each place.

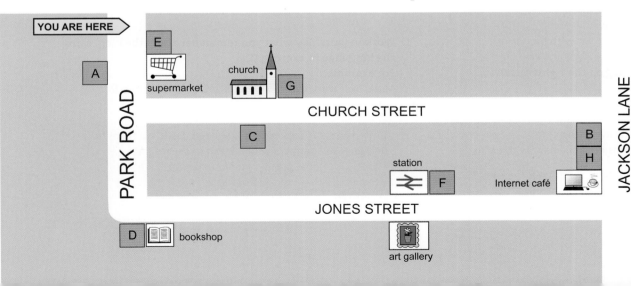

YOU ARE HERE

E
A
supermarket
church
G
PARK ROAD
CHURCH STREET
C
station
F
Internet café
B
H
JACKSON LANE
factory
JONES STREET
D   bookshop
art gallery

A Which rooms are the things in the box usually in?

a sofa	a cupboard	a mirror
a TV	an alarm clock	plates
shampoo	the sink	a table
a fridge	a bed	towels

B Where do you do the things in the box? Look up any words you don't know in the *Vocabulary Builder*. Then discuss your ideas in pairs.

do the washing-up	check your emails	put on make-up
watch DVDs	cut vegetables	wash your clothes
brush your teeth	get dressed	

C How often do you do the things in exercise B? Tell a partner.

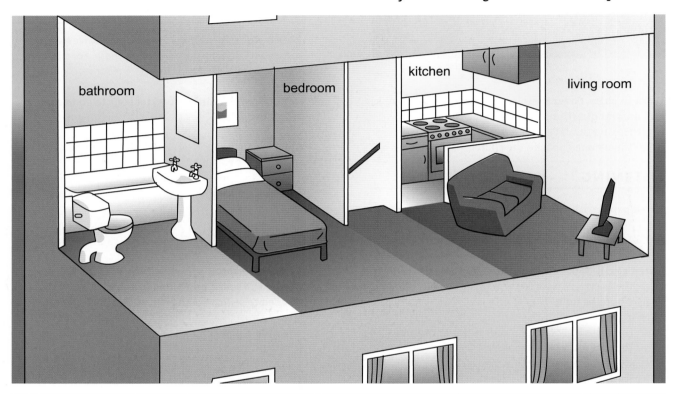

READING

You are going to read about a young Greek woman, Maria. She describes where she lives.

A Work in groups. Say one good thing and one bad thing about:
- living at home with your parents.
- living on your own.
- sharing a house / flat with friends.

B Read Maria's blog on the right. Answer these questions.
1 Where does she live?
2 What is good / bad about each place?
3 Who does she live with?
4 What problems does she have with each person?

C Match the verbs with the words they go with in the blog.

1	live	a	an hour to drive there
2	study	b	a room with my sister
3	take	c	hours putting on her make-up
4	share	d	with my sister and brother
5	annoy	e	me
6	spend	f	Business Management

D Work in pairs. Say what you remember about the blog, using the language in exercise C.
For example:
Maria lives with her sister, Dimitra, and her brother, Costa.

LANGUAGE PATTERNS

Write the sentences in your language. Translate them back into English. Compare your English to the original.
She spends hours putting on her make-up.
He spends hours checking his emails every day.
I spend about an hour a day practising the piano.
They spend a lot of time working.

SEARCH BLOG   FLAG BLOG   NEXT BLOG

My name's Maria and I live in Thessaloniki. It's a great city. There are lots of things to do. I live with my sister, Dimitra, and my brother, Costa. They both work here, and I study – English and Business Management. We usually stay in the city during the week and then sometimes, at the weekend, we go back to our family house in the mountains near Askós. It takes about an hour to drive there. It's a beautiful place, but the village is very quiet and small. There's not much to do there.

In our family home, I have a big bedroom with my own TV. My sister's room has its own bathroom as well, but I prefer mine. It's nice and quiet and I can relax, listen to music, read, do whatever I want there.

Our flat in Thessaloniki is very small. I share a room with Dimitra, but Costa has his own room. Ours is nice and tidy, but his is really messy! Men!

We take turns to cook and clean and do the washing-up. I love living with my family, but sometimes my sister annoys me. She spends hours putting on her make-up and washing her hair – and we only have one bathroom!

GRAMMAR
Possessive adjectives and pronouns

> **Use possessive adjectives before nouns. Examples of possessive adjectives are *my* and *your*.**
> I live with *my* sister, Dimitra, and *my* brother, Costa.
>
> **A possessive pronoun can replace a possessive adjective + noun. Examples are *mine* and *yours*.**
> My sister's room has its own bathroom as well, but I prefer *mine* (= my room).

A Complete the table.

Subject	Object	Adjective	Pronoun
I	me	my	mine
you	you	your	yours
he	him		his
she	her	her	
we	us	our	
they	them		

B Choose the correct word.

1 *Your / Yours* house is really nice.
2 *Their / Theirs* house is next to the sea, but *our / ours* is about ten minutes away.
3 She shares a flat with *her / hers* sister.
4 My room is OK, but I prefer *your / yours*.
5 They come to *our / ours* house a lot, but we don't visit *their / theirs* very often.
6 This isn't *my / mine* dictionary. Is it *your / yours*?
7 It's a nice photo. Are those *your / yours* sisters?
8 A: Are these scissors *your / yours*?
    B: No, they're *her / hers*. *My / Mine* are in *my / mine* bag.

▶ **Need help? Read the grammar reference on page 150.**

SPEAKING

A Think about your answers to these questions.
- What is good / bad about where you live?
- Who do you live with?
- Do you ever have any problems with the person / people you live with? What?

B Work in groups. Discuss your answers.

LISTENING

You are going to hear three conversations in someone's home.

A Match the sentences 1–8 to the pictures a–h.

1 I can't concentrate.
2 I can't reach.
3 I can't hear it.
4 I can't find my keys.
5 I'm cold.
6 I'm hot.
7 It's a mess.
8 It's very dirty.

B Work in groups. Discuss these questions.

- Which of the problems in exercise A do you have in your home?
- In your language, what do you say or ask next in each of the eight situations in exercise A? Use a dictionary to try and say it in English.

C ✇ 3.2 Listen to the three conversations. Match each one to a situation in exercise A.

D Listen again. Complete the sentences with ONE word in each gap.

1 a I .... walk across it and not break something!
  b Can you .... it, please?
2 a What temperature is the air-conditioning .... ?
  b Can you .... it down? I'm cold.
  c It's .... cold.
3 a What did he .... ?
  b Can you turn it .... ?
  c Is that .... for you?

VOCABULARY Collocations

> We call words that go together 'collocations'. For example, *watch TV*.
> ....
> When you learn a noun, learn a verb or adjective that goes with it. For a new verb, learn some nouns that go with it. The *Vocabulary Builder* helps you with this.

A Look at the collocations from the *Vocabulary Builder* for this unit. Match the verbs in the box to 1–6.

turn down	share	wash	put on	brush	cut

1 .... : ~ my jacket, ~ your shoes, ~ some make-up
2 .... : ~ yourself, ~ some vegetables, I can't ~ it, I need some scissors to ~ it, ~ my hair
3 .... : ~ the TV, ~ the air-conditioning, ~ the music, ~ the sound
4 .... : I just need to ~ my hair, ~ my teeth, ~ the dog
5 .... : I need to ~ my hands, ~ some dirty clothes, ~ my hair, ~ the plates
6 .... : ~ a flat with two other people, ~ a room with my sister, ~ a sandwich, ~ a pizza, ~ your things

Match the nouns in the box to 7–12.

table	air-conditioning	cupboard
towel	alarm clock	sink

7 .... : need a ~ to dry myself, have a clean ~, the ~'s wet, leave your ~ on the floor after you use it, a beach ~
8 .... : is the ~ on?, turn the ~ on, turn up the ~, turn down the ~, turn off the ~
9 .... : put the things in the ~, it's in the ~, put it back in the ~, the kitchen ~, the bedroom ~, a big ~, a small ~, the ~ under the sink
10 .... : it's on the ~, the kitchen ~, set the ~ for dinner, clean the ~
11 .... : the kitchen ~, wash your hands in the ~, leave the dirty plates in the ~, the cupboard under the ~
12 .... : do you have an ~?, set the ~ for seven, hear the ~

B Say things about you and people you live with by adding *always / usually / hardly ever / never*.
For example:
My mum always washes my clothes.
My brother hardly ever washes his hands before dinner.

- wash my clothes
- wash ... hands before dinner
- put milk back in the fridge
- leave dirty plates in the sink
- set the table for dinner
- hang up towels after using them
- set the alarm clock
- turn up the air-conditioning

GRAMMAR *can / can't*

> To say something is impossible, use *can't* + verb.
> *I can't reach.*
> *He can't hear it.*
> ....
> To ask to do something, use *Can I / you*, etc. + verb?
> A: *Can you turn* the TV *down*, please? I can't concentrate.
> B: OK, sorry.
>
> A: *Can I use* this towel? I want to have a shower.
> B: Of course. It's there for you.

A Put the words into the correct order.
1 sleep I can't .
2 you can me help ?
3 use I can bathroom your ?
4 up you turn can music the ?
5 book find I can't my .
6 can clothes wash some I ?
7 week can't we next come .
8 moment can't he drive at the .

B 🎧 **3.3 Listen and check your answers.**

> *Can* is pronounced /kæn/ or /kən/.
> *Can't* is pronounced /kɑːnt/.

C Listen to the sentences again. Practise saying them.

D Write questions with *Can I ...?* or *Can you ...?* and the words in brackets.
1 I can't see the TV. (move)
2 I need to do some shopping. (take me in the car)
3 I can't speak now. (talk to you later)
4 Dinner's ready. (set the table)
5 I'm hot. (open the window)
6 I need to eat something. (make a sandwich)

▶ Need help? Read the grammar reference on page 151.

E Work in pairs. Have short conversations using your questions from exercise D.

> I can't see the TV. Can you move?
>
> Yes, sure.

SPEAKING

A Work in pairs. Write short conversations based on the pictures in *Listening*, exercise A on page 34.

B Remember what you wrote. Act your conversations for another pair.

04 HOLIDAYS

In this unit, you learn how to:
- talk about what you did
- pronounce past forms
- express your feelings about what people tell you
- talk about dates and months
- ask and answer questions about holidays

Grammar
- Past simple – regular / irregular verbs
- Past simple negatives
- Past simple questions

Vocabulary
- Months, seasons, dates
- Going on holiday

Reading
- A holiday in Ireland

Listening
- Did you have a nice weekend?
- Public holidays around the world

LISTENING

You are going to hear four conversations about last weekend.

A Look at what four people did last weekend. Which weekend activities do you think were *great*, *OK* or *bad*?

1 I was ill. I had a bad cold.
2 We went to a rock festival.
3 Some friends came to visit, so I showed them the city.
4 Nothing much really. I did some shopping on Saturday.

B ♪ 4.1 Listen and put sentences 1–4 in exercise B into the order you hear them. Was each weekend *great*, *OK* or *bad*?

C Listen again and match a–f below to conversations 1–4.
1 ......   3 ...... , ...
2 ......   4 ...... , ...

a We went for a picnic in the park.
b I saw The Specials on Saturday night. They were good.
c I stayed in bed all weekend.
d I cooked lunch for everyone.
e I played tennis, watched TV... the usual things.
f I didn't sleep much.

D Work in pairs. Discuss whether you like:
- a busy weekend or a quiet weekend.
- going to markets or cooking.
- showing people round your town / area.

GRAMMAR The past simple

> The past simple form is usually verb + *-ed* or *-d* (if the base form of the verb ends in *-e*).
> I *played* tennis and *watched* TV.
> I *wanted* to go out yesterday.
> She *smiled* to herself.
>
> A lot of other common verbs are irregular:
> | | | |
> |---|---|---|
> | see – *saw* | take – *took* | spend – *spent* |
> | get – *got* | read – *read* | buy – *bought* |

A Look at these verbs in the past simple from *Listening*. Write the base form.

1 went – *go*   6 showed – ....
2 did – ....   7 cooked – ....
3 had – ....   8 stayed – ....
4 was / were – ....   9 played – ....
5 came – ....   10 watched – ....

B Work in pairs. Test each other.
Student A: say a verb.
Student B: say the past simple form.

C Complete the sentences about things people did last weekend with the past simple forms of the verbs in the box.

stay	go	be	spend
come	get	have	watch

1 I .... lunch with my grandparents.
2 I .... to the beach with some friends.
3 We .... at home and relaxed.
4 I .... a football match on Saturday.
5 There .... a free concert in town.
6 Some friends .... to our house for dinner.
7 I went shopping and I .... some new shoes.
8 I .... all weekend studying for an exam.

▶ Need help? Read the grammar reference on page 152.

D Write three things you did in the past that were great, and three things you did that were bad or boring.

DEVELOPING CONVERSATIONS
That sounds …

> **We often give our feeling about what people say using *That sounds* + adjective. For example:**
>
> A: Some friends came to visit, so I showed them round the city.
> B: *That sounds nice.*

A Write a comment about these sentences using *That sounds* + an adjective in the box.

nice	great	bad	interesting

a I went for a walk in the countryside.
b We rented a boat and went on the lake.
c I had a headache, so I stayed at home.
d I went shopping with my mum.
e I saw a documentary about crime.
f We had a party at home.

B Practise the conversations.

> **What did you do?**
>
> **We rented a boat and went on the lake.**
>
> **That sounds great.**

PRONUNCIATION Past simple forms

A 🔊 4.2 Listen. Circle the form of the verb or verbs you hear in each sentence.

1 visit / visited
2 visit / visited
3 play / played
4 try / tried; play / played
5 want / wanted; rain / rained
6 meet / met; chat / chatted
7 walk / walked; chat / chatted
8 walk / walked; have / had

> **With verbs ending in -*t*, the pronunciation of the past ending is /ɪd/.**
>
> | wanted | chatted | visited |
> |--------|---------|---------|
> | /ˈwɒntɪd/ | /ˈtʃætɪd/ | /ˈvɪzɪtɪd/ |
>
> **With other verbs, you hear a /d/ or /t/ sound.**
>
> | rained | played | walked |
> |--------|--------|--------|
> | /reɪnd/ | /pleɪd/ | /wɔːkt/ |

B Look at the audioscript on page 173. In pairs, practise reading the conversations from *Listening*.

CONVERSATION PRACTICE

A Think about last weekend. Did you have a nice weekend? Choose an answer from the list below.
Yeah, it was great.
It was OK.
Not really.

Write down two or three things you did.

B Have conversations with different people in your class. Use these two questions:
Did you have a nice weekend?
What did you do?

Comment on people's answers about their activities with *That sounds …*

C With a partner, decide which person in the class had the best weekend. Why?

VOCABULARY Months, seasons, dates

A Put the months in the correct order.

August	June	January	December
February	May	October	September
April	July	March	November

B Work in groups. Discuss these questions.
- Do you have the four seasons in the photos in your country?
- What months are they?
- Did you go on holiday this / last year?
- What season was it? What month?

> When we say dates we use ordinal numbers.
> We say:
> March the *first*, May the *second*, June the *third*,
> July the *fifth*, August the *twelfth*.
>
> To make ordinal numbers, add *'th'* to the
> number: *fourth, fifth, sixth, seventh, eighth,
> ninth, tenth, eleventh,* etc. Then *twenty-first,
> twenty-second,* etc.

C ✿ 4.3 Listen. When are these public holidays?

1	New Year's Day, UK	1st Jan
2	Mother Theresa Day, Albania	....
3	Women's Day, Russia	....
4	Day of the Dead, Mexico	....
5	San Juan's Day, Catalonia and Alicante	....
6	Martin Luther King Day, USA	....

D Work in pairs.
Student A: look at File 4 on page 167.
Student B: look at File 11 on page 169.

E Work in groups. Discuss these questions.
- Which of the public holidays in exercises C and D do you have in your country?
- Do you have any public holidays to celebrate famous people? When? Who is the person?
- Who has a birthday next in your class?

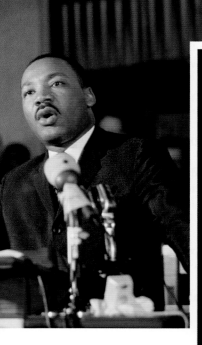

LISTENING

You are going to hear three stories about what people did in the public holidays from *Vocabulary*, exercise C.

> When you listen, you often can't hear every word people say. Don't worry! Use the words you can hear to guess what they said.

A ◈ 4.4 **Listen. Which public holidays do they talk about? Listen for dates, months and days.**

B **Look at these words and check you understand them.**
1 night – beach – fire – songs – swam – warm – slept
2 missed – work – nice – presents – flowers – said – room
3 three – drove – clear – cloud – views – traffic – two

C **In your own language, think about what each person did. Then listen again and check.**

D **Listen again. Complete the sentences with ONE word in each gap.**
1 a We .... a fire on the beach.
  b We .... songs and laughed.
  c Some of my friends swam in the ....
2 a I wasn't in Russia, so I missed the ....
  b On Women's Day, men usually .... us very well.
  c I didn't get any flowers. .... said nice things to me.
3 a We .... on Saturday at three in the morning.
  b We drove to the ....
  c It was very clear and sunny. There wasn't a cloud in the ....

E **Work in pairs. Use the words in exercise B to remind you, and say what each person did on the last public holiday. Then compare your ideas with the audioscript on page 173.**

GRAMMAR Past simple negatives

> **For the verb *be*, past simple negatives are *wasn't / weren't*.**
> I *wasn't* in Russia in March. I was in London for work.
> People *weren't* very friendly.
>
> **For other verbs, use *didn't* + verb.**
> I *didn't go out* for dinner. I *didn't get* any flowers. Nobody said nice things to me. Some of my friends swam in the sea, but I *didn't*.

A **Write the negative form of the past simple verbs in brackets.**
1 I .... much on Sunday. (did)
2 I .... till 11. (got up)
3 I wanted to have breakfast, but there .... any coffee or bread. (was)
4 I went to the shop, but I .... my keys. (took)
5 The shops .... open. It was a holiday! (were)
6 I tried to call my neighbour, but he .... (answered)
7 I went to a café and I had a coffee, but then I saw that I .... any money! (had)
8 I went back to my flat. I broke a window to get in. I .... again after that. (went out)

> **We often use *not very* + adjective / adverb.**
> It was*n't very warm*.
> We did*n't* go *very far*.

B **Replace the words in *italics* using *not very* + the words in brackets.**
1 We went to bed *early*. (late)
  We didn't go to bed very late.
2 The hotel was *expensive*. (cheap)
3 We got back *late*. (early)
4 People were *unfriendly*. (friendly)
5 There was *nothing* to do. (much)
6 We bought *few* things. (many)
7 We stayed a *short* time. (long)
8 My parents were *annoyed*. (happy)

▶ Need help? Read the grammar reference on page 152.

SPEAKING

A **Write answers to these questions. Then work in groups and say what you've written.**
• What's your favourite public holiday? What do you normally do?
• When was the last public holiday? What did you do?

VOCABULARY Going on holiday

> **go on holiday:** If you go on holiday, you stop working and go away to a different place to relax, usually for a few days or more.

A Match the verbs 1–6 to the groups of words they go with in a–f.

1 fly
2 stay
3 take
4 spend
5 rent
6 go

a a day in Rome / the week relaxing / lots of money
b to Helsinki / with British Airways / first class
c the train / the bus / a taxi
d with friends / in a hotel / in a bed and breakfast
e sightseeing / out for dinner / swimming
f a car / a boat / a flat

B Work in groups. Discuss these questions.
- How often do you / does your family go on holiday?
- Do you usually go to the same place or do you go to different places?
- What do you usually do when you are on holiday?

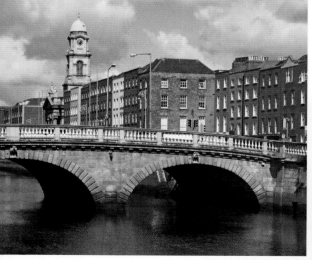

READING

You are going to read an email from a Danish man to his Italian friend.

A Read the email on the opposite page. Answer these questions.
1 Where did Nicklas go?
2 Did he go on his own?
3 How long was he there for?
4 Was the weather good?
5 What did he do there?

B Complete the sentences with ONE word in each gap. Look at the email if you need help.
1 We .... to Dublin.
2 We .... a week there.
3 It's a .... city.
4 I was .... about the weather, but it didn't rain once!
5 My .... place was the west of the country.
6 We went .... in the mountains.
7 We didn't see .... on the first day!
8 How .... your summer?
9 .... you go on holiday anywhere?

LANGUAGE PATTERNS

Write the sentences in your language. Translate them back into English. Compare your English to the original.

We didn't see anyone the first day.
I didn't go anywhere last weekend.
I didn't do anything last night.
We didn't try any of the food.

SPEAKING

A Work in pairs. Tell each other the best place in your country:
- to go sightseeing.
- to go walking.
- to go swimming.
- to spend a week relaxing.
- for nightlife.
- for driving around.

To: mauro1990@shotmail.it

Subject: Re: Ireland

Hi Mauro,

How are you? I hope you and your family are well. How was your trip to Korea? I'm sure it was great.

Helena and I spent three fantastic weeks in Ireland and had a really great time. We flew to Dublin, the capital, and spent a week there. It's a beautiful city. We went sightseeing every day and saw all the old buildings. Then in the evenings, we went out and enjoyed the nightlife. It's a fun city! You'd love it.

Next, we rented a car and spent two weeks driving round the country. It's really beautiful! I was worried about the weather, but it didn't rain once. We stayed in little bed and breakfasts and met some really lovely people.

My favourite place was the west of the country. We went walking in the mountains in County Mayo for a few days. It was lovely and quiet. We didn't see anyone on the first day!

Anyway, now we're back in Copenhagen and back at work! How was your summer? Did you go on holiday anywhere? Did you have a good time?

Please write and tell me everything!

Your friend,
Nicklas

GRAMMAR Past simple questions

For the verb *be*, make questions with *was / were*.
How *was* your summer?
How long *were* you there for?

For other verbs, use *did*.
Where *did* you go?
Did you have a good time?

A Use the notes below. Write past simple questions you could use to ask a friend about their holiday.
1 you / go on holiday anywhere?
2 where / go?
3 who / go with?
4 have a good time?
5 how long / there for?
6 where / stay?
7 it very expensive?
8 the weather good?
9 the food good?

B Match the answers a–i to the questions in exercise A.
a Yes, I did. It's a great country.
b Yes, great. They eat lots of fruit, lots of rice. It's lovely.
c I stayed with friends in Rio and then in a hotel.
d Yes, I did. I went to Brazil.
e Two weeks.
f I went on my own.
g No, not really. Most things are quite cheap there.
h Rio de Janeiro and Salvador in the north-east.
i It was great, yes. Really hot and sunny.

▶ Need help? Read the grammar reference on page 153.

SPEAKING

A Choose one of the things below to talk about.

last weekend
the last public holiday
the last time you went on holiday
your last birthday
a special day in your life

B Write five past simple questions for your partner to ask you about your day / weekend / holiday.

C Work in pairs. Swap questions and interview each other.

CONVERSATION PRACTICE

Work in pairs. Do one of these *Conversation practice* activities.

Home, Unit 3, page 31.
Holidays, Unit 4, page 37.

ACT OR DRAW

Work in pairs. One person acts or draws the words. *Don't* speak. Your partner guesses the words. Then change roles.

close	a fire	a shirt	a picnic
hear	boots	keys	a cupboard
dirty	eat	rain	a headache
reach	a cold	laugh	a fridge
cook	break	sing	a lake

QUIZ

Work in groups. Answer as many questions as possible.
1 Which season(s) do you have **warm** weather in?
2 What do you buy in a **chemist's**?
3 What date is **New Year's Day**?
4 Say three things you can **put on**.
5 Where do you go to **send a package**?
6 Where do you go to have a **steak**?
7 What do you do in a **sink**?
8 What room do you normally have **a sofa** in?
9 When do you use a **mirror**?
10 Where do you normally **brush your teeth**?
11 Why can't someone **reach a cupboard**?
12 Say three **seasons**.
13 Say three places you can **stay** on holiday.
14 When do you give someone **a present**?
15 What do you do if you are **ill**?

FAST WRITER

Work in groups. See who is quickest to write each of 1–6.
1 Five kinds of shops or facilities.
2 Six months.
3 Four questions with *Can ...?* that you ask at home.
4 Four negative sentences in the past.
5 Four sentences with an irregular past verb.
6 Four sentences about where things are near your home.

PRONUNCIATION Consonants and air

Look at the consonants in the table below. The ones in the top two lines all use a lot of air to make the sound.

/θ/ bath	/f/ fun	/p/ past	/t/ turn
/tʃ/ change	/s/ miss	/ʃ/ wash	/k/ key
/ð/ the	/v/ very	/b/ boat	/d/ drive
/dʒ/ job	/z/ use	/ʒ/ Asia	/g/ get

A R 2.1 **Listen and repeat the words and sounds in the two top rows.**

B R 2.2 **Listen and repeat the sounds /p/, /f/, /t/, /tʃ/, /k/. Put a piece of paper in front of your mouth. Try to move the paper when you say these sounds.**

C **Work in pairs. Try to say these words.**
1 /pʊt/
2 /kʌt/
3 /ˈsəʊfə/
4 /ʃəʊ/
5 /mætʃ/
6 /θɪŋk/
7 /ˈfəʊtəʊ/
8 /pleɪts/

D R 2.3 **Listen and check.**

E **Work in pairs. Practise saying the sentences. Who has good pronunciation? Which sounds are difficult for you?**
1 Sorry, I can't reach.
2 Set the table for six people, please.
3 Can you put the plates in the kitchen sink, please?
4 I think this cup's clean.
5 She took a taxi to the post office!
6 A fun photo is a nice present.

LISTENING

You are going to hear four conversations.

A ⏺ R 2.4 **Listen. Match each conversation to one picture.**

B **Listen again and check.**

[... / 8]

a   b   c

d   e   f

GRAMMAR

A **Choose the correct words.**
1 There's a café *on / in* the corner of this road.
2 Our house is *front / next to* a school.
3 *My / Mine* parents live on this road.
4 It's not his car, it's *her / hers*.
5 I'm sorry, I *can't / can* see the board.
6 I *wasn't / didn't* do anything yesterday.
7 Did you *went / go* out last night?
8 They *were / was* both ill at the weekend.

[... / 8]

B **Write the past simple form of the verbs in brackets.**

We ¹........................ (have) a great holiday in Greece.
We ²........................ (fly) to Athens and ³........................
(spend) three days there and ⁴........................ (see) all
the famous sights. After that, we ⁵........................ (take)
a boat to Mykonos and we ⁶........................ (stay) in a
small hotel near the beach.

[... / 6]

C **Write the questions using the words in *italics*.**
1 A: *be / there* a book shop near here?
   B: Yes, there's one on High Road.
2 A: *you / have* a nice weekend?
   B: Yes, I went to a concert on Saturday night.
3 A: Oh yes? *be / it* good?
   B: Yeah, it was great. I really enjoyed it.
4 *you / help me*? I don't understand this.

[... / 4]

ADJECTIVES

Replace the adjectives in 1–6 with their opposites on the right.
1 Do you have any *dirty* clothes?   messy
2 It's very *hot* in here.   cold
3 His room's normally very *tidy*.   unfriendly
4 It's quite *sunny* today.   wet
5 Is that towel *dry*?   cloudy
6 The people were quite *nice*.   clean

[... / 6]

COLLOCATIONS

Match the verbs in the box to the groups of words they go with in 1–8.

wash	share	turn up	cut
show	close	change	set

1 ~ a flat with a friend / ~ a pizza / ~ your ideas
2 ~ the window / ~ the door / the shop ~s at six
3 ~ some money / ~ your clothes / ~ places
4 ~ the table / ~ your alarm clock / ~ a rule
5 ~ the vegetables / ~ yourself / ~ it with scissors
6 ~ your hair / ~ your hands / ~ the plates
7 ~ the air-conditioning / ~ the TV / ~ the temperature
8 ~ me on the map / ~ us round town / ~ him what to do

[... / 8]

VOCABULARY

Complete the text with the words in the box.

sing	prefer	view	fun	house
drive	annoy	visit	clear	nightlife

We live in a small ¹........................ in the mountains. I
²........................ to work in the nearest town every day
and also take my kids to school there. It takes an hour
to get there. We ³........................ to live in the countryside.
It's quiet and we have no neighbours to ⁴........................
us. There's no ⁵........................ here, but we watch DVDs
or play games or ⁶........................ songs together. We have
a lot of ⁷........................ . It's also fantastic to get up in
the morning when the sky is ⁸........................ because we
have a great ⁹........................ – you can see the sea from
here. Friends often come to ¹⁰........................ us because
they think it's so nice here.

[... / 10]

    [Total ... /50]

05 SHOPS

In this unit, you learn how to:
· point and describe what you want
· talk to a shop assistant
· say numbers better
· talk about things happening now
· follow directions in a shop
· talk about prices and shops

Grammar
· *this, that, these, those*
· Present continuous

Vocabulary
· Describing what you want to buy
· Department stores

Reading
· Sale!
· A famous department store

Listening
· *Who's next?*
· *Do you sell...?*

VOCABULARY Describing what you want to buy

A Work in groups. Complete the table with the words in the box. Use a dictionary if you need to.

green	yellow	short	square
wood	shirt	cake	jeans
round	cheese	plastic	fish
dress	leather	cotton	brown

colour	material	clothes	food	shape
red	wool	jacket	fruit	long
white		shoes	meat	small

B How many of the words in exercise A can you see in the photos? Who found the most?

LISTENING

You are going to hear three conversations in places in the photos.

A 🔊 5.1 Listen. Decide which place they are in.

B Listen again.
1 Which thing(s) do they buy?
2 How much is it / are they?

C Work in groups. Discuss these questions.
· Do you think they make good choices?
· Do you think the shops are expensive?
· What would you choose?

GRAMMAR *this, that, these, those*

a This apple's nice.

b Give me that cake, please.

c I like these shoes.

d I like those jeans over there.

A **Based on what you see in the pictures above, choose the correct word.**
1 *That / Those* cake looks nice.
2 Do you like *this / these* shoes? I bought them yesterday.
3 Can you pass me *this / that* newspaper over there on the table?
4 *This / These* apple tastes great. Where did you get it?
5 How much are *these / those* jeans in the window?
6 Is *this / these* yours? It's not mine.
7 *This / That* salad tastes lovely. How's your pasta? It looks nice.

▶ Need help? Read the grammar reference on page 154.

B **Work in groups. Ask each other the name in English for different things in the classroom. Ask *What's this / that?* or *What are these / those?***

DEVELOPING CONVERSATIONS
Questions in shops

> Learning common questions for particular situations will help you have conversations.

A **Who usually asks the questions 1–8: shop assistants or customers?**
1 Who's next?
2 What are those made of?
3 How much are the apples?
4 Can I have some ...?
5 Which one(s)?
6 How much would you like?
7 How many would you like?
8 Anything else?

B **Match each pair of answers to a question in exercise A.**
1 a Sure. How much?
   b Of course – how many do you want?
2 a 50p each.
   b One forty-nine a kilo.
3 a Me.
   b This lady, I think .
4 a That much.
   b Half a kilo.
5 a Those ones have fish in them and the others have meat.
   b Cotton.
6 a No thanks, that's all.
   b Yeah, can I have some of that, please?
7 a Five or six.
   b Just one.
8 a The blue one.
   b The things next to the apples.

C **Spend two minutes remembering one answer for each question in exercise A. Then work in pairs.**
Student A: ask questions.
Student B: close your book and give an answer.

CONVERSATION PRACTICE

Have similar conversations to the ones in *Listening*.

A **Work in pairs. Choose a shop from the pictures.**
Student A: You are the shop assistant. Hold your book open for Student B to see.
Student B: You are the customer. Buy two different things in the picture. Use as much of the language from this page as you can.

B **Choose a different picture. Change roles and repeat exercise A.**

PRONUNCIATION Numbers

A 🔊 **5.2 Listen to these numbers and mark the main stress.**

thirteen	fourteen	sixteen	thirty	forty	sixty

B 🔊 **5.3 Listen and write the numbers.**

C Work in pairs.
Student A: say one of the numbers in each of a–f.
Student B: point to the number.

a	14	40	d 513	530
b	15	50	e 16,000	60,000
c	118	180	f 17,000	70,000

READING

You are going to read about two women who work in shops. The shops are having a sale.

A Before you read, discuss these questions in groups.
- Where was the last sale you went to? Did you buy anything?
- Tell a partner about something you found cheap in a sale, using sentences like these:
  - I bought *a coat*. It was *30 euros*, reduced from *60*.
  - I bought a *mountain bike*. It was reduced by *50%*.
- Who in your group got the best price?

B Work in two groups.
Group A: read about Emily and answer questions 1–6.
Group B: read about Dalena and answer questions 1–6.

1 Where is she from?
2 What does she do?
3 Where does she work?
4 Why is the shop having a sale?
5 How's she feeling? Why?
6 What does she want to do in the future?

C Compare answers with someone in your group.

D Now find a person from the other group. Ask each other the questions in exercise B to learn about your partner's text.

NATIVE SPEAKER ENGLISH

bargain
We say something is a *bargain* when it is good and cheap.

Everyone is happy when they find a bargain.
There are some great bargains in the sales.
That's a bargain.

SOLDES

SCHLUSSVERKAUF

REBAJAS

РАЭПРОДАЖБА

SALDI

EMILY, GERMANY

We're having a sale because we're closing the shop. It's sad, because my grandfather opened it 60 years ago. When I was small, I came here on Saturday mornings and sat and read the children's books.

When my grandad retired, I managed the shop. Now there's a sale, lots of people are buying things, but it's normally very difficult. There are lots of very big bookshops now, which sell every book a customer can want. They also have a café and famous writers give talks at the shop. We can't do that, so we're not getting many customers and we're losing money.

I'm looking for a job at the moment, but I don't really know what I want to do in the future. I don't really want to work in another bookshop after I leave here.

販売

出售

SALE

بيع

NIŽANJE

INDIRIM

bis zu
50%

DALENA, SLOVAKIA

I'm a sales assistant at an S&A store. The store opened last year and it's doing very well. We're having our summer sale at the moment, so I'm working really hard. The shop is staying open late. I'm tired, but I like it. I like helping people find nice clothes and, of course, everyone is happy when they find a bargain.

I want to continue working with S&A and maybe become a floor manager and then a shop manager. I think it's a good company, and they are growing at the moment and opening new stores, so I think there are lots of opportunities. Maybe I can get a job in one of their shops in the UK and improve my English!

SPEAKING

A Work in pairs. Discuss these questions.
- Do you know any shops that are closing? Do you know why?
- Are any shops opening where you live? What kind of shops? Are you happy about it?
- Do you prefer small shops or big shops? Why?
- Do you think working in a shop is a good job? Why? / Why not?

GRAMMAR Present continuous

> The present continuous is formed using *am / are / is + -ing*. For example:
> We*'re having* a sale.
> How's she *feeling*?
> Their new clothes *are not selling* very well.
>
> Use the present continuous to talk about things happening around now which are temporary and not finished.

A Look at both texts and find ten examples of the present continuous.

B Complete the sentences with *am / are / is*, but use the short form where you can.
1 They...... having a sale at a shop in town.
2 I...... not working very hard at the moment.
3 My mother's not here. She...... doing the shopping.
4 The economy...... growing fast at the moment.
5 My football team...... doing very well now.
6 I hope you...... enjoying this class.
7 Some friends ...... staying with me at the moment.
8 My brother...... studying at university.

▸ Need help? Read the grammar reference on page 154.

C ⬥ 5.4 Listen and repeat the sentences.

D Work in pairs. Which sentences in exercise B are true for you?

E You are a 'receptionist' and you answer the phone. The caller wants to speak to the people in the box, but the people don't want to / can't talk now. Write a reason using the present continuous.

your mum or dad	Susie (your sister)
The President	David (a friend)
Mr Smith (your boss)	you

Now have conversations like this using your sentences:
A: Hello. Can I speak to your mum or dad?
B: Sorry. Can you call back later? *They're watching a film.*
A: Sure. Thanks

VOCABULARY Department stores

A Match the pictures in 1–8 to the departments in the box.

Home Entertainment	Toys
Accessories	Beauty
Computing and Gaming	Sports
Womenswear	Menswear

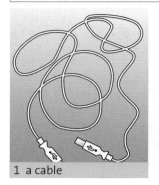

1 a cable

2 a dress

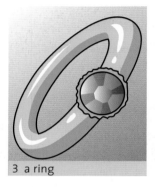

3 a ring

4 face cream

5 a doll

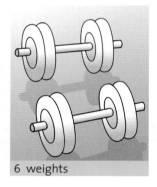

6 weights

7 a suit

8 a radio

B Work in groups. Try to think of one more thing you can buy in each of the departments above.

C Which words from the box can you see in the pictures below?

the basement	the second floor	the stairs
the ground floor	the bottom shelf	the lifts
the main entrance	the first floor	the escalator
the changing rooms	the top shelf	the till

D Work in pairs. Answer these questions using words from exercise C.
1 Where do you try clothes on?
2 What do you go up or go down?
3 Where do you go in and go out of the store?
4 Where do you ask 'Are you going up?' or say 'Fourth floor, please'?
5 What can be difficult to reach?
6 Which floor do you always go down to?
7 What floor is the main entrance usually on?
8 What do you walk up or down?
9 Where do you pay?

LISTENING

You are going to hear three conversations in a department store.

A 🔊 **5.5 Listen and answer these questions.**
1   What does each customer ask for?
2   Where are the things they want?

B **Listen again. Complete the sentences with ONE word in each gap.**
1   a   They're over there, ... the till.
    b   There they are. .... the bottom shelf.
    c   I walked .... them a minute ago.
2   a   .... the second floor.
    b   Go .... the escalator.
    c   Turn right .... the top.
3   a   It's .... the Sports department.
    b   You can take the lifts from .... there.
    c   When you get .... the lift, it's on the left.

C **Look at the audioscript on page 174 and choose four useful words or expressions to remember.**

D **Tell a partner. Did they choose the same?**

LANGUAGE PATTERNS

Write the sentences in your language. Translate them back into English. Compare your English to the original.
Have a nice day.
Take a seat.
Have a good time.
Don't worry.
Don't get angry.

E **You are going to have similar conversations to the ones you heard. Write five things you want to buy in your local department store. Use a dictionary to help you, if you need to.**

F **Take turns asking and answering questions about where the things are. Use one of the following to start your conversations:**

Excuse me. Can you help me? I'm looking for ...

Excuse me. Do you sell ...?

SPEAKING

A **Read the text. Then discuss the questions in groups.**

The biggest department store in northern Europe is Stockmann. There are seven stores in Finland, six in Russia, one in Latvia and another one in Estonia. The company started in Helsinki in 1862 and slowly grew. Different departments soon opened, followed by new stores. Stockmann also bought a bookshop, a sports company, a fashion company and more.

Stockmann now makes a lot of money from online sales, but continues to sell everything from clothes to cheese, from TVs to furniture. It also has its own fitness centre!

- What's the biggest department store where you live?
- Do you ever shop there? If yes, how often do you go there? What for? Can you remember what's in the basement? On the top floor? On other floors? Tell a partner.
- What do you know about the company? When did it start? Is it growing? Do they have stores in other countries? Do they sell things online?
- What things do you buy online? Why?
- In your country, are there shops that foreign companies own? Which country or countries are the companies from?
- What's your favourite shop? Why?

06 STUDYING

In this unit, you learn how to:
- name school and university subjects
- talk about studying at university
- explain your feelings about courses
- talk about your school system
- talk about languages and learning
- give opinions

Grammar
- Modifiers: *quite, very, really*
- Comparatives

Vocabulary
- Subjects
- School, university and college
- Languages

Reading
- Bilingual's better!

Listening
- *What are you studying?*
- A Russian education

VOCABULARY Subjects

A Look at the pictures and decide:
1 which subjects are arts subjects.
2 which subjects are science subjects.
3 which subject(s) are only school subjects not university subjects.
4 which subject(s) are only university / college subjects not school subjects.

B Work in groups. Discuss which subject(s):
- you think are interesting.
- you think are boring.
- you think is most / least important.
- you think are easy / difficult.
- you are good at.

Maths

Chemistry

PE

IT

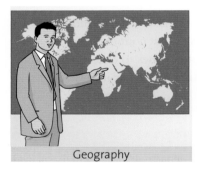
Geography

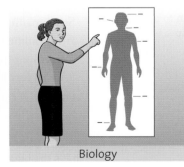
Biology

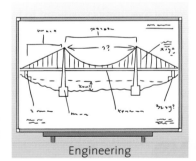
Engineering

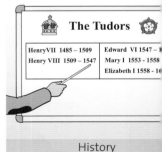
History

Marketing

Literature

Medicine

Law

LISTENING

You are going to hear three conversations about studying.

A 🔊 **6.1 Listen and complete the table.**

	Subject	Year	How's it going?
1			*Really well.*
2		*2nd*	
3			

B Listen again and choose the correct words.
1 a I'm *doing / making* a degree in Marketing.
   b I'm really *enjoying / liking* it.
2 a I'm a student *at / of* university.
   b Not very well. It's quite *boring / bored*.
3 a It's a lot of *work / works*!
   b Good luck *with / for* it.

C Work in pairs. Discuss these questions.
- Do you know anyone at university / college at the moment?
- What are they studying?
- What year are they in?
- Are they enjoying it?

PRONUNCIATION *are*

> We often pronounce *are* /ə/.

A 🔊 **6.2 Listen. Repeat the questions you hear.**

B Listen again and write what you hear.

C Work in pairs. Ask and answer the questions.

DEVELOPING CONVERSATIONS
How's the course going?

> We can ask *How's the course / it going?* to find out if someone is enjoying their course or not.
>
> A: *How's the course going?*
> B: Really well. It's great. I'm really enjoying it.

A Here are nine answers to the question *How's the course going?* Add *Really well*, *OK* or *Not very well*.
1 .... , but it's quite difficult.
2 .... It's quite boring.
3 .... It's really interesting.
4 .... , but it's a lot of work.
5 .... I don't really like my teachers.
6 .... The other students are really nice and friendly.
7 .... I did very well in my exams. I found them easy.
8 .... I think I chose the wrong subject!
9 .... , I suppose, but I'm not sure it's what I really want to do.

B Work in groups. Discuss these questions.
- How's your course going?
- What's good about it?
- Is there anything you don't like?

NATIVE SPEAKER ENGLISH

How's it going?
We also use *How's it going?* instead of *How are you?*

A: *Hi, how's it going?*
B: *Fine, thanks. How are you?*
A: *Yeah, not too bad.*

CONVERSATION PRACTICE

A Work in pairs. Have four conversations like the ones in *Listening*. Take turns asking and answering the questions below. Give different answers each time.

So, what do you do?

What're you studying?

How's the course going?

What year are you in?

VOCABULARY School and university / college

A Translate these adjectives into your language.

friendly
nice
lazy

varied
boring
difficult

helpful
patient
strange

popular
expensive
modern

B Match the nouns in the box to the group of adjectives in exercise A that describe them.

| a course | a classmate | a teacher | a university |

C Work in pairs. Add one more adjective to each group in exercise A.

D Which adjectives describe your school / university / college life? Tell a partner.

LISTENING

You are going to hear an interview with a Russian student, Irina. She is talking about the Russian school system.

A 🔊 6.3 Read the questions and check you understand them. Then listen to the interview and put the questions in the order the interviewer asks them. The first is done for you.

a ...... How much homework do you get?
b ...... And how long each day do you study at school?
c ...... And when can you leave school?
d ...... What kind of subjects do you study?
e ...... What's your favourite subject?
f ...... And when does the school day begin?
g ..*1*.. What age do you start school?
h ...... How many breaks do you get?

B Work in pairs. Match each number or number expression with a question in exercise A.

...... two
...... seven
...... ten or more
...... 16 or 18
...... half past eight
...... six or seven
...... 45 minutes
...... five
...... between an hour and a half and three hours

C Listen again and check your answers. What other things do you hear Irina say?

D Listen to the interview again and complete the sentences with ONE word in each gap.

1 Most children .... some kind of pre-school classes.
2 You can then get a job or go to a special college to learn a ....
3 Each class .... 45 minutes.
4 Quite a lot! It .... on the age of the student.
5 We do a lot of writing and a lot of .... for class.
6 We do English and maybe one other .... language.

LANGUAGE PATTERNS

Write the sentences in your language. Translate them back into English. Compare your English to the original.
Each lesson lasts 45 minutes.
The breaks last between 15 and 25 minutes.
The meeting didn't last very long.
How long does your course last?

GRAMMAR Modifiers

> *Very, really* and q*uite* are modifiers. They go before adjectives.
> *Very / really* mean *'a lot'*.
> It's *very interesting*. I love it.
> It's *really expensive*. You need a lot of money to go there.
> ···
> We often make adjectives negative by adding *not very*.
> I'm *not very good* at History.
> ···
> *Quite* means 'a little'.
> It's *quite good*, but it's not great.

A **Choose the correct words.**

1 Some of my classmates aren't *very / quite* friendly.
2 The course is *quite / really* difficult! I don't understand anything!
3 It's a great university. It's *very / not very* popular.
4 She's nice, but she's *quite / not very* lazy.
5 Most of the students are really friendly, but one or two aren't *really / very* nice.
6 It's a good course. It's *quite / not very* varied.
7 He's a good teacher, but he's not *very / quite* patient.
8 It's a great university, but it's *quite / really* expensive! I can't study there.

▶ **Need help? Read the grammar reference on page 155.**

B **Work in groups. Tell each other about things – or people – that you think are:**

a really expensive.
b very popular at the moment.
c quite strange.
d not very modern.
e quite boring.

SPEAKING

A **Think about the education system in your country or the school you went / go to. Answer the questions from *Listening*, exercise A. Discuss your ideas with a partner.**

VOCABULARY Languages

A Look at the languages in the box and say what country each language comes from. Which language isn't based on the name of a country?

French	Spanish	Japanese	Finnish	English
Chinese	Arabic	Turkish	German	Russian

B Work in pairs. Discuss these questions.
- How important are these languages in the world:
  - very important?
  - quite important?
  - not very important?
- Which of these languages sound nice to you?

SPEAKING

A Read the short article and answer the questions.

PRIMARY SCHOOL OF LANGUAGES IN EAST LONDON

Well done

Vizuri sana

Good afternoon

ari ya mchana

A primary school in London has students who speak over 40 languages! Each month, one of the children at Newbury Park Primary teaches other children some words of the language that they speak at home. A teacher films the student speaking in the foreign language and asks how to say simple things like *hello* and *thank you*. They show the film to the other pupils in the school and the pupils learn the words. In January and February, they learned some Turkish and Japanese. This month, they're learning Romanian.

In the UK, one in seven children now speaks a language other than English at home.

- What do you think of the article? Is it good news or bad news?
- Do / Did you have people from different countries at your school? Where are / were they from?
- Do / Did you know any bilingual people (people that speak two languages) at your school? What languages do / did they speak?
- Are there any bilingual schools in your country? Do you think they are good? Why? / Why not?

READING

You are going to read an article with information and opinions about growing up bilingual.

A Before you read, work in pairs. Decide what the words in **bold** mean.
1 I'm quite a **creative** person. I'm good at arts subjects.
2 I'm a very **sensitive** person. I'm good at listening to other people and understanding their problems.
3 I'm not very **flexible**. I like doing things my way.
4 I sometimes **caused** problems at school and my teacher got angry with me.
5 I'm good at **solving** problems. People often ask me for help.
6 I'm a good student. I got **high grades** at school.
7 I'm a very **positive** person. I always try and think about good things.
8 I'm quite an **emotional** person. I always show how I'm feeling.

B Discuss which of the sentences in exercise A are true about you.

C Read the article on page 55. Decide which opinions the writer agrees with.
1 Kids in the UK who don't speak English at home are bad at science.
2 Speaking two languages is normal for most people in the world.
3 Learning two languages when you're young is good.
4 Bilingual children are good at thinking of new ideas.
5 Bad experiences can affect how kids learn at school.
6 People are wrong to worry about children speaking different languages at home and school.
7 What they're doing at Newbury Park Primary School in *Speaking* is good.

D Compare your ideas. Explain your choices.

E Work in pairs. Discuss these questions.
- Did you find any of the ideas surprising? Which ideas?
- Do you think *everything* the writer says is true? If not, what do you thing is untrue?

GRAMMAR Comparatives

> **You can compare how good two things are using *better than*.**
> Growing up with two languages is *better than* only knowing one language.
>
> ....
>
> **We often then use other comparatives to explain why.**
> Bilingual children are *more flexible* and get *higher* grades.
> She finds French *easier* than Spanish.

A Choose the correct comparative.
1 Her English is better than mine. She gets *higher / lower* grades.
2 This computer is better than mine. My one's *slower / faster*.
3 Mr Platt is a better teacher than Mrs Jones. He's *funnier / more boring*.
4 I think Biology is better than English. It's *more interesting / more difficult*.
5 They're better students than me. I'm *more helpful / lazier*.
6 He's *taller / shorter* than me. I'm 1.85 and he's 1.80.

B Work in pairs. Discuss when we add *-er / -ier / more …* to make a comparative. Talk in your own language if you like.

▶ Need help? Read the grammar reference on page 155.

C Choose a partner. Compare yourself to your partner, using the comparative forms of the adjectives below.
- I am *tall / short* than you.
- My school was *big / small* than yours.
- I'm a *good / bad* student than you.
- My house is *near to / far from* the school than yours.
- I find Maths *easy / difficult* than you.
- My mobile was *cheap / expensive* than yours.

D Tell your partner your ideas. Does your partner agree? Ask questions to decide who is right.

SPEAKING

A Choose five things from the box. Decide if they are better or worse now than before. Spend two minutes thinking of one or two reasons why. Use a dictionary if you need to.

schools	transport	old people
exams	the economy	young people
universities	the weather	parents
hospitals	sport	teachers

B Work in groups. Say your ideas. What do the other people in your group think?

BILINGUAL'S BETTER!

Some people in the UK worry that children speak a language other than English at home. They say it causes problems at school: it is more difficult for the teacher; children cannot learn Science or other subjects well because they do not speak English well.

In fact, 70% of the world's population is bilingual. Most research also says growing up with two languages is better than only knowing one language. Normally, children who speak different languages at home and school:
- are more flexible;
- are more creative;
- are better at solving problems;
- are more sensitive towards other children;
- get higher grades at school – including in their second language!

Sometimes families had bad experiences before and after they moved to the UK from a different country. Maybe they saw a war, or a parent died, or they lost their home, or they have little money. These experiences can cause emotional problems, which makes learning difficult. Children possibly need help with that, but it is wrong to see their language and culture as a problem, because it isn't. In fact, the results are even better if students can do some things at school in their first language, because students feel positive about both school and their language.

REVISE TOGETHER

CONVERSATION PRACTICE

Work in pairs. Do one of these *Conversation practice* activities.
Shops, Unit 5, page 45.
Studying, Unit 6, page 51.

ACT OR DRAW

**Work in pairs. One person acts or draws the words.
Don't speak. Your partner guesses the words. Then
change roles.**

cake	a till	meat	round
fish	an apple	die	go down
jeans	cheese	science	top shelf
square	a lift	a dress	face cream
stairs	a lady	worry	customer

QUIZ

Work in groups. Answer as many questions as possible.
1   What's the opposite of **difficult**?
2   Say three **sizes** of shirt.
3   Where's the **main entrance** of a building?
4   How old is someone who is **retired**, normally?
5   When are prices usually **reduced** in a shop?
6   Say the names of three pieces of **furniture**.
7   What's the opposite of **make money**?
8   Say three kinds of **material**.
9   Where can you get a **degree**?
10 Is it good to be **lucky**?
11 What's the opposite of **the top**?
12 How long does a football match usually **last**?
13 If something **improves**, does it get better or worse?
14 Who gives you **grades**?

FAST WRITER

Work in groups. See who is quickest to write each of 1–5.
1   Six colours.
2   Six subjects people study at school or university.
3   Four present continuous sentences using *I, he, we, they*.
4   Four sentences comparing you with your mum, a
    brother or sister, or a friend.
5   Four sentences about where you live, using *really, very,
    quite* and *a bit*.

PRONUNCIATION Vowel sounds

We make vowel sounds by small changes to the
tongue and mouth. The mouth gets rounder for the
sounds towards the right of the chart.

/iː/ seat	/ɪ/ fish	/ʊ/ put	/uː/ true
/e/ bread	/ə/ agree	/ɜː/ first	/ɔː/ store
/æ/ match	/ʌ/ luck	/aː/ half	/ɒ/ wrong

A ◈ R 3.1 **Listen and say the words and vowel sounds.**

B **Touch the end of your tongue and say the sounds.**

◈ R 3.2 **Listen and say** /iː/, /ɪ/, /ʊ/, /uː/. **The tongue
moves back.**

Then listen and say /iː/, /e/, /æ/. **The tongue moves
down.**

C **Practise saying the other sounds. Go from left to
right and then top to bottom in the chart above.**

D **Work in pairs. Try to say these words.**
1 /pliːz/   5 /ɪmˈpɔːtənt/
2 /aːt/   6 /ekˈsæm/
3 /gʊd/   7 /ˈwʌrɪ/
4 /luːz/   8 /ˈkɒlɪdʒ/

E ◈ R 3.3 **Listen and check.**

F **Work in pairs. Practise saying the sentences. Who
has good pronunciation? Which sounds are difficult
for you?**
1   It's a very good school.
2   Young people have positive ideas.
3   Do you want a piece of bread with your meat?
4   Give me three or four red apples, please.
5   I had fish and chips for breakfast.
6   The first teacher we had was more patient.

LISTENING

You are going to hear four conversations.

🔊 R 3.4 Listen and choose two correct sentences.

1 a She buys apples and oranges.
   b She buys apples and plums.
   c They cost £3.13.
   d They cost £3.30.
2 a She manages a shop.
   b She works in a clothes shop.
   c She reads a lot because she gets free books.
   d She doesn't have much free time.
3 a She's a primary school teacher.
   b She's a student.
   c She doesn't enjoy it.
   d She finishes this year.
4 a She has an English mother.
   b All the classes at her school are taught in English.
   c She wants to study in Italy.
   d She wants to study Engineering.

[... / 8]

GRAMMAR

A Choose the correct words.

1 A: Can you pass me *that / those* cups over there?
   B: Sure. Here.
2 A: *You are / Are you* waiting to pay?
   B: No. Go ahead.
3 A: How's the course going?
   B: Badly. It's much *more hard / harder* than last year.
4 A: Hello. Can I speak to Greg, please?
   B: Sorry, *he watches / he's watching* a film.
5 A: What *does your brother do / is your brother doing*?
   B: He's a doctor. He works in a clinic near here.
6 A: Did you enjoy the film?
   B: It was *quite / very* good, but not great.
7 A: Do you want to try some of *this / that* soup?
   B: Oh, it's really nice. It's *more good / better* than mine.

[... / 7]

B Complete the sentences with ONE word in each gap. Contractions (*He's, don't* etc.) are one word.

1 I lost my job. I'm .... working at the moment.
2 I can't help you now. .... doing my homework.
3 What .... all those people looking at?
4 Do you have a coat? .... raining outside.
5 I love .... shoes. They're .... nice.
6 A: I can't do .... exercise. Can you help me?
   B: Sure. It is a .... difficult.
7 A: Are you .... this book?
   B: Yes I am, but .... not very good. Her last book was much .... interesting than this one.

[... / 11]

ADJECTIVES

Choose the best adjective.

1 Lots of people do it. It's very *popular / helpful / special*.
2 She's 1.84 m. She's quite *high / slow / tall*.
3 It's an interesting course. It's very *friendly / varied / boring*.
4 Our teacher's nice. He's very *lazy / patient / easy*.
5 I like art. I'm quite *little / normal / creative*.
6 His cat died. It was really *sad / important / modern*.
7 I found a bargain. I was very *sensitive / happy / young*.
8 I'm good in difficult situations. I'm *wrong / flexible / stupid*.

[... / 8]

COLLOCATIONS

Match the verbs in the box to the groups of words they go with in 1–8.

give	cause	look for	go up
pay	leave	improve	have

1 ~ a fire / ~ a headache / ~ problems
2 ~ the service / ~ my grades / ~ my English
3 ~ a talk / ~ him a present / ~ me some help
4 ~ my job / ~ school / ~ home
5 ~ my keys / ~ a new job / ~ a new flat
6 ~ at the till / ~ for the shopping / ~ the taxi driver
7 ~ a bad experience / ~ a break / ~ a sale
8 ~ the escalator / ~ the stairs / ~ the mountain

[... / 8]

VOCABULARY

Complete the text with the words in the box.

found	own	online	positive
started	grew	plastic	continues

I have my [1]........................... business. I sell cheap [2]........................... things. I sell everything from toys to radios to kitchen things. I also sell things [3]........................... from my website. I [4]........................... the business five years ago. The first year, I lost money. The second year, I was OK, but then, two years ago, shops had bad economic problems. Most [5]........................... it difficult to sell, but it was the opposite for me – it was very [6]........................... . Sales [7]........................... by 500% last year, so I'm making good money now. I hope it [8]........................... .

[... / 8]

 [Total ... /50]

07 FAMILY AND FRIENDS

In this unit, you learn how to:
· talk about your family
· express surprise
· give opinions about family life
· explain things that are (not) necessary
· talk about people you know

Grammar
· Auxiliary verbs (*be, do, can*)
· *have to / don't have to*

Vocabulary
· Relationships
· Jobs and activities in the home
· Describing people

Reading
· Debate of the week: working parents
· With a little help from your friends

Listening
· *Do you have any brothers or sisters?*
· Different kinds of friends

VOCABULARY Relationships

A **Complete the table with the words in the box.**

sister	grandmother	daughter	
mum	husband	girlfriend	uncle

male	female
grandfather	
	wife
dad	
son	
	aunt
boyfriend	
brother	
cousin	

NATIVE SPEAKER ENGLISH

Grandma and Grandad
Different people use different names for their grandparents. For example: *Grandma, Gran, Granny* for a grandmother; *Grandad, Grandpa* for a grandfather.

B **Complete the sentences with words from exercise A.**
1 Pat is my uncle. He's my mum's ....
2 Clare is my .... She's my aunt Stella's daughter.
3 Larry is my cousin. He's my uncle Matthew's ....
4 Tina's my younger .... I'm two years older than her.
5 Granny P is my .... and my mum's ....
6 Mel is my brother's .... They met six months ago.

C **Write the names of six people in your family. Then tell a partner who they are.**

LISTENING

You are going to hear three short conversations about families.

A 🔊 7.1 **Listen. Which relationships from *Vocabulary* do they mention?**

B **Listen again. What do you learn about the family members?**

C **Work in pairs. Discuss your ideas. Then read the audioscript on page 175 to check.**

GRAMMAR Auxiliary verbs

We use auxiliary verbs (e.g. *be, do, have, can*) when we don't want to repeat the main verb and / or words that follow it. For example, short answers:

A: *Did you go out* yesterday?
B: Yeah, *I did ~~go out~~.*

A: So, *are you married*, Ted?
B: Yes, *I am ~~married~~.*

A Complete the answers with the correct auxiliary verbs.

1 A: Do you have any brothers or sisters?
   B: Yeah, I ....
2 A: Is he married?
   B: Yes, he ....
3 A: Does she have a boyfriend?
   B: Yes, she ....
4 A: Do your children still live with you at home?
   B: My son .... , but my daughter
   ....
5 A: Are you very similar?
   B: Yes, we ....
6 A: Are your grandparents still alive?
   B: My mum's parents .... , but my dad's
   ....
7 A: Did you do anything nice at the weekend?
   B: Yes, I ....
8 A: Did it rain?
   B: No, it ....

B Work in pairs. Take turns reading the questions, but this time give opposite answers. For example, for number 1:

> Do you have any brothers or sisters?

> No, I don't.

▶ Need help? Read the grammar reference on page 156.

DEVELOPING CONVERSATIONS
Adding information

In conversations, we don't normally just give short answers to questions. We try to add comments.

A Match the extra comments to the questions and short answers in *Grammar*, exercise A.

1 Luckily! It was a bit cloudy, but it stayed dry.
2 My grandad had his 80th birthday party.
3 A younger brother.
4 They died a few years ago.
5 She's studying in the United States.
6 We're sisters, but we're best friends too.
7 The wedding was last month.
8 He's a really nice guy. I like him.

B Work in pairs. Practise reading the conversations in *Grammar*, adding the comments above.

C Write short answers and then add comments to these questions. Then ask and answer the questions in pairs.

• Do you live near here?
• Have you got any aunts or uncles?
• Are you married?
• Did you go anywhere during the holidays?

PRONUNCIATION *Really?*

A 🔊 7.2 Listen and repeat *Really?* three times.

We often say *Really?* to show surprise / interest. The intonation goes up high and then down.

Really?

B 🔊 7.3 Listen to six sentences. Say *Really?* if the information is surprising or interesting. Say *Oh, OK* if it's not unusual.

CONVERSATION PRACTICE

You are going to have conversations about families.

A Write five questions about families that you want to ask other students in your class.

B Ask your questions to different partners. Try to add comments when you answer their questions. Say *Really?* when you hear interesting or surprising things.

VOCABULARY Jobs and activities in the home

A Match 1–5 to a–e and 6–10 to f–j.

1	look after	a	my son play basketball
2	tell	b	songs together
3	sing	c	my baby brother
4	repair	d	jokes to each other
5	watch	e	a light switch
6	feed	f	my daughter from school
7	pick up	g	a story at bedtime
8	play	h	the dishwasher
9	empty	i	the dog
10	read	j	games together

B Say which jobs and activities in exercise A you think are:
- essential.
- bad or boring.
- nice to do.

C Do you do any of the jobs and activities in exercise A?

SPEAKING

A Work in pairs. Read the introduction to a discussion board on a website. Discuss the three questions at the end.

Debate of the week: Working parents

Family life is changing. In the past, women stayed at home and looked after the children. They did all the housework and men earned money and maybe repaired a few things in the house. Now, both parents often have full-time jobs. Who does all the housework? How does both parents working affect the kids and family life? Is it a good thing?

READING

A Read the comments on the message board and match the words below to the people. One word is not necessary and one is done for you.

a grandmother	....	a grandfather	....
a father	....	a mother	*Hannah*
a nanny	....	a daughter	....
a son	....	an uncle	....

B Read again and decide if the people think both parents working is a good thing, a bad thing, or both good and bad.

C Work in pairs. Say if you like what each person wrote or not.

My son Travis brings the kids to my house three days a week. They're a bit difficult sometimes, but I love being with them. We sing songs and play games. I also admire my son's wife. She has a very full life. It's great that she has a job and doesn't have to stay at home all the time.
Bertha, Canada

I'm happy both my parents work because they can buy me nice things.
José, Chile

Martha feels guilty about not being with her children. I feel the same! My son is often at home on his own and sometimes I can't watch him play soccer or help him with his studies. I do those things with Martha's kids! It's crazy!
Lourdes, USA

We have a dishwasher and I have to fill it and empty it. Mum and Dad say they don't have time. It's not fair! My friends don't have to do jobs in the home. Their parents do them or they employ a cleaner!

Sophie, Germany

I recently started work again after I had my baby, Lianna. My husband takes her to the day nursery at nine and I pick her up at five. I then have to do housework and feed Lianna. I also have to get up at night if she wakes up. It's difficult, but I still want to work. I love my job and I feel like a more important part of society.

Hannah, Australia

I think it's better to have one parent at home, but it doesn't have to be the woman. My wife had a better job than me so I left my job to stay with our kids.

Roberto, Italy

Of course both parents want to work. Send your kids to live in a private school. My brother does that and everyone's happy. The kids always have friends and get a good education. The family spends the holidays together.

David, England

GRAMMAR *have to / don't have to*

> ***Have to*** shows something is necessary
> (= you need to do it).
> ***Don't have to*** shows something is not necessary
> (= you can choose).
>
> We have a dishwasher, and I *have to* fill it and empty it.
> My friends *don't have to* do jobs in the home. Their parents do them.

A **Choose the correct words.**
1 Sorry, I can't stay. I *have to / don't have to* pick up my little brother from school.
2 My mum and dad say I wanted the dog, so I *have to / don't have to* feed it and take it for walks.
3 My dad often *has to / doesn't have to* work at the weekends.
4 I set the table earlier, so you *have to / don't have to* do it now.
5 I think it's good that we eat together as a family. We chat and *have to tell / tell* jokes to each other. It's nice.
6 Tell Simon he *has to / doesn't have to* pick me up. I got a taxi.
7 I can't repair it. You *have to / don't have to* take it to a shop.
8 We *have to / don't have to* play cards, if you don't want to. We can do something else.

▶ Need help? Read the grammar reference on page 156.

B **Work in groups. Say things you have to do at home.**

SPEAKING

A **On your own, decide if it is *good*, *bad* or *doesn't matter*:**
- if both parents have to work.
- if families eat together.
- if parents set lots of rules for children.
- if kids don't have to do jobs in the home.
- if kids watch TV.
- if parents send their kids to bed at eight o'clock.
- if kids have to do lots of homework.
- if parents don't go out on their own.

B **Work in pairs. Take turns saying your ideas. Reply using one of the phrases below.**

> It doesn't matter if both parents have to work.

> I agree.   I don't agree.   It depends.

C **Write two more opinions you have about family life.**

D **Tell different students your ideas. See if they agree.**

SPEAKING

A Read the text on the right. Then discuss the questions in groups.
- Which kind of friend is most / least important? Why?
- What do you talk about with each kind of friend?
- Which kind of friend do you meet / talk to the most?
- What other different kinds of friends can you think of?

LISTENING

You are going to hear four people talking about people they know.

A ⊙ 7.4 Listen and decide what kind of friend each person is describing.

B Listen again. Correct two mistakes in each summary.
1 He met Johan at university. Johan lives in New York now. He's a doctor.
2 Her husband studies with Miguel. She doesn't get on well with Miguel. Miguel is 21.
3 He's a student. He met Claire when he was on holiday. Claire wants to come to England.
4 Liu is her grandmother. Liu is stupid. She lives in Shanghai.

C Read the audioscript on page 176 to check your ideas.

LANGUAGE PATTERNS

Write the sentences in your language. Translate them back into English. Compare your English to the original.
She made me feel good about myself.
I made her cry.
She makes me laugh.
He makes me happy.
They make me really angry sometimes.
It made me really sad.

D Work in pairs. Discuss these questions.
- What makes you laugh?
- What makes you happy?
- What makes you angry?
- What makes you sad?

A LITTLE HELP FROM YOUR FRIENDS

Some friends last a lifetime, but often we make friends for particular reasons at particular times. Here, we look at a few of the different kinds of friends we make during our lives.

The old friend
Old friends are friends you met a long time ago and that you are still close to. You have a shared history. You enjoy talking about the past and always stay in contact.

The friend of the family
These friends can be useful. People that our parents or brothers or sisters know can often teach us things or help us to find a job.

The online friend
Many people make 'friends' through the Internet. Sometimes these friendships move into the real world, but usually they don't.

The 'friend' you don't really like very much
Perhaps it's a friend from your past who is different now. Maybe it's a friend of your friend / wife / husband. The problem is you don't get on with them, but you have to see them and be nice to them.

VOCABULARY Describing people

A Translate the eight adjectives in the pictures into your language.

B Work in pairs. Which adjectives do you think are positive and which are negative? Why?

C Complete the sentences with the adjectives. in exercise A

1 She's a very .... woman. She always makes me laugh.

2 He's really .... He goes running every day and plays basketball twice a week as well.

3 He's quite .... He doesn't say very much.

4 She's very .... She's an engineer, she speaks five languages and she's very good with computers!

5 He's so .... ! When he's talking, it's difficult for anyone else to say anything!

6 My dad's quite .... If I come home late or don't do well at school, he gets angry.

7 She's very .... She always does what she says. You can trust her.

8 She's really .... She knows what she's good at and she knows what she can do.

D Work in groups. Discuss these questions.

- Which adjectives describe people in your family / people you know? Explain why?
- Which adjectives do you think describe you?

SPEAKING

A Think of four people you know – not family members. Write their names and think about the answers to the questions below for each person.

How did you meet each other?
We were in the same class at secondary school.

What kind of person is he / she?
He's great. He's very funny and very clever.

How often do you talk?
Two or three times a week. We talk on the phone a lot.

How often do you go out together?
Maybe once or twice a month. We go out for dinner or for a drink.

B Work in groups. Ask and answer questions about the people you know. Start like this:
I have a friend called ...

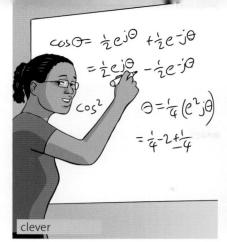
clever

confident

fit

funny

loud

quiet

reliable

strict

08 PLANS

In this unit, you learn how to:
- talk about people's plans
- make suggestions
- talk about things you want to do
- talk about government plans
- give opinions and reasons

Grammar
- *be going to* + verb
- *would like to* + verb

Vocabulary
- More common activities
- For and against

Reading
- Government plans

Listening
- *What're you doing now?*
- *I'd really like to …*

VOCABULARY More common activities

A Match the verbs in the box to the groups of words they go with in 1–8.

do	get	go	go for
go to	have	play	write

1 ~ the library / the doctor's for a check-up
2 ~ a meeting with a client / ~ a romantic dinner
3 ~ a few emails / ~ a letter
4 ~ a walk in the park / ~ a run
5 ~ home / ~ fishing
6 ~ some shopping / ~ my homework
7 ~ tennis / ~ baseball
8 ~ something to eat / ~ a taxi home

B Work in pairs. Look at exercise A and find:
a two things people do at work.
b two things students do.
c two things people do if they feel ill.
d two things people do to keep fit.
e two things you did yesterday.
f two things you are planning to do soon.

LISTENING

You are going to hear three conversations about plans.

A 🔊 8.1 Listen and decide which conversation happens:
1 at work.
2 at university.
3 on holiday.

B Compare your ideas with a partner. How did you decide?

C Discuss in which conversation someone:
1 is going to go to a restaurant.
2 arranges where to meet.
3 asks someone out on a date.
4 is going to tell some colleagues about something.
5 doesn't want to meet.
6 is going to fly somewhere soon.

D Listen again and check your ideas.

LANGUAGE PATTERNS

Write the sentences in your language. Translate them back into English. Compare your English to the original.

What're you doing now?
What're you doing after class?
What're you doing this afternoon?
What're you doing tonight?
What're you doing this weekend?

GRAMMAR *be going to* + verb

> We use *be (not) going to* + verb to talk about definite plans and decisions for the future.

> *I'm going to study* in the library.
> *We're not going to come* to the party tonight.
> Where *are you going to eat*?

A Complete the sentences with the correct form of *be going to* + the verbs in brackets.

1 We .... something to eat. (get)
2 I .... to class tonight. I have to work! (not / come)
3 Can I phone you later? I .... running in a minute. (go)
4 My boyfriend and I .... a romantic dinner tonight because it's my birthday. (have)
5 .... you .... at home tonight? (be)
6 I've got a bad back so I .... tennis for a while. (not / play)
7 When .... he ....? (retire)
8 When .... you .... the dishwasher? (repair)

▶ **Need help? Read the grammar reference on page 157.**

> We often pronounce *going to* as /ɡəʊɪŋtə/.

B 🔊 **8.2 Listen. Write the sentences you hear.**

C **Listen again and repeat what you hear.**

D **Tell a partner which things below you are going to do today / tomorrow / this week. Say when.**

a watch TV
b clean the house
c write some emails
d buy some new clothes
e go to bed early
f do some cooking
g do some English homework

DEVELOPING CONVERSATIONS
Making suggestions

> We often make suggestions using *How about ...?*

> A: Do you want to meet somewhere?
> B: Yes, OK. Where?
> A: *How about in the main square at eight?*

A **Put the sentences in the correct order to make a conversation.**

a How about in the main square, under the big clock?
b Is six OK?
c Oh, sorry. Well, how about seven thirty?
d What're you doing later? Are you busy?
e Perfect! See you later. Bye.
f Yes. Great. Where?
g No. Why? Do you want to meet somewhere?
h It's quite early.
i Yes, fine. What time?

B 🔊 **8.3 Listen and check your ideas.**

C **Now have two similar conversations, using places in your town / city.**

D **Respond to the sentences below, making suggestions with *How about ... ?***

1 What do you want to see at the cinema?
2 What are we going to get her for her birthday?
3 What do you want to eat tonight?
4 Do you know a good place to have a party?

CONVERSATION PRACTICE

You are going to have a similar conversation to the ones in *Listening*.

A **Work in pairs. Decide who is A and who is B.**

B **Now have a conversation about your plans. Use these ideas.**

Student A	Student B
What're you doing now?	I'm going to ... What about you?
I'm going to ...	What're you doing later? Do you want to go out somewhere?
Yes, great. Where?	How about ...?
Yes, fine. What time?	How about ...?
Perfect. See you. Bye.	

LISTENING

You are going to hear four people talking about things they want to do.

A The four pictures below show things the people want to do. With a partner, discuss these questions.
- What can you see in each picture?
- What do you think the four people want to do?

B 🔊 8.4 Listen and match each speaker to one of the pictures. Then compare your ideas with a partner.
Speaker 1: Picture ......
Speaker 2: Picture ......
Speaker 3: Picture ......
Speaker 4: Picture ......

C Listen again. Tick ✓ the sentences that are true.
1 a He's from Manchester.
   b He already does kung fu.
2 a She's planning to leave her job this year.
   b Her business is more important to her than having children.
3 a He thinks that retiring is going to be good.
   b He wants to grow flowers.
4 a She wants to be rich.
   b She wants to learn how to drive.

D Read the audioscript on page 176 to check your answers. <u>Underline</u> the words that helped you decide.

E Would you like to do any of the things the people talk about?

a

b

c

d

GRAMMAR *would like to + verb*

We use *would like to* + verb to talk about things we want to do – or hope to do – sometime in the future.
I'd really like to learn Spanish.
I'd like to go to Iran one day. I'm sure it's interesting.

The negative form is *wouldn't like to* + verb. The question form is *Would you / he / she / they like to* + verb.
I wouldn't like to do his job! (= I don't want to do it)
I wouldn't like to live there.
Would you like to go out with me? (= Do you want to?)
Would you like to try some of this food?

A **Complete the sentences with the pairs of words in the box.**

get + lose	leave + get	save + buy
learn + go	retire + relax	start + become

1 I'd like to .... fitter and maybe .... some weight.
2 I'd like to .... sometime in the next ten years and then I'd just like to .... more.
3 I'd like to .... Arabic and .... to Syria.
4 I'd like to .... my own business and .... a successful business person.
5 I'd like to .... home and .... my own apartment.
6 I'd really like to .... some money and .... a car.

B **Work in pairs. Discuss which of the things in exercise A you would like to do. Why?**

Would you like to get fitter?

Yes, I would. I'm really unfit!

No, I wouldn't. I don't need to!

Remember that we use *like / love + -ing / noun* to talk about things we always enjoy or think are good.

We use *would(n't) like / love* + noun or *would(n't) like / love to* + verb to talk about things we want (to do) in the future .

I really like playing volleyball. (= generally)
I'd really like to play tennis this weekend. (= I want to)

I love travelling. (= generally)
I'd love to travel round Europe. (= I want to do this sometime in the future)

C **Choose the correct form of the verbs.**

1 *I'd like to buy / I like buying* a new car sometime soon.
2 *I'd love to go / I love going* shopping. I go every Saturday!
3 *I'd really like to learn / I really like learning* how to play the guitar sometime in the future.
4 *I'd really like to go / I really like going* fishing. I go most weekends. I find it very relaxing.
5 England is OK for a holiday, but *I wouldn't like to live / I don't like living* there. I'm happy here in Italy.
6 *I wouldn't like to shop / I don't like shopping* for food! It's boring, but I know I have to do it.
7 A: *Do you like / Would you like* classical music?
   B: No, not really. I prefer soul and jazz.
8 A: *Would you like / Do you like* a cup of tea?
   B: Oh, yes please. I'd love one.

▶ **Need help? Read the grammar reference on page 157.**

SPEAKING

A **Work in groups. Discuss which of the things below you'd like to do sometime in the future.**
a buy my own house
b have kids
c move to a different country
d speak really good English
e buy a motorbike
f travel round the world
g get married
h eat less meat
i write a book

B **Now tell each other about:**
• a place you'd really like to visit.
• a person you'd really like to meet.
• something you'd really like to do.
• something you'd like to learn.
• something you'd like to stop doing.

READING

You are going to read some short news stories about government plans.

> When you read, you will see words you don't know. Don't worry! Notice words you know and look at other things like numbers and pictures to help you understand the words you don't know.

A Match the headlines below to the news stories on the right. Don't use a dictionary. Use the underlined words you know to help you.

GOVERNMENT TO REDUCE <u>TAX</u>

COUNCIL TO CUT SERVICE FOR <u>YOUNG PEOPLE</u>

GOVERNMENT TO EXPAND <u>AIRPORT</u>

GOVERNMENT TO INTRODUCE <u>NEW ROAD</u> LAWS

COUNCIL TO DEVELOP <u>CITY'S</u> HISTORIC <u>AREA</u>

B Work in pairs. Compare your answers.

C Read the news stories again. Match the words in blue in the texts and headlines to pictures 1–6 or meanings 7–12.

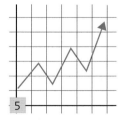

7   make something bigger
8   make something lower / stop spending money on it
9   change something and make it better
10 make something and start it
11 do / have / give something for people
12 help

D Check your answers in a dictionary.

E Work in pairs. Imagine you live in the different places in the news stories. Do you think the plans are good or bad? Try and say why.

1

The government is going to build a new terminal at Moorline. They want to increase the number of flights from 150 to 300 a day. Local people who are against the plan are going to protest tomorrow outside the Department for Transport. They say the expansion is going to cause more noise and pollution.

2

The government is planning to reduce the speed limit on roads from 80 km/h to 60 km/h. It would also like to stop drivers from listening to music in their cars and stop children under 12 sitting in the front seat.

3

The government is going to cut tax for people earning over $100,000 from 50% to 40%. They are also going to make it cheaper for people to buy cigarettes and alcohol.

4

Tapton Council is going to close its three youth centres. The centres provide sports and arts activities for children in the area and also advice for children with problems. The council says it is going to save £1.5 million a year.

Camberhill Council is going to change the old part of the town by knocking down 50 houses and building a park and arts centre. Many of the houses are over 200 years old and the council says they are dangerous. It says the plan is going to improve the city.

5

VOCABULARY For and against

If you are *for* a plan, you think it's good. If you are *against* a plan, you don't like it. We often give a reason:
Local people say it's going to cause more noise and pollution.

In sentences like this, *be going to* shows the results we predict for the future.

A Do 1–10 show people are for or against the plans?
1   It's going to cause more crime.
2   It's going to create jobs.
3   It's not going to save any money.
4   It's going to improve safety.
5   It's going to help business.
6   The government's going to lose money.
7   It's going to provide a service to the community.
8   It's not going to work and it's going to be bad for the environment.
9   It's going to attract tourists.
10 It's going to make people richer.

B Work in pairs. Which sentences in exercise A comment on the government plans in *Reading*?

C Now cover exercise A and complete the verbs.
1   I think it's a good idea. It's going to pr............................ help for a lot of people.
2   I'm against it. It's going to ca............................ a lot of problems.
3   I'm against the idea. It's going to b............................ bad for the environment because of the pollution.
4   It's bad. It's not going to im............................ the economy.
5   I'm against the plan. The city's going to l............................ tourists.
6   I'm for it. It's going to at............................ new businesses.
7   If the plan w............................ , it's going to s............................ money.
8   I'm really for the development. It's going to cr............................ jobs and m............................ the place look nicer.

D Work with a new partner. Discuss your opinions of the plans you talked about in *Reading*, exercise E. Say if you are for or against each one – and explain why.

SPEAKING

A Decide which plans and ideas below you are for and which you are against. Write why.
1   The council would like to build a shopping centre in your area with 100 shops and a car park.
2   The government is going to build high-speed trains.
3   The government is going to increase taxes to improve education.
4   The council wants to cut jobs to save money.
5   The government is going to introduce a law to stop people smoking.
6   The government would like people to retire at 70.

B Work in groups. Discuss your opinions the plans. For example:

I'm for the shopping centre. It's going to create jobs.

Yes, me too. It's going to attract business. And it's going to provide a service for us.

I'm against it. It's going to cause more traffic.

REVISE TOGETHER

CONVERSATION PRACTICE

Work in pairs. Do one of these *Conversation practice* activities.
Family and friends, Unit 7, page 59.
Plans, Unit 8, page 65.

ACT OR DRAW

Work in pairs. One person acts or draws the words. *Don't* speak. Your partner tries to guess the words. Then change roles.

a baby	pollution	protest	a party
a light	fishing	wake up	feed
a dog	a letter	a flight	strong
cry	dangerous	noise	build
run	cigarettes	a clock	repair

QUIZ

Work in groups. Answer as many questions as possible.
1 Who is your **uncle**?
2 Who do you see for a **check-up**?
3 Say two things you can **grow**.
4 Say three examples of **housework**.
5 Why do people tell **jokes**?
6 What's the opposite of **put on weight**?
7 If you **develop** something, is it better or worse?
8 Say two things you can do in a **library**.
9 What's the opposite of **fill** (a bag or dishwasher)?
10 What does a **nanny** do?
11 If you are **for** a plan, do you agree with it?
12 Why do governments sometimes **cut** services?
13 What's the difference between **a colleague** and **a client**?
14 If you **expand** a service, is it bigger or smaller?
15 If a school is **private**, what do you have to do?

FAST WRITER

Work in groups. See who is quickest to write each of 1–6.
1 Six *female* relatives.
2 Six adjectives to describe someone's character.
3 Four questions about future plans.
4 Four sentences with *I / she / we / they + be going to*.
5 Four sentences with *would like*.
6 Two sentences with *have to* and two with *don't have to*.

PRONUNCIATION Diphthongs

We saw in Review 1 that some vowels are two sounds together. They're called diphthongs.

/eɪ/	/aɪ/	/ɪə/	/eə/
date	driver	career	area
/ɔɪ/	/aʊ/	/əʊ/	/ʊə/
noise	cloudy	soul	tourist

A **♪ R 4.1** Listen and say the words and the sounds.

B **♪ R 4.2** Listen and say the single sounds, then the diphthongs. Touch your lips. They move when you say the diphthong.

1 /e/	/ɪ/	/eɪ/
2 /æ/	/ɪ/	/aɪ/
3 /ɪ/	/ə/	/ɪə/
4 /e/	/ə/	/eə/
5 /æ/	/ʊ/	/aʊ/
6 /ɔ/	/ɪ/	/ɒ/
7 /ə/	/ʊ/	/əʊ/
8 /uː/	/ə/	/ʊə/

C **Work in pairs. Try to say these words.**
1 /laʊd/
2 /feə/
3 /tʊə/
4 /klɪə/
5 /enˈdʒɔɪ/
6 /ˈnəʊtɪs/
7 /əˈreɪndʒ/
8 /ˈklaɪənt/

D **♪ R 4.3** Listen and check the words in the audioscript on page 176. Listen again and repeat the words.

E **Work in pairs. Practise saying the sentences. Who has good pronunciation? Which sounds are difficult for you?**
1 I can't find my flight details.
2 Wait outside the hotel in the main square.
3 I'm going to the protest against the new airport.
4 We only employ reliable people here.
5 I do a fair share of the housework.
6 I went on a romantic tour round Paris with my boyfriend.

LISTENING

You are going to hear four conversations.

R 4.4 Listen and choose the correct words for each of the four conversations. Listen twice if you want.

1 The woman *is working / worked* for a car company. She has a daughter who is *18 / six* months old.
2 The man is going to meet her *older / younger* brother. The woman *isn't / is* going to meet him.
3 The photo is of the woman's *brother / cousin*, James, and his girlfriend. James' girlfriend is very *funny / friendly*.
4 They *don't agree / agree* about the government's plan. The man thinks it's going to *cause problems / be good* for business.

[... / 8]

GRAMMAR

A Complete with ONE word in each gap.

1 A: Are you going to .... here for lunch?
   B: Yes, I .... I'm going to leave .... about four o'clock.
2 A: Do you have to work at the weekends?
   B: No, I ....
3 A: Who's going to make the dinner?
   B: We ....
4 A: Your grandad's 98! Can he .... walk?
   B: Yes, he .... , but he's very slow.
5 A: .... you like singing?
   B: Not really.
6 I can't talk. I have .... speak to my boss.
7 I don't speak much English, but my wife ....
8 I .... like to visit Chile next year, but it's very expensive to get ....

[... / 12]

B Make the sentences into negatives (-) or questions (?).

1 I'm going to see him today. (-)
2 She has to come to the meeting. (-)
3 You'd like to be famous someday. (?)
4 I'd like to work for that company. (-)
5 He's going to stay here. (?)
6 I have to wait. (?)

[... / 6]

VERBS

Complete the texts with the verbs in the boxes.

provide	reduce	save	stop

The government wants to [1]........................... the speed limit in cities to 40 km/h. It says the change is going to [2]........................... accidents and [3]........................... money in the health service. The government would also like to [4]........................... more bus services.

create	increase	make	work

The government is going to [5]........................... taxes. It wants to [6]........................... 100,000 new jobs with the money. A lot of people are against the plan because they say it's not going to [7]........................... and it's going to [8]........................... people poorer.

[... / 8]

ADJECTIVES

Complete the adjectives with the missing letters.

1 My dad's very f_ _. He ran a marathon last year.
2 My sister's very c_ _ver. She always gets A grades.
3 My mum was very a_ _ _yed with me yesterday because I didn't clean my room.
4 He's very quiet. He's not very c_ _fi_ _ _t.
5 My brother is very s_ _ _ _tive and he helps me a lot.
6 My grandad is very f_ _ _y. We laugh a lot together.
7 She's very s_ _ _ct with her kids. They can't do anything!
8 It's very l_ _d! Can you turn it down?

[... / 8]

COLLOCATIONS

Match the verbs in the box to the groups of words they go with in 1–8.

attract	check	have	pick up
work	give	repair	stay

1 ~ my email / ~ my flight details / ~ that she's OK
2 ~ a meeting / don't ~ time / ~ a baby
3 ~ my child from school / ~ a friend from the airport
4 ~ business / ~ tourists / ~ people
5 ~ part-time / ~ full-time / ~ late
6 ~ my car / ~ a broken chair / ~ a window
7 ~ in contact / ~ for three nights / ~ in a hotel
8 ~ your opinion / ~ a presentation / ~ it to me

[... / 8]

 [Total ... /50]

09 EXPERIENCES

In this unit, you learn how to:
- talk about your experiences
- share opinions and experiences
- describe good and bad things that happen
- join words together when you speak

Grammar
- Present perfect 1
- Present perfect 2

Vocabulary
- Good and bad experiences
- Describing experiences

Reading
- Put it down to experience

Listening
- On holiday in Turkey
- Different kinds of experiences

SPEAKING

A Work in groups. Look at the photo and discuss the questions.
- Do you know anyone who travels like this?
- Which countries would you like to visit? Why? How would you like to travel?

GRAMMAR Present perfect 1

To find out if someone has a particular experience or not, use the present perfect (*have* + past participle):

A: *Have you been to* Brazil?
B: *Yes (I have). Have you (been there)?*

A: *Have you seen* the Pyramids?
B: *No, (never / I haven't). Have you (seen them)?*

A Complete 1–3 with ONE word in each gap.
1 A: Have you .... to Poland?
   B: No. .... you?
   A: Yes.
2 A: Have you .... that new Clooney film?
   B: Yes, I .... Have .... ?
   A: No. Is it good?
   B: Yes.
3 A: .... you been .... Mexico?
   B: No, we ....
   A: Me neither, but I'd like to go one day.

▶ Need help? Read the grammar reference on page 158.

B Work in pairs. Have similar conversations about countries or cities and / or different films.

When you answer present perfect questions, use the past simple to add details about the experience, such as the time or how you felt.

A: *Have you been* to Budapest?
B: Yes. ~~I've been~~ I went there *last year*.

A: *Have you seen* 'The President's Son'?
B: Yes, I have. ~~I've seen~~ I saw it *on Saturday*. ~~I haven't liked~~ I didn't like it very much.

C Translate the conversations in the box above. Do you use the same tenses in your language?

D Add details in the past simple using the ideas in *italics*.
1 A: Have you ever been to Japan?
   B: Yes, I have. *I / go there last year.*
2 A: Have you been to Moscow before?
   B: Yes. *I / come here a few years ago.*
3 A: Have you ever seen 'The Exorcist'?
   B: I have, but *I / not like it*. I don't like horror films.
4 A: Have you seen 'Mystery Car'?
   B: Yes. *I / see it a few weeks ago. It / be great!*
5 A: Have you been to the cathedral?
   B: Yes, *we / go yesterday. We / love it!*

E Change partners. Have similar conversations to the ones in exercise B, but this time, add details when you answer.

LISTENING

You are going to hear a conversation in Istanbul between a tourist and someone who lives there.

A 🔊 **9.1 Listen. Put the questions in the order you hear them.**

... How long did you spend there?

... Have you been to Topkapi Palace?

... What are you doing later?

... Did you go up the Galata Tower?

_1._ Have you been to Istanbul before?

... Have you seen that film _Berlin_?

... Where have you been?

... When did you arrive?

B **Work in pairs. Discuss what you remember about the answers. Then listen again and take notes.**

C **Work in groups. Discuss these questions.**
- Would you like to go to Istanbul?
- Which tourist places in your country have you never been to?

DEVELOPING CONVERSATIONS
Me too / Me neither

> You can show you share the same opinion, experience, etc. by saying _Me too_. To respond to a negative sentence, say _Me neither_.
>
> A: I want to see it. C: I've never been to Mexico.
> B: _Me too._ D: _Me neither._

A **Work in pairs. Take turns saying the sentences below. Respond with _Me too_ or _Me neither_.**
1 I've been to Thailand.
2 I've never seen _Meet the Parents_.
3 I didn't do anything yesterday.
4 I have to work today.
5 I'm not going to come to class next week.
6 I can speak a few words of German.
7 I can't drive.
8 I'm going to the cinema tonight.

B **Work in groups of three. Find eight opinions, experiences, facts about yourself, etc. that you all share. Don't use questions.**

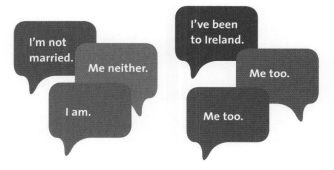

CONVERSATION PRACTICE

You are going to have similar conversations to the one in _Listening_.

A **Work in pairs. Write a list of places to visit or go to at night in the area or country you are studying in.**

B **On your own, imagine you are a visitor. Think of your answers to the questions below about your area / country using some of the places on your list.**
- Have you been here before?
- When did you arrive?
- Where have you been?
- Did you like it?
- Have you been to ... ?
- What are you doing later?

C **Now have your conversations.**
Student A: you are a local person. Ask the questions in exercise B.
Student B: you are the visitor. Answer, using your ideas.

D **Change roles and repeat exercise C.**

VOCABULARY
Good and bad experiences

A Match the experiences 1–9 to the pictures a–i.

1 I failed my exam.
2 I lost the match.
3 Someone stole my bike.
4 My cat died.
5 I forgot to lock the door.
6 I fell off the wall.
7 I broke a window.
8 I criticised my boss.
9 I got divorced.

B Decide if the experiences in 1–9 in exercise A are:
- very serious.
- quite serious.
- not very serious.

C Replace the verbs in 1–9 with the opposites in the box.

supported	climbed onto	found
was born	remembered	passed
repaired	married	won

D Say five things that have happened in the last year using some of the verbs from exercises A and C.
For example:
My brother passed his driving test.

READING

You are going to read a magazine article about what the writer's father told him when he had a bad experience.

A Work in pairs. Before you read, discuss if you agree with each of the sentences 1–4.

1 We all have bad experiences, but it's best to forget them.
2 We need to teach children to be positive and to only talk about success.
3 It's important to have good and bad experiences and it's bad to worry a lot about making mistakes.
4 Children are bad now because they can do what they want and their parents don't criticise them.

B Now read and decide which sentence in exercise A best explains the writer's argument.

PUT IT DOWN TO EXPERIENCE

When I was young and something bad happened to me – I failed an exam, I lost a football match, my cat died, someone stole my bicycle – my dad never criticised me or said I was stupid if I cried. He didn't say, 'It doesn't matter' or 'Forget about it'. He said, 'Put it down to experience'. It was a good expression and I thank my dad for it. 'Put it down to experience' means 'think about everything that happens – both good and bad – as a useful experience'. Negative experiences matter and it's not stupid to feel bad or sad.

You need to remember them so you don't repeat mistakes, but you also need to continue to enjoy life and be open to new experiences.

Unfortunately, in our society, many people think that only good experiences and success are important: passing exams; winning a match; earning lots of money. We only talk about the good things that we have done. At the same time, we criticise every mistake that other people make and try to limit every possibility of bad experiences; parents don't let their children

C Work in groups. Explain your choice. Was there any part of the article you didn't understand? Can your partners help you?

D Work in pairs. Did you like what the writer said? Which of his opinions below do you agree with? Why?
- If people 'forget about it', they repeat their mistakes.
- All experiences are useful.
- In our society, only good experiences and success are important.
- It's not a good idea to try to limit every possibility of bad things happening.
- Politicians and managers do a better job when they have had lots of different experiences.
- Society is better if people feel OK about making mistakes.

LANGUAGE PATTERNS

Write the sentences in your language. Translate them back into English. Compare your English to the original.

Their parents don't let them climb trees.
I don't let my son go out on his own.
They don't let me smoke in the house.
My sister lets me play on her computer sometimes.
My dad let me drive his car when I was younger.

SPEAKING

A Work in groups. Discuss these questions.
- Do you protect your house / flat a lot? How?
- What do / did your parents not let you do?
- What have you learnt from bad experiences?
- Do your parents have a phrase they often say? Can you translate it into English?

play outside and climb trees, or walk to school on their own; and we stay with what we know, living in flats with locked doors and bars on the windows, behind walls with guards.

It's not good. Our politicians, our managers are better when they have had a range of experience, good and bad, in different jobs, with different people. Society is better if people criticise less, worry less and feel OK about making mistakes.

GRAMMAR Present perfect 2

The present perfect is *have* + past participle. Most past participles are the same as the past simple form of the verb:
Have you ever *played* baseball?
(play – played – played)
I've never *had* any success.
(have – had – had)
. . . .
Some past participles have different forms to the past simple:
Have you ever *stolen* something?
(steal – stole – stolen)

A Test each other. Take turns to say the verbs in the box. Your partner should say all three forms.

lose	cry	fail	steal	make
work	win	do	break	fall

B Complete the questions with the correct form of the verbs in exercise A.
1 A: Have you ever .... a prize?
  B: Yes, I came first in a cycle race when I was ten.
2 A: Have you ever .... any bones?
  B: Yes, I broke my arm when I fell down the stairs.
3 A: Have you ever .... something really important?
  B: Yes. Once I left the tickets for my flight in a taxi!
4 A: Have you ever .... off something high?
  B: No, I haven't, but my sister once fell three metres out of a window!
5 A: Have you ever .... an exam?
  B: No, never. I always pass them!
6 A: Has anyone ever .... anything from you?
  B: Yes, someone stole my car a few years ago.
7 A: Do you know anyone who has .... abroad?
  B: Yes, my cousin once had a job in the UK.
8 A: Have you ever .... in public?
  B: Yes. When Michael Jackson died. It was really sad.
9 A: What's the best thing you've ever .... ?
  B: That's a difficult question. Maybe going to Disneyland.
10 A: What's the worst mistake you've ever .... ?
  B: Getting divorced!

▶ Need help? Read the grammar reference on page 158.

C Choose five questions from exercise B and write answers that are true for you.

D Work in pairs. Write the numbers of the questions you have answered. Give them to your partner. Then ask and answer each other's questions.

E Write two more present perfect questions to ask other students in the class. Then ask them.

VOCABULARY Describing experiences

A Match the sentences 1–8 to the pictures a–i.
1 It was really relaxing.
2 It was really annoying.
3 It was really boring.
4 It was really sad.
5 It was really embarrassing.
6 It was really exciting.
7 It was really scary!
8 It was really stressful.

B Work in pairs. Discuss which adjectives in exercise A describe good experiences and which describe bad experiences.

C Which of the adjectives in exercise A can you use to describe these experiences?
a I've met her a few times, but last night I forgot her name!
b I had a nice, long bath last night.
c I nearly fell off my motorbike.
d Someone broke one of my car windows.
e Our dog died last month.
f I had five exams in three days.
g My football team won a really important match.
h I had a four-hour class this morning – without a break.

LISTENING

You are going to hear two people describing experiences they have had.

A 🔊 9.2 Listen and decide which adjective from *Vocabulary*, exercise A best describes each experience.

B Compare your ideas with a partner. Explain your choice.

C Look at these words and check you understand them.
1 countryside – university – lovely – stress – late – breakfast – hills – lucky – warm – outside
2 late – dark – car window – traffic light – jumped – gun – shoot – poor – cash – alive

D In your own language, think about what each person did. Then listen again and check.

E Listen again. Complete the sentences with ONE verb in each gap.
1 a I .... a house in the countryside.
  b We .... a really lovely time.
  c We .... up late every day.
  d We .... nice long breakfasts.
  e We .... outside and chatted until late.
2 a I .... work late.
  b It was very hot, so I .... my car window.
  c I .... at a traffic light.
  d They took me to a poor .... of town.
  e They .... my car, all my cash and my credit cards.

F Work in pairs. Describe each person's experience using the words in exercise C to remind you. Then compare your ideas with the audioscript on page 177.

NATIVE SPEAKER ENGLISH

nice and ...
We often say a noun was *nice and* + a positive adjective.

It was nice and sunny.
It was nice and warm.
The area was nice and quiet.
The people there were nice and friendly.
The test was nice and easy.

PRONUNCIATION Joining words together

> When one word ends in a consonant sound – b, c, d, m, n, p, etc.
> – and the next word starts with a vowel sound – a, e, i, o, u, etc.
> – we join the sounds together.
> **For example:**
> six o'clock.

A **Work in pairs. Decide which words in 1–10 you can join together.**
1 I stopped at a traffic light.
2 A poor part of town.
3 It was awful, but I'm still alive.
4 I rented a house.
5 We sat outside and chatted until late.
6 I can speak a few words of Italian.
7 It was about a week ago.
8 He had an awful accident.
9 It was a really stressful experience.
10 She fell out of a window.

B 🔊 9.3 **Listen and check your ideas. Practise saying the sentences.**

SPEAKING

You are going to describe an experience you have had.

A **Choose one of the sentences in *Vocabulary*, exercise A to describe your experience. Plan what you want to say about this experience. Use a dictionary or ask your teacher for help, if you need to. Think about:**
- when it happened
- where you were
- who you were with
- what happened first, second, etc.

B **Work in groups. Tell each other your stories. Can the other students guess what kind of experience it was?**

10 TRAVEL

In this unit, you learn how to:
- talk about train travel
- buy tickets
- talk about the time
- talk about transport where you live
- recommend places

Grammar
- *too, oo much, too many*
- Superlatives

Vocabulary
- Trains and stations
- Transport

Reading
- *Taxi!*

Listening
- Buying a train ticket
- Asking for recommendations in a hotel

VOCABULARY
Trains and stations

A Check you understand the words in **bold**. Then match the questions 1–8 to the answers a–h.
1. Would you like a **single** or **return**?
2. I'm a student. Do I get a **discount**?
3. Which **platform** is it?
4. Is it a **direct** train?
5. What's causing the **delay**?
6. Which stop do we **get off** at?
7. How would you like to pay?
8. How much is a **first class** ticket?

a. In **cash**.
b. No, you have to change in Munich.
c. 67 pounds – and second class is 39.
d. A return, please, coming back tomorrow.
e. Not the next one, but the one after that.
f. Platform three.
g. There's an animal on the **line**.
h. Yes, you get 15% off.

B Work in pairs. Who usually asks the questions in exercise A – someone travelling or someone who works for the train company?

C Work in pairs. Practise reading the questions and answers in exercise A.

LISTENING

You are going to hear a conversation in a train station in Amsterdam, Holland.

A 🔊 10.1 Listen and answer these questions.
1. What kind of tickets do the passengers buy?
2. How much are the tickets?
3. How do they pay?
4. What time is their train?
5. Which platform do they need?

B Listen again. Complete the sentences with ONE word in each gap.
1. .... can I help?
2. The .... train is at 12.25.
3. It's probably .... to buy two singles.
4. Please .... your pin. Great.
5. You have to .... at Hilversum.
6. How long does the journey .... ?
7. You .... around three o'clock.
8. Thanks for your ....

C Work in groups. Discuss these questions.
- Are trains good or bad in your country? Why?
- Do you have a favourite train journey?
- Are there any train journeys you'd like to make?

LANGUAGE PATTERNS

Write the sentences in your language. Translate them back into English. Compare your English to the original.
How long does the journey take?
The drive usually takes about an about and a half.
It usually takes me half an hour on the train.
It took me three hours to get here today!

PRONUNCIATION *to*

When we use *to* between other words, we often pronounce it /tə/.

A 🔊 10.2 Listen. Write the words you hear.

B Listen again and repeat what you hear.

CONVERSATION PRACTICE

A Work on your own. Decide where you want to go, what kind of tickets you want and when you are going to travel.

B Work in pairs.
Student A: you are buying tickets.
Student B: you are selling tickets.
Make sure you talk about:
- times.
- prices.
- how to pay.
- how long the journey is.
- the platform number.

Now have a similar conversation to the one in *Listening* on the opposite page.

C Change roles and repeat exercise B.

DEVELOPING CONVERSATIONS
Telling the time

We can say times in two different ways. For example:
12.25: *twenty-five past twelve* or *twelve twenty-five*
11.45: *quarter to twelve*   or *eleven forty-five*

Both ways are very common.

A **Match the times to the pictures.**
1 Half past three.
2 Quarter to four.
3 Four fifteen.
4 Five to nine.
5 Five past nine.
6 Six twenty-five.
7 Nine o'clock.
8 Two thirty.

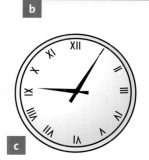

B **Work in pairs. Cover 1–8 in exercise A. Say the times in the pictures a–h in two different ways.**

C **Work in groups. Discuss these questions.**
- What time is it now?
- What time did your class start?
- What time does it finish?
- What time do you usually get up?
- What time did you go to bed last night?
- What time do you usually catch the bus / train in the morning? And what about going home?
- What time do you usually get home?
- What time do you usually have dinner?

VOCABULARY Transport

A Match the words in the box to the group of words they go with in 1–6.

flight	bike	bus	taxi	car	bus

1. get the ~ / the 73 ~ / get off the ~ / wait at the ~ stop / the ~es run all night
2. go in the ~ / get in the ~ / park the ~ / my ~ broke down / they're repairing my ~ / have a sports ~
3. catch a ~ / get the 8.20 ~ / a direct ~ / miss my ~ / pick me up from the ~ station
4. ride my ~ / lock my ~ / fall off my ~ / have a mountain ~ / someone stole my ~
5. get a ~ / stop a ~ / pay the ~ driver / the ~ driver charged too much
6. book my ~ / miss my ~ / the ~'s delayed / ~ FR09 to Rome

B Work in groups. Discuss these questions.

- Do you ever get the bus? What number? Where are the stops you usually get on / off?
- Do you have a bike? What kind? Is it safe to ride a bike where you live? Do people often steal bikes there? Have you ever fallen off a bike?
- Do you have a car? What kind? Is it easy to park where you live? Has your car ever broken down?
- How often do you fly? Have you ever missed a flight? What airlines have you used?

READING

You are going to read some facts and stories about taxis.

A Work in pairs. Before you read, discuss what is good about taxis and taxi drivers.

B Read the texts. Decide if they are true or false.

C Work in pairs. Discuss your ideas. Then check in File 2 on page 166 to see if you were right.

D Work in pairs. Say what you remember about these things, places and numbers in the texts.

1. the hippocampus
2. Puebla
3. 320 and 25%
4. Uzbekistan
5. South Africa and 2,000
6. 7,000 and 300
7. Olden and 550
8. Seoul and 17
9. Europe and one

E Read again and check.

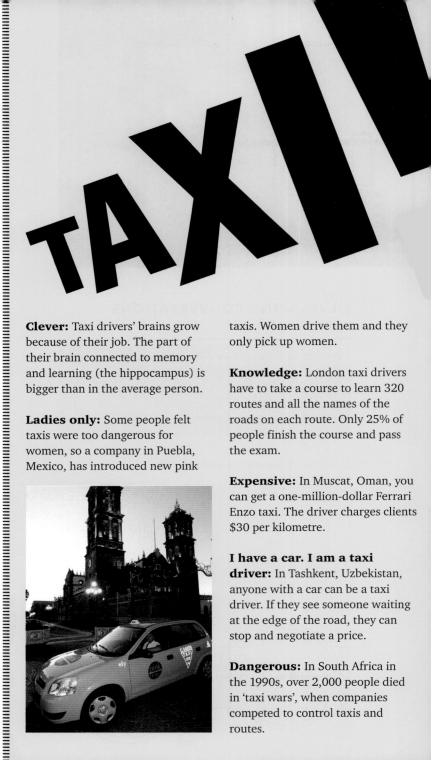
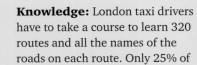

Clever: Taxi drivers' brains grow because of their job. The part of their brain connected to memory and learning (the hippocampus) is bigger than in the average person.

Ladies only: Some people felt taxis were too dangerous for women, so a company in Puebla, Mexico, has introduced new pink taxis. Women drive them and they only pick up women.

Knowledge: London taxi drivers have to take a course to learn 320 routes and all the names of the roads on each route. Only 25% of people finish the course and pass the exam.

Expensive: In Muscat, Oman, you can get a one-million-dollar Ferrari Enzo taxi. The driver charges clients $30 per kilometre.

I have a car. I am a taxi driver: In Tashkent, Uzbekistan, anyone with a car can be a taxi driver. If they see someone waiting at the edge of the road, they can stop and negotiate a price.

Dangerous: In South Africa in the 1990s, over 2,000 people died in 'taxi wars', when companies competed to control taxis and routes.

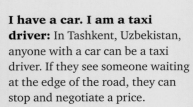
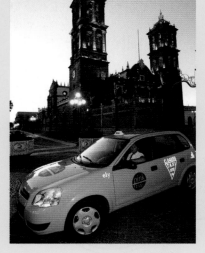

The longest journey: Two old ladies in Australia in 1930 took a taxi on a 7,000-mile trip across the desert, with taxi driver Charles Heard. The trip cost around £300.

Lost in translation: A Spanish couple had to pay $3,000 when they got a taxi in Norway. They wanted to go to Olden but the driver understood Halden – over 550 kilometres further away!

That's better: The city of Seoul, South Korea, provides a translating service in 17 languages for foreigners taking a taxi. Customers can phone a number and get a free translator to speak to the driver.

They're the best: A recent report said Britain has some of the worst transport problems in Europe. It said there's too much traffic; there are too many delays on public transport; and it's too expensive. However, the UK is number one for taxis. International tourists voted on a website. They said Britain's taxi drivers are friendly and reliable: in fact, the best in the world!

GRAMMAR *too, too much, too many*

> ***too* shows something is bad – it's more than we want.**
>
> There's *too much* traffic.
> There are *too many* delays on public transport and it's *too* expensive.
> People drive *too* fast here. It's dangerous.

A Match 1–3 with a–c, based on the examples above.
1 Use *too many* +   c singular / uncountable noun
2 Use *too much* +   b adjective / adverb
3 Use *too*   +   a plural noun

B Choose the correct words.
1 The trains are *too / too many* slow. They need to go faster and run more often.
2 The government says there are *too / too many* accidents in the city, so it wants to reduce the speed limit.
3 I always travel by car. There's *too much / too many* crime on public transport.
4 The buses stop running *too / too much* early. You have to get a taxi after 11 in the evening.
5 *Too many / Too much* people are flying these days. Flights are *too / too much* cheap.
6 There are *too / too many* cars on the road. Travelling to work takes *too / too many* long.

C Work in groups. In three minutes, see how many sentences you can say using *too / too much / too many* about the picture. Which group got the most?

▶ Need help? Read the grammar reference on page 159.

SPEAKING

A Work in groups. Talk about where you live. Think about the things in the box and the questions below.

trains	drivers	pollution	roads and motorways
buses	cyclists	traffic	parking spaces
taxis	flights	accidents	airports

- Are there too many / Is there too much of anything?
- Are these things good or bad in your city? Why?
- How can they be better?

DEVELOPING CONVERSATIONS
Recommending places

> If you recommend a place, you tell someone that you think it's good.

A Match the questions 1–8 to the answers a–h.
1 Where's the best place to eat?
2 Where's the best place to stay?
3 Where's the best place to change money?
4 Where's the best place to go shopping?
5 Where's the best place to go dancing?
6 Where's the best place to go cycling?
7 Where's the best place to get some exercise?
8 Where's the best place to get a haircut?

a Try the park. There are **bike lanes** there, so it's very safe.
b Try Melati's. It's small and friendly, and it has a really nice **atmosphere**. The food is great as well.
c Try Embassy. It's always really busy and the music's great. They have **live bands** every Friday as well.
d Try the post office. They usually give you a good **rate**, especially for dollars.
e Try the Natural Fitness Centre. There's a good gym there and a really nice **swimming pool**.
f Try the big department store in town. They sell a good **selection** of different things.
g It depends what **style** you want.
h Try the Imperial. The rooms are nice and it's not expensive. It's **good value for money**.

B Work in pairs. Discuss what you think the words in **bold** in exercise A mean.

C Now practise having conversations.
Student A: you are a tourist. Ask questions 1–8 in exercise A.
Student B: recommend places you know in your town / city.

LISTENING

You are going to hear a conversation in a hotel. Two guests are talking to a receptionist.

A 🔊 10.3 Listen and answer these questions.
- Which two questions from *Developing conversations*, exercise A do the guests ask?
- Which places does the receptionist recommend?

B Choose the words you heard. Then listen again to check your ideas
1 How *can I / I can* help you?
2 *We like / We'd like* to go out for dinner.
3 It's not the *cheapest / cheaper* place in town.
4 *Need we / Do we need to* book?
5 *Which / What* time would you like your table?
6 What's the *easy / easiest* way to get there?
7 It *takes / spends* about half an hour to walk there.
8 *Do / Would* you like me to book one for you?
9 There's a nice market *in / at* the main square.
10 No problem. *It's my / It was* pleasure.

C Work in pairs. Discuss these questions.
- Are you happy to go to a more expensive restaurant if the food there is very good?
- How much fish do you eat?
- Do you prefer walking or taking a taxi? Why?
- How often do you buy presents for other people?
- What was the last present you bought?

NATIVE SPEAKER ENGLISH

You're welcome
When someone says *Thank you* to us, we often respond by saying *You're welcome*. We often say *No problem* too.

A: *Thanks for everything.*
B: *You're welcome.*

A: *Thanks for your help.*
B: *No problem. You're welcome.*

GRAMMAR Superlatives

> **To compare more than two things, use *the* + superlative adjective.**
>
> **For short adjectives, add *-est*. If they end in *-y*, change to *-iest*.**
> It's not *the cheapest* place in town.
> What's *the easiest* way to get there?
>
> **For longer adjectives, use *the most* + adjective.**
> It's *the most expensive* hotel in town.
>
> **There are also some irregular superlative adjectives.**
> It's *the best* film of the year.
> It's *the worst* club in town.

A Complete the table with superlative forms.

adjective	comparative	superlative
good	better	
bad	worse	
fast	faster	
small	smaller	
early	earlier	
hot	hotter	
boring	more boring	
interesting	more interesting	

▶ **Need help? Read the grammar reference on page 159.**

B Complete the conversations with the superlative form of the adjectives in brackets.

1 A: What's .... way to get back to our hotel? (quick)
   B: Take the underground. It's only two stops away.
2 A: How was Vienna?
   B: Amazing. It's one of .... cities I've ever been to. (beautiful)
3 A: Is it an expensive hotel?
   B: Well, it's not .... place to stay, but it's not .... either. (cheap, expensive)
4 A: Is the crime bad there?
   B: Yes. It's one of .... cities in the world! (dangerous)
5 A: How was your journey?
   B: It was awful – one of .... flights I've had. (bad)
6 A: How's your course going?
   B: It's impossible! It's .... thing I've taken! (difficult)

SPEAKING

A Work in groups. Make questions by changing the words in *italics* into superlatives.

1 Where's *good* place to live in your town / city?
2 And where's *bad* place to live?
3 Where's *old* part of your town / city?
4 What's *easy* way to get around your town / city?
5 Where's *cheap* place to eat?
6 What's *big* city in your country?
7 What's *beautiful* part of your country?
8 What are *popular* places for tourists?
9 Who's *famous* person from your country?
10 What's *important* day in your country?
11 What's *delicious* food from your country?
12 What's *good* time of year to visit your country?
13 And what's *bad* time to visit?

B Now discuss your answers to the questions. Do you agree with the other people in the group?

REVISE TOGETHER

CONVERSATION PRACTICE

Work in pairs. Do one of these *Conversation practice* **activities.**
Experiences, Unit 9, page 73.
Travel, Unit 10, page 79.

ACT OR DRAW

Work in pairs. One person acts or draws the words.
***Don't* speak. Your partner tries to guess the words. Then change roles.**

fall	go up	a platform	find
sign	a cat	a motorway	brain
steal	a race	a bone	climb
a bike	a wall	a mistake	shoot
jump	lock	smoke	break

QUIZ

Work in groups. Answer as many questions as possible.
1 What happens if you **fail** an exam?
2 Which is bigger – a **hill** or a **mountain**?
3 Where do you **wait for a bus**?
4 What causes **delays** to a train or flight?
5 Say two ways you can **pay for** something.
6 Who gets a **discount** on public transport?
7 Say the names of two **airlines**.
8 If a service is **reliable**, is it good or bad? Why?
9 What thing(s) can be **delicious**?
10 Does **good value** mean expensive?
11 What transport can you **miss**?
12 Is it **dark** at night or in the day?
13 What colours are **traffic lights**? What do you do when you see each colour?
14 What's the opposite of **alive**?
15 What does a **guard** do?

FAST WRITER

Work in groups. See who is quickest to write each of 1–5.
1 Six adjectives to describe experiences.
2 Four things you say when you buy train tickets.
3 Four sentences with a superlative.
4 Four present perfect questions.
5 Three things you've done and one you haven't.

PRONUNCIATION
Voiced and unvoiced consonants

In Review 2 we saw that some consonants are said with lots of air (unvoiced). The others in the box below may sound a bit lower because they are said from the throat (voiced).

/θ/	/f/	/p/	/t/	/tʃ/	/s/	/ʃ/	/k/
bath	off	trip	let	catch	bus	cash	lock
/ð/	/v/	/b/	/d/	/dʒ/	/z/	/ʒ/	/g/
the	alive	bike	died	edge	bars	Asia	gun

A ⏺ R 5.1 Touch your throat. Listen and say the words and sounds in the chart. For the words in the bottom row, feel the sound in your throat. Remember to use lots of air for words in the top row.

Remember, with /f/ and /v/, the top teeth touch the bottom lip.
··
With /p/ and /b/, the lips come together.

B ⏺ R 5.2 Listen and say the words with /p/, /b/, /f/ and /v/.

C Work in pairs. Try to say these words.
1 /bɔːn/   5 /dʒʌmp/
2 /kɔːz/   6 /ˈvɪzɪtə/
3 /kɔːs/   7 /ˈfɜːðə/
4 /gɑːd/   8 /dɪvɔːst/

D ⏺ R 5.3 Listen and check the words in the audioscript on page 178. Listen again and repeat the words.

E Work in pairs. Practise saying the sentences. Who has good pronunciation? Which sounds are difficult for you?
1 I travel there first class, or I drive.
2 They have big discounts for old people.
3 The bus broke down in the middle of the road.
4 I can't find a space to park the car.
5 There's a good range of live bands at that bar.
6 Forget about it – it doesn't matter.

LISTENING

You are going to hear four conversations.

R 5.4 Listen and choose the best words. Listen twice if you want.

1 The couple arrived *two / three* days ago. They're having a *relaxing / stressful* time.
2 The customer buys a single ticket. He's *annoyed / happy*. He pays £32.45 *by credit card / in cash*.
3 The woman wants to be at the airport by *6.00 / 7.45*, so she *doesn't have / has* time to go to the museum.
4 The man had a bad experience because *the airline lost / someone stole* his bag. He also broke *a bone / his mobile phone*.

[... / 8]

GRAMMAR

A Put the verbs in the questions in the present perfect and the answers in the past simple.

1 A: *you / ever / be* to Brazil?
  B: Yes. *I / go* there last year on holiday.
2 A: *your son / see* the new Disney film?
  B: Yes. *He / see* it at the weekend.
3 A: *they / visit* America before?
  B: Yeah, *they / come* to see us here two years ago.
4 A: *she / meet* your parents yet?
  B: Yes. *We / have* lunch with them on Sunday.
5 A: *you / try* Indian food?
  B: Once, in London, but *I / not like* it.

[... / 10]

B Correct the mistake in each sentence.

1 That's her goodest book.
2 He have done this hundreds of times.
3 The most easy way to get there is by taxi.
4 I've never readed anything by Günter Grass.
5 His books are too much long.
6 There are too much guns in our society.
7 The Alhambra is most beautiful building in Spain.
8 I've played a really good computer game yesterday.

[... / 8]

ADJECTIVES

Replace each *adjective* in sentences 1–8 with its opposite from the second column.

1 The mountains are quite *far*.   stressful
2 We had a very *relaxing* week.   poor
3 It's a very *exciting* film.   simple
4 It's quite a *rich* area.   near
5 It was a *serious* mistake.   happy
6 The weather was *awful*.   impossible
7 I was very *sad* to leave.   boring
8 It's *easy* to park the car there.   amazing

[... / 8]

COLLOCATIONS

Match the verbs in the box to the groups of words they go with in 1–8.

repair	remember	arrive	lose
repeat	get off	book	charge

1 ~ my car / ~ a broken window / ~ the dishwasher
2 Can you ~ that, please? / ~ the mistake / ~ an exam
3 ~ in London at eight / ~ late / the train ~s at nine
4 ~ a flight / ~ a table / ~ a return ticket
5 ~ the bus / ~ at the next stop / ~ the train
6 I ~ seeing it / I don't ~ his name / ~ to lock the door
7 ~ a lot / they don't ~ for the service / ~ €10 an hour
8 ~ my keys / ~ the match / ~ money

[... / 8]

VOCABULARY

Complete the words in the text.

My grandad was [1]bo...... in 1900 and he died in 2000, one day after his 100th birthday. He had several jobs in his life – he was a taxi [2]dr...... , a teacher and, for 20 years, he was a politician. He had quite a lot of success. He always [3]sup...... public transport and [4]cyc...... , when other people wanted more cars and to build [5]mot...... . He introduced the first bike [6]la...... in the country. Many people criticise politicians, but I think our [7]soc...... is safer and better because of people like my grandad. Unfortunately, he was less lucky in his private life. He got married four times. Two of his wives died and he got [8]div...... twice.

[... / 8]

 [Total ... /50]

11 FOOD

In this unit, you learn how to:
- order and pay in restaurants
- check things
- name different foods
- explain how to cook things
- make offers and invitations

Grammar
- *a lot of, some, any, much, many* and *a bit of*
- Invitations and offers

Vocabulary
- Restaurants
- Food

Reading
- Vegetarians live longer

Listening
- A restaurant in France
- Dinner for friends

SPEAKING

A Work in groups. Discuss these questions.
- How often do you eat in restaurants?
- Do you have a favourite restaurant?
- What do you usually eat when you go out for a meal?
- Who usually pays?

VOCABULARY Restaurants

A Use the extra information in 1–6 to guess the meanings of the words in **bold**. Translate the sentences into your language. Then check in the *Vocabulary Builder*.

1 A: Can we see the **menu**, please?
   B: Yes, of course. Here you are.
   A: Wow! It all looks great.

2 A: Can we have the **bill**, please?
   B: Yes, of course. Here are you.
   A: Thank you. Oh! It's quite expensive. Does this include **service**?
   B: Yes, we add 10%.
   A: OK. So we don't need to leave a **tip**.

3 A: What would you like for **starters**?
   B: Nothing, thank you. I'd just like a **main course**. I'd like a steak, please.

4 A: Can we have a **table** for two, please?
   B: Have you **booked**?
   A: No, I'm afraid not.

5 A: Would you like any **dessert**?
   B: Yes, please. Can I have the ice cream?

6 A: Are you ready to **order**?
   B: Not yet. We're still trying to decide what we want.

B Work in pairs. For each of 1–6 above, decide whether A is the waiter / waitress or the customer. Then put 1–6 in the order you usually hear / say them.

LISTENING

You are going to hear two English people in a restaurant in France.

A 🔊 11.1 Listen. Which six questions from *Vocabulary*, exercise A do you hear? In which order?

B Work in pairs. Discuss these questions.
1 What three problems do they have?
2 What do they order?
3 Do you think they are going to leave a tip? Why? / Why not?

C Listen again and read the audioscript on page 178 to check your ideas.

D Work in pairs. Discuss these questions.
- What do you know about French food? Have you ever tried it? What did you have?
- When you go out for dinner, do you usually have a starter and a dessert as well as a main course?
- Is it better if restaurants include service in the bill or if you can choose how much to leave as a tip? Why?

NATIVE SPEAKER ENGLISH

Can I get ...?
We often say *Can I get ...?* instead of *Can I have ...?* or *I'd like ... .*

Can I get a steak, please?
Can I get some more water, please?
Hi. Can I get a cappuccino, please?
Can we get the bill, please?

DEVELOPING CONVERSATIONS
Checking

> To check things, we can use negative sentences as questions. Our voice goes up when we say these sentences.
> ···
> A: Can we see the menu, please?
> B: Of course.
> A: Ah. *You don't have* English menus?
> B: We don't. I'm sorry, but I can help you.

A Write negative sentences using the verbs in brackets.

1 A: I'm a vegetarian.
  B: Oh really? .... meat? (eat)

2 A: It's cash only, I'm afraid.
  B: .... cards? (take)

3 A: I'm really full.
  B: Yeah? .... any dessert? (want)

4 A: We're very, very busy tonight.
  B: So .... any free tables? (have)

5 A: I'd just like something non-alcoholic.
  B: OK. So .... alcohol? (drink)

B Match A's answers a–e to 1–5 above.

a No, I'm fine. Really. I can't eat anything else.
b No. No meat, no fish. Nothing that moves!
c Not at the moment. Can you wait ten minutes?
d No. I don't like the taste.
e No, I'm afraid not. We don't have a machine.

C ◉ 11.2 Listen and check. Then practise the conversations with a partner.

CONVERSATION PRACTICE

You are going to have a similar conversation to the one in *Listening*.

A Work on your own. Using your own language, write a menu for a restaurant in your country. Include starters, main courses and desserts.

B Work in pairs.
Student A: you are a customer.
Student B: you are a waiter / waitress.

Use the menu you wrote and the plan below for your conversation. Spend three minutes deciding what to say. Then have the conversation.

Student A	Student B
Ask for a table.	Ask if Student A has booked.
Answer.	Show Student A to a table. Give your menu.
Ask about different foods on the menu.	Explain the different foods.
Order.	Invent a problem with Student A's order.
Change your order.	Ask if Student A would like a dessert.
Decide if you want a dessert. Ask for the bill.	

C Now change roles and repeat exercise B.

VOCABULARY Food

A Match the kinds of food in the box to the pictures.

meat	dairy products	fruit	nuts	drinks
fish	vegetables	beans	seafood	

 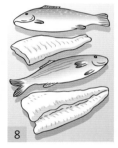 

B Work in pairs. Decide which word does not go in each group in 1–8. Use the sentences below 1–8 to explain why. For example:

1 *They're all things you add for flavour, except water.*

1 salt / sugar / pepper / spices / ~~water~~
2 potatoes / pasta / cream / rice / bread
3 wine / milk / cheese / butter / cream
4 apples / oranges / eggs / kiwis / bananas
5 juice / coffee / carrots / tea / beer
6 lemons / onions / garlic / potatoes / spinach
7 tomatoes / beef / lamb / pork / steak
8 red beans / peas / soya / chicken / broad beans

- They're all basic foods except …
- They're all vegetables except …
- They're all things you add for flavour except …
- They're all drinks except …
- They're all kinds of meat except …
- They're all kinds of beans except …
- They're all dairy products except …
- They're all kinds of fruit except …

C Which of the foods in 1–8 can you see in the pictures?

D Work in pairs.
Student A: look at the pictures in File 6 on page 167.
Student B: look at the pictures in File 8 on page 168.

Take turns to describe the food and draw it for your partner. For example:

It's a kind of seafood. It's pink. It looks like this.

Your partner should write down the name of each food in their own language. When you finish, look at each other's pictures and say if you wrote down the correct names.

E Find out what tastes you and your partner share. Use the patterns below.

I don't like potatoes.	I love apples.
Me neither. / Oh, I do.	Me too. / Oh, I don't.

READING

You are going to read an article about people who don't eat meat.

A Before you read, look at these quotes from famous people. Tell your partner which you think are:
- sensible.
- not very sensible.
- stupid.

'Animals are my friends and I don't eat my friends.'
George Bernard Shaw, writer and Nobel Prize winner

'A human can be healthy without killing animals.'
Leo Tolstoy, writer

'By continuing to eat a vegetaria diet, my weight is under control I like the way I look.'
Carl Lewis, winner of nine Olympi gold medals

'Being vegetarian is the way to go. One of the leading causes of global warming is factory farming.'
Pamela Anderson, actress

B **Read the article below and decide if the sentences are true or false.**

1 Vegetarians have less risk of dying from some cancers than meat eaters.
2 Gandhi was a vegetarian.
3 Most people become vegetarians because it's healthier.
4 The WHO recommends becoming vegetarian.
5 Most Britons eat more than 400 g of fruit and vegetables a day.
6 Some British people eat no fruit or vegetables.

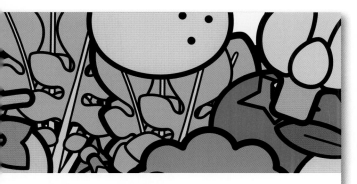

VEGETARIANS LIVE LONGER

A report has shown that a vegetarian diet reduces the risk of dying from heart disease and some cancers by up to 20%. The writer of the report, Andy Bond, looked at a hundred articles in scientific publications such as *The British Medical Journal* and *Cancer*.

The Vegetarian Society of Great Britain, which paid Mr Bond to write the report, started in 1847. The society has had Gandhi and Nobel Prize winners as members. It says that the majority of people become vegetarians for moral reasons: they don't like the way farms keep animals, or they don't approve of killing animals, or they are worried about how eating meat affects the environment. However, the society says it is important to prove that a vegetarian diet is good for your health.

Since 1991, the World Health Organization (WHO) has recommended that people should eat a minimum of five portions (400 g) of fruit and vegetables every day to improve health. The WHO also recommends controlling how much red meat we eat and having good levels of fish oils in our diet.

In Britain, only around 30% of people eat the recommended amounts of fruit and vegetables and a few don't eat any.

GRAMMAR
a lot of, some, any, much, many and *a bit of*

> **We use *a lot of, some* and *any* before nouns to show quantity.**
>
> I eat *a lot of* meat.
>
> I eat quite *a lot of* meat.
>
> I eat *some* meat.
>
> I don't eat *a lot of* meat.
>
> I don't eat *any* meat.
>
>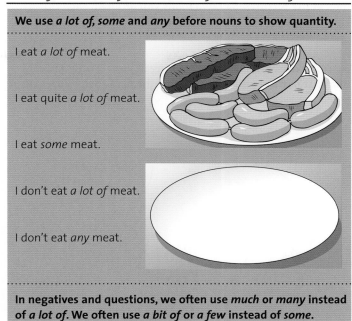
>
> In negatives and questions, we often use *much* or *many* instead of *a lot of*. We often use *a bit of* or *a few* instead of *some*.

A **Decide if the words in *italics* show the same or a different quantity. Where the quantities are different, which quantity is less?**

1 I use *a lot of / a bit of* salt in my cooking.
2 I don't put *much / any* sugar in my coffee.
3 Do you eat *many / any* sweets?
4 I have *some / a bit of* fat in my diet, but not much.
5 I don't drink *a lot of / many* cups of coffee a day.
6 I eat *quite a lot of / some* eggs.

B **Work in pairs. Complete the rules with words from exercise A.**

1 .... , *some* and *any* can go before plural and uncountable (singular) nouns.
2 *A few* and .... only go before plural nouns.
3 *A bit of* and .... only go before uncountable (singular) nouns.

▶ Need help? Read the grammar reference on page 160.

C **Replace the words in *italics* with *much, many, a bit of* or *a few*.**

1 I don't eat *a lot of* sweet things.
2 I read *some* non-fiction, but I mainly read novels.
3 I like *some* of their songs.
4 He doesn't eat *a lot of* fat in his diet.
5 Do you watch *a lot of* TV?
6 We had *some* drinks.

D **Work in groups. Tell each other how much / many of these things you eat or drink.**
For example:
I eat a lot of fruit. I have three or four pieces a day.

fruit	fish	vegetables	sweets
red meat	coffee	chicken	soft drinks

E **Decide who has the best diet.**

VOCABULARY Cooking

A Look at the pictures. Say two foods you often do each thing to. Then compare your ideas with a partner. Did you think of the same foods?

B Work in pairs. Who does the cooking in your family / home? Tell your partner which cooking methods in the pictures they:
- use every day.
- sometimes use.
- don't use very often.
- never use.

C Work in pairs.
Student A: act the eight ways of cooking.
Student B: close your book. Say the words.

D Now change roles and repeat exercise C.

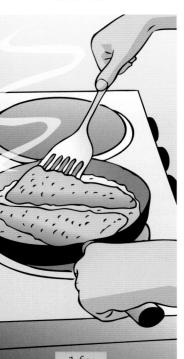

1 fry

2 grill

3 boil

4 roast

5 stuff

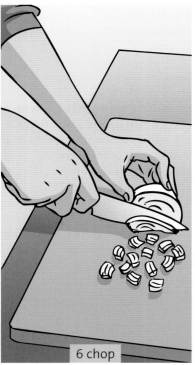

6 chop

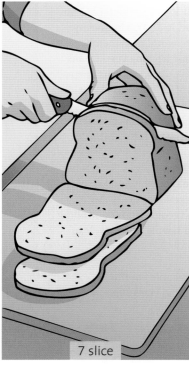

7 slice

8 stir

LISTENING

You are going to hear three friends at someone's house. They are talking about what they have had for dinner.

A 🎧 **11.3 Listen and answer these questions.**
1 What two dishes did they have?
2 Which four cooking verbs from *Vocabulary* did you hear?

B Put the sentences in the order you heard them. Compare your ideas with a partner. Then listen again and check.
a Fry *them* for ten or 15 minutes.
b Would you like me to put the plates in the kitchen?
c Slice each *one* into five or six pieces.
d *They* were really, really good.
e You make *it* sound easy.
f Just put *them* in the sink.
g Would you two like to come?
h Add some salt and pepper – and *it's* ready to eat.

C Work in pairs. Discuss what the six words in *italics* in exercise B refer to. Then read the audioscript on page 179 to check your ideas.

D Work in groups. Discuss these questions.
• Do you think Nicoletta's food sounds good?
• Could you cook it?
• Do you ever invite friends to your home for a meal? When was the last time? What did you cook?

LANGUAGE PATTERNS

Write the sentences in your language. Translate them back into English. Compare your English to the original.
Would you like me to email you the recipe?
He emailed me the address last week.
I emailed the files to you yesterday.
I can send you the details later, if you want.
They sent me a Christmas card last year.
I sent a letter to the hotel last month.

GRAMMAR Invitations and offers

To invite someone to do something, we can use *Would you like to ...?*
Would you like to come to my birthday party next week?

To offer to do something for someone, we can use *Would you like me to ...?*
Would you like me to put the plates in the kitchen?
Would you like me to help with that?

We often offer food / drink by asking *Would you like ...?*
Would you like any more?
Would you like any bread?
Would you like a drink?

A Complete the questions with *Would you like, Would you like me to* or *Would you like to*.
1 .... try a piece of this cake?
2 .... do the washing-up?
3 .... go out for dinner sometime?
4 .... a starter?
5 .... cook for you one evening?
6 .... a cup of coffee?

▶ Need help? Read the grammar reference on page 160.

B Match the answers a–f to the questions 1–6 above.
a Oh, yes, please. I've never tried Iranian food before.
b No, thank you. It stops me sleeping!
c No, thanks. I'm just going to have a main course.
d Yes, OK. Where do you want to go?
e No, it's OK. Don't worry. I can do it later.
f Yes, please. It looks delicious. Did you make it yourself?

C 🎧 **11.4 Listen and check your answers. Then practise asking and answering the questions in pairs.**

SPEAKING

You are going to have a similar conversation to the one you heard in *Listening*.

A Spend five minutes thinking how to cook your best dish or a typical dish from your country. Use as many of the words from this unit as you can.

B Work in pairs. Decide who is the cook and who is the guest. Have a conversation about the meal. Start like this:

> Mmm. This is delicious. How did you cook it?

12 FEELINGS

In this unit, you learn how to:
- talk about health problems
- give advice
- reject advice or offers
- talk about feelings

Grammar
- *should / shouldn't*
- Present perfect 3

Vocabulary
- Health problems
- Feelings

Reading
- Economics and happiness
- Three newspaper articles

Listening
- *Are you OK?*
- A mixed day

LISTENING

You are going to hear five conversations with people who have different health problems.

A Look at the pictures and say which person has a problem with each of these parts of the body.

arm	foot	back	leg	hand	stomach	head

B 🔊 **12.1** Listen to the five conversations and match them to the pictures. There is one picture you don't need.

C Work in pairs. Decide which pair of words goes with which conversation. Try to explain what they said.
1. sick / fresh air
2. doctor / a bad cough
3. hurts / lie down
4. play / stiff
5. broken / cancel

D Listen and read the audioscript on page 179 to check your ideas.

LANGUAGE PATTERNS

Write the sentences in your language. Translate them back into English. Compare your English to the original.

It'll be fine in a couple of days.
I'll be fine in a moment.
It'll be fine by the weekend.
I'll be fine after I have something to eat.
I'll be fine after I warm up.

VOCABULARY Health problems

A Complete the sentences with the words in the box.

burnt	stiff	cut	infection	sick
cough	hurts	cold	headache	hungry

1 Do you have any aspirin? I've got a ....
2 I .... my arm frying an egg.
3 My legs are .... after my run yesterday.
4 That's a bad .... You should stop smoking.
5 I'm going to take the day off. I have a .... I don't want anyone else to get it.
6 You shouldn't carry that if your back ....
7 The doctor said I have a chest ....
8 I .... my foot on a piece of glass.
9 I haven't eaten all day. I'm really ....
10 I feel really ill. I think I'm going to be ....

B Work in groups. Discuss these questions.

- Have you hurt / cut / burnt yourself recently? How?
- Have you ever broken a bone? Which one? How?
- When was the last time you were sick or had a cold / cough / headache? Did you go to the doctor?

GRAMMAR *should / shouldn't*

> We use *should(n't)* + verb to give advice. *Should* shows we think it's a good idea to do the action. *Shouldn't* shows we think it's a bad idea.
>
> You *should stop smoking*.
> You *shouldn't carry* that.

A Work in pairs. Say the advice the speakers gave in the five conversations in *Listening*.

B Work in pairs. Give more advice for each person in the pictures in *Listening*. Use *should / shouldn't*.

▶ Need help? Read the grammar reference on page 161.

DEVELOPING CONVERSATIONS
Rejecting advice and offers

> When we reject an offer or a piece of advice, we often give a reason. We often then ask *Are you sure?*
> ....
> A: Maybe you should lie down.
> B: No, it's OK. I think I'm just hungry.
> A: *Are you sure?*
> B: Honestly, I'll be fine after I have something to eat.

A Write four similar conversations starting with the advice / offers 1–4. Reject the advice / offers and add ideas from the table.

1 Maybe you should go to hospital.
2 Would you like any more?
3 Maybe you should take the day off.
4 You should come out with us.

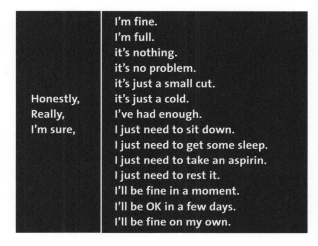

Honestly, Really, I'm sure,	I'm fine.
	I'm full.
	it's nothing.
	it's no problem.
	it's just a small cut.
	it's just a cold.
	I've had enough.
	I just need to sit down.
	I just need to get some sleep.
	I just need to take an aspirin.
	I just need to rest it.
	I'll be fine in a moment.
	I'll be OK in a few days.
	I'll be fine on my own.

B Read your conversations in pairs.

CONVERSATION PRACTICE

A Have conversations with different students. Follow the plan below. For each new conversation, change partner and choose a different problem.

Student A	Student B
Are you OK? / How are you?	Say your problem
Maybe you should / shouldn't ...	Reject the advice
Are you sure?	Yes + reason

VOCABULARY Feelings

A Decide if the words in the box describe positive or negative feelings.

angry	annoyed	excited	happy
relaxed	sad	stressed	tired

B Complete the sentences with words from exercise A.

1 I heard some friends are getting divorced. I was very .... about it. I cried when I heard.
2 On my way to work yesterday, someone almost hit my car. We had an argument. I shouted at him. I was very ....
3 I'm really .... I passed my driving test.
4 I worked from six till seven today, so I was very .... when I got home. I fell asleep watching TV.
5 I was a bit .... because the shop didn't have the book I wanted.
6 I have to do a lot of work this week, and my boss isn't very patient, so I'm feeling very .... at the moment.
7 It's nice to be on holiday – lying on the beach and doing nothing. I feel so ....
8 I'm going to go to France with my school. I'm really .... because it's my first time away without my parents. I'm really looking forward to it.

C Work in pairs. Take turns to act the different feelings in exercise A and to guess the words.

D Which emotion(s) are the words in the box connected with?

cry	look forward to	do a test
fall asleep	smile	lie on a beach
shout	have to wait	

E Tell a partner about the last time you did four of the things in exercise D.

LISTENING

You are going to hear a woman talking about what she did yesterday.

A ⏺ 12.2 Listen to the nine different things that she did and choose how she felt.
1 tired / happy / annoyed
2 angry / sad / excited
3 stressed / tired / relaxed
4 happy / angry / bored
5 positive / annoyed / stressed
6 bored / angry / surprised
7 worried / happy / annoyed
8 excited / relaxed / tired
9 bored / tired / stressed

B Why did she feel each emotion? Compare your answers in pairs.

C Listen again and check.

NATIVE SPEAKER ENGLISH

upset
We say someone is _upset_ if they are sad, worried or annoyed about something that happened.

I was a bit upset, but I tried not to cry.
He was a bit upset that I forgot his birthday.
Don't get upset about it. It's not a big problem.
She was upset because I said I didn't like her idea.

D Work in groups. Describe what you did yesterday.
• Who did you talk to?
• How did you feel about each thing you did?
• Who had the best day.

You are going to read a short article about economics and happiness.

A Read the article and decide what you think is:
- surprising.
- not surprising.
- a good idea.
- a bad idea.

B Work in groups and discuss your ideas.

ECONOMICS AND HAPPINESS

The economist Daniel Kahneman interviewed women in Texas to compare how happy different things made them feel. They were less happy at work, doing housework and, worst of all, travelling to and from work. But, they enjoyed spending time with relatives like aunts and uncles more than spending time with their children!

Another economist, Richard Leyard, has suggested governments should worry less about trying to make the country richer and do more to make people happy. Here are some of his ideas:

- Increase taxes on high salaries so that people don't want to work so hard.
- Don't let children under 12 see adverts because it makes them want things they can't have.
- Provide more help for people who have depression.
- Don't change education, healthcare, etc. too much, because a lot of change worries people.
- Have lessons at school on how to be a good parent.

C Make a list of the four things that make people happiest.

D Work in pairs. Discuss your ideas and try to agree on the same choices.

SPEAKING

A Read the text. Then discuss the questions in groups.

Positive News is an international newspaper that comes out every three months. As you can tell from its name, the paper looks at good news stories and tries to tell the general public about people who are working to improve the world. The paper also has special youth pages, so young writers can tell young readers about what they are doing to change society and the environment for the better.

The paper has offices in the UK, USA, Hong Kong, Spain and Argentina, and now has over a quarter of a million readers. It is free, but any readers who want to offer money for it, can!

- Do you think Positive News is a good idea?
- Would you like to read it? Why? / Why not?
- Can you remember the last positive news story you heard or read?
- Why do you think positive news stories don't appear more often in normal newspapers or on the TV news?

READING

You are going to read three short newspaper articles.

A Before you read, match the headlines below to the groups of words 1–3.

HEAVY RAIN

FAST-FOOD FIGURE GOES FAST

LOST MAN FINDS HIS MISSION

1 got lost – looked after – raised more than one million dollars – education – bridges
2 sailors – court – statue of Ronald McDonald – threw – arrested
3 floods – escape – government – rise – worse

B Work in pairs. Explain your decisions. Discuss what you think each article is about, using the groups of words.

C Now read the articles on the opposite page and see if you guessed correctly.

D Work in pairs. Say what happened in each story, using the words in exercise A.

E Work in pairs. Say which articles you think describe positive news. Explain why.

GRAMMAR Present perfect 3

We can use the present perfect to talk about actions that happened sometime before now, but have a present result. We don't use it with past time expressions (e.g. *yesterday*, *a few days ago*).

Over 1,000 families *have left* their homes. (now they have nowhere to live)

A Find six more examples of the present perfect in the articles.

B Complete the sentences with the present perfect form of the verbs in the box.

| arrest | die | escape | raise |
| go up | send | save | start |

1 Sailors .... the lives of more than 100 people in the Indian Ocean.
2 The wives of hundreds of policemen .... letters to the government, saying their husbands need more money.
3 Talks between the US and China .... in Beijing.
4 Six people .... on the roads today following heavy snow last night.
5 House prices .... by 150%.
6 Police .... a man for stealing 200 metres of train line.
7 Three dangerous men .... from a police station.
8 A little boy .... over £500,000 in six months.

▶ Need help? Read the grammar reference on page 161.

SPEAKING

A Work in pairs. Choose one of the sentences from *Grammar*, exercise B, and write a news story about it. Start with the sentence you have chosen.

B Work with another pair. Read your news stories.

In 1993, Greg Mortenson got lost trying to climb the mountain K2 in Pakistan. Some village people found him and looked after him until he was well. Greg thinks they saved his life. To say thank you, he decided to help them by starting a charity to build schools. He has raised more than one million dollars and has helped more than 30,000 children to get a better education. His organisation has opened over 80 schools and it has also helped to build roads, bridges and health centres.

At least 15 people have died after heavy rains caused floods in southern Thailand. Over 1,000 families have left their homes to escape the waters and the government has closed several schools in the area. Water levels are continuing to rise and the situation is probably going to get worse.

Two British sailors appeared in court in Chile yesterday after they stole a plastic statue of Ronald McDonald from outside a McDonald's in Valparaiso – and threw it into the sea. The sailors' boat stopped in the city on Monday and police arrested the men later that day. They had to pay £350 and have now left the country!

CONVERSATION PRACTICE

Work in pairs. Do one of these *Conversation practice* activities.
Food, Unit 11, page 87.
Feelings, Unit 12, page 93.

ACT OR DRAW

Work in pairs. One person acts or draws the words. *Don't* speak. Your partner tries to guess the words. Then change roles.

kill	rest	throw	lie down
stiff	hit	a flood	hungry
smile	fry	grill	a bridge
burn	chop	slice	a disease
a bird	juice	order	a cough

QUIZ

Work in groups. Answers as many questions as possible.
1 Say two things you often **carry**.
2 If you **recommend** something, is it good?
3 If something **rises**, does it go up or down?
4 Who **arrests** people, and why?
5 What don't **vegetarians** eat?
6 Say two things that make people **stressed**.
7 What do you take if something **hurts**?
8 Say the names of two **courses** you have at dinner.
9 Where do you leave **a tip**? What for?
10 What do people feel and do if they have **an argument**?
11 If you come first in a race, what **medal** do you get?
12 What do you **roast** food in?
13 Do **soft drinks** have alcohol?
14 Say three things you **add** to improve taste.
15 How do you feel if you're **looking forward to** something?

FAST WRITER

Work in groups. See who is quickest to write each of 1–6.
1 Eight parts of the body.
2 Six kinds of food.
3 Six questions a waiter or customer asks in a restaurant.
4 Two sentences with *should* and two with *shouldn't*.
5 Four sentences with the present perfect.
6 Four offers with *Would you like ...?*

COLLOCATIONS

A **One student reads a group of collocations from Unit 11 of the *Vocabulary Builder*. Where there is a '~', say 'blah'. Your partners guess the word. Who guesses the most?**

Watch *blah*, have a big *blah*, turn on the *blah*, a *blah* programme.

TV?

That's right.

B **Now do the same with Unit 12 of the *Vocabulary Builder*.**

PRONUNCIATION Long vowel sounds

Some single vowel sounds are a bit longer than others. In a dictionary, these sounds are marked with the symbol ː.

/iː/ meat	/ɪ/ sick	/ʊ/ foot	/uː/ youth
/e/ leg	/ə/ cancel	/ɜː/ hurt	/ɔː/ warm
/æ/ hand	/ʌ/ rush	/ɑː/ arm	/ɒ/ cough

A ✿ R 6.1 Listen and say the words and the sounds.

B ✿ R 6.2 Listen and say the first sound and then say the second one. Make sure the second one sounds longer. Then say the words.

C **Work in pairs. Try to say these words.**
1 /stɜː/
2 /pɔːk/
3 /əˈsliːp/
4 /fɑːmɪŋ/
5 /ˈɪntəvjuː/
6 /ˈsiːfud/
7 /ˈstætʃuː/
8 /əˈpruːv/

D ✿ R 6.3 Listen and check the words in the audioscript on page 180. Listen again and repeat the words.

E **Work in pairs. Practise saying the sentences. Who has good pronunciation? Which sounds are difficult for you?**
1 They serve big portions.
2 I hurt my arm and burnt my hand.
3 We eat beef and chips on Tuesdays.
4 They appeared in court for stealing a statue.
5 We asked for pork with cream sauce.
6 Warm up well before you start to play.

LISTENING

You are going to hear four conversations.

♻ R 6.4 Listen and decide if the sentences are true or false. Listen twice if you want.

1 a The man's at someone's house.
   b He has a potato and seafood soup and some water.
2 a They are eating a vegetarian dish.
   b He roasted the food in the oven.
3 a The woman feels ill.
   b She's going to go to the doctor.
4 a He's nervous because he has exams.
   b He's studying medicine.

[... / 8]

GRAMMAR

A Complete with the present perfect form of the verbs in brackets.

1 He's in hospital. He .... his leg. (break)
2 They .... one million pounds to build schools. (raise)
3 I .... anything yet. What would you like? (not order)
4 .... they .... a service charge? (include)
5 .... you .... any salt or pepper? (add)
6 We .... the day off. (take)

[... / 6]

B Choose the correct words.

1 I need to send *a few / a bit of* emails.
2 There's not *many / much* risk of rain today.
3 Would you like *us to drive / that we drive* you there?
4 We don't use *a lot of / much* spices in our cooking.
5 I don't eat *any / much* pork because it's against my religion.
6 I*'ve had / had* a chest infection last month but I'm better now.

[... / 6]

C Complete the sentences with ONE word in each gap.

1 A: I have a headache.
   B: Maybe you .... lie down.
2 A: Would you like .... to get you a glass of water?
   B: Please.
3 A: What .... you done to your leg?
   B: I fell over yesterday and cut it.
4 I think there are too .... adverts on TV.
5 I feel a bit sick. I need to get .... fresh air.
6 I didn't have .... money, so I couldn't buy it.

[... / 6]

ADJECTIVES

Complete the sentences with words from the box.

delicious	excited	scientific	high
annoyed	healthy	bored	full

1 The film was really slow and I got quite ....
2 I can't eat anything else. I'm really ....
3 Our company does a lot of .... research.
4 I'm .... about the trip. It's going to be great!
5 How did you make this soup? It's ....!
6 I have quite a .... diet.
7 I was .... because he criticised us.
8 Doctors don't get very .... salaries in my country, so a lot of them move abroad.

[... / 8]

COLLOCATIONS

Match the verbs in the box to the groups of words they go with in 1–8.

boil	prove	escape	stop
save	leave	affect	cancel

1 ~ the floods / ~ from prison / ~ from the war
2 ~ some water / ~ the potatoes / ~ for 10 minutes
3 ~ it's healthy / ~ it causes cancer / ~ it wrong
4 ~ money / ~ his life / ~ 100 people from the flood
5 ~ the country / ~ a tip / have to ~ your home
6 ~ your health / ~ the environment / ~ us
7 ~ smoking / ~ for a rest / ~ me sleeping
8 ~ the meeting / ~ my flight / ~ my credit card

[... / 8]

VOCABULARY

Complete the words in the text.

I'm trying to keep my ¹we...... under control. I don't fry my food – I usually ²bo...... it or eat things like salad with a little olive ³o...... . I eat lots of fruit and ⁴ve...... and I don't eat red meat, because it has too much ⁵f...... . I don't have too much salt either because I read a ⁶rep...... that said it can cause heart ⁷dis...... . You need to look ⁸a...... yourself here because healthcare is very expensive.

[... / 8]

 [Total ... /50]

13 NATURE

In this unit, you learn how to:
- talk about the weather
- talk about possibilities in the future
- ask for details
- talk about the countryside and cities
- talk about animals
- talk about national symbols

Grammar
- *might* and *be going to*
- Passives

Vocabulary
- Weather
- Country and city
- Animals

Reading
- Six reasons not to ...

Listening
- *What's the forecast?*
- National symbols

VOCABULARY Weather

A Describe the weather in the photos below with the words in the box.

hot	snow	rain	ice	sunny	cloudy
wet	warm	cold	dry	windy	storm

B What kind of weather do you think goes with these seasons?

autumn	winter	spring	summer

C Which parts of your country have the best / worst weather? Why?

LISTENING

We ask about the weather by saying *What's the forecast for today / tomorrow etc.?* We start the reply with *It / They said ...*

A: *What's the forecast for today?*
B: *They said* it's going to rain.

You are going to hear three conversations in which people decide what to do.

A 🔊 **13.1** Listen. Find out the forecast and what the people decide to do.

B Work in pairs. Practise reading the conversations in the audioscript on page 180.

GRAMMAR *might* and *be going to*

We use *might* + verb and *be going to* + verb to talk about the future. *Might* shows possibility. *Be going to* shows certainty.

It *might rain* this morning, but *it's going to be* dry this afternoon.

A Complete the sentences with *might* or the correct form of *be going to*.

1   A: What are you doing later?
    B: I .... go shopping, but I'm not sure.
2   A: What are they doing to that church?
    B: They're knocking it down. They .... build some flats there.
3   A: What are you going to do when you leave school?
    B: I'd like to continue studying, but I .... have to get a job. Our family needs the money.
4   A: What's the forecast for tomorrow?
    B: They said it .... possibly snow! It .... definitely .... be cold, though.
5   It said on the news it .... continue to rain for the next two days. There .... possibly be some flooding.

▶ Need help? Read the grammar reference on page 162.

B Work in pairs. Say the forecast for today / tomorrow / the weekend. Use *might / be going to*.

C Write four things you might do in the next week, month or year. Why are they just possibilities – because of the weather / money / other people / some other reason?

D Work in groups. Explain your ideas to each other.

LANGUAGE PATTERNS

Write the sentences in your language. Translate them back into English. Compare your English to the original.
Why don't we just relax this morning?
Why don't we go to the swimming pool?
Why don't you talk to him about it?
Why don't you go to the doctor?
Why don't I do it for you?

DEVELOPING CONVERSATIONS
Short questions

In conversation, we often use short questions without verbs.

A: Why don't we go to the swimming pool?
B: We could do. *Which one?*
A: The open-air one.

A Read the conversations. Choose the best short question to complete each one.

1 A: Why don't we go and see a film?
   B: Maybe. *Where? / What film? / What time?*
   A: There's a showing at 8.40.
2 A: I might go for a walk later.
   B: Really? *Who with? / When exactly? / Where?*
   A: Just on my own – unless you want to come.
3 A: Do you want to go into town later?
   B: Maybe. *How? / What for? / What time?*
   A: To have a drink or something.
4 A: Why don't we take a holiday?
   B: We could do. *How long for? / When? / Where?*
   A: Just a few days.
5 A: Why don't you invite some friends for dinner?
   B: *Who? / Why? / When?*
   A: Do you need a reason? It's a nice thing to do!
6 A: Why don't we go to the beach?
   B: We could do. *Which one? / What time? / How?*
   A: We can get a bus.

B Work in pairs. Practise the conversations.

C Change partners. Say the first line of the conversations. Your partner uses a different short question. Then give a different answer.

CONVERSATION PRACTICE

You are going to have similar conversations to the ones you heard in *Listening*.

A Work in pairs. Look at the plan below and think about what you are going to say for one minute.

B Have a conversation. Then change roles.

Student A	Student B
What / want to do?	What / forecast?
Answer	Why don't … ?
Ask a short question	Answer
OK, let's do that!	

READING

You are going to read a blog called *Six reasons not to ...*

A Read the introduction and complete the title.

SEARCH BLOG

SIX REASONS NOT TO ...

Cities are man's greatest invention. They are creative places; they are places where you can be who you want to be; they are even good for the environment. So why do people want to live in the countryside? Here are six reasons why you shouldn't.

B Work in groups. Discuss these questions.
- Do you agree that cities are a great invention?
- How are they good for the environment?
- What reasons do you think the writer is going to give?

C Read the rest of the blog on the right and find out the six reasons she gives.

D Decide if the sentences are true or false, according to the blog.
1. Everything in the country is natural.
2. The author is scared of cows.
3. All the shops close early.
4. It's easy to make good friends in the countryside.
5. It's difficult to keep your clothes clean.
6. The scenery isn't varied enough in the country.

E Work in pairs. Say which reasons you think are:
- funny   - wrong
- stupid   - interesting
- true   - strange

NATIVE SPEAKER ENGLISH

Not a hope
We use *not a hope* to say something is totally impossible.

Can you buy milk at eight o'clock in the evening? Not a hope!
A: Do you think you can finish the work by tomorrow?
B: No. Not a hope!
They don't have a hope of winning

SEARCH BLOG

THE SMELL

People say the country has fresh air, but don't breathe too deeply! The country is full of animals: pigs, cows, horses. They all smell bad and none of them use a toilet or wash their hands. And farmers put chemicals in the fields. The country's not fresh – it's horrible!

Evil eyes

THE COWS

I once walked across a field, and a group of cows started following me. It made me nervous – their big eyes looking at me, following me. There was a wall at the end of the field and the cows were following me – and their eyes! I couldn't escape. I started running. I jumped onto the wall. And they were still there – those huge eyes: the cows, looking at me. I still have nightmares about it. I don't like cows.

THE SHOPS

The country may be full of cows, but can you buy milk at eight o'clock in the evening? Not a hope! And if you want to buy anything during the day, you have to travel half an hour by car to get it!

THE PEOPLE

You often live quite a long way from other people and your choice of friends is limited, so living in the country means spending a lot of time with your family. I love my family, I really do, but I don't want my best friends to be my mum and my dog!

THE DIRT

The countryside is covered in soil and grass, and it rains a lot – not a good combination if you want to wear white clothes or nice shoes!

THE SCENERY

OK, I like mountains. I wouldn't like to climb one, but they're nice to look at. They're impressive. The problem is, the countryside doesn't have enough mountains. Travelling by train, you look out of the window, what you see is a field, another field, another field, a few trees, a field, another field, a farmer in a field, field, field, cows (argghhhh!), field, field. It's just very, very boring!

No people, no shops, just fields

Recent posts

SIX REASONS NOT TO ...

… have a boyfriend.
… take the bus.
… like *Friends*.
… watch sport.
… vote.
… drink beer.

VOCABULARY Country and city

A Work in pairs. Put the words into two groups – country and city. There should be 12 in each group.

agricultural	fields	noisy
traffic lights	a factory	hills
a block of flats	a cottage	a horse
crime	hunting	grass
convenient	slow	traffic
a farm	soil	crowded
a shopping centre	crops	polluted
entertainment	a park	peaceful

B Work in pairs. Take turns to act or draw the words. Your partner says the word.

C Complete the two descriptions with words from exercise A.
1 I live on the second floor of a [1]......................... near the centre of town. It's quite crowded and noisy, but it's [2]......................... for shops and work. I walk everywhere. There's also a huge choice of [3].........................: live sport and music, theatres, cinemas, shopping centres, bars, restaurants – everything.
2 We live in a little [4]......................... in a village in the north. City life is too fast for me. I prefer a more [5]......................... life. It's a big [6]......................... area. The soil's very good. The main [7]......................... they grow are potatoes and other kinds of vegetables. There are also some dairy farms. It's usually nice and quiet, but occasionally people go [8]......................... in the fields near here. They shoot birds and rabbits.

D Work in groups. Discuss these questions.
- Which place do you prefer in exercise C?
- Is your life slow or fast? Why?
- How convenient for shops / work is the place where you live?
- What entertainment is there where you live? Are you good at making your own entertainment?
- What's the countryside like in your country? What are the main crops? Where do they grow?
- Are there any factories near you? What do they produce?
- Have you ever ridden a horse? Did you like it?
- What hills or mountains are there near where you live? Have you been to the top of any of them?

VOCABULARY Animals

A Work in groups. Look at the animals in File 7 on page 168. Discuss these questions.
- Do you know anybody who has any of these animals?
- Which animals are common in your area?
- Which animals hunt?
- Which can run fast?
- Which eat meat?
- Which animal makes the best pet? Why?
- Which do you normally find in the wild?

B Close your books. Can you remember all nine animals?

LISTENING

You are going to hear two people talking about the national symbols in the photos.

A Look at the words in the box and check you understand them. Work in pairs. Discuss which words you think are connected to which photo and why.

cut down	protected	the desert	protein
dye	a radar	entertainment	valuable
leather	a violin bow		

B ⊘ 13.2 Listen and check your ideas. Discuss with a partner which words are connected to which photo – and how.

Kuwait - camel

Brasil - Pau Brasil tree

C Listen again and complete the notes below.

CAMELS

Three ways camels are better than horses:
1 Need less [1].................... and [2].................... .
2 Can carry more.
3 They're [3].................... and more intelligent.

Three things camels provide:
1 Milk - very good for you.
2 Meat - low in [4].................... .
3 [5].................... - used to make leather.

Camel racing popular, but debate about the use of [6].................... to ride them.

PAU BRASIL TREE

Can grow up to [7].................... high.

In the past, the tree was found all along the [8].................... .
Beautiful wood - an [9]....................- [10].................... colour.

Production of chemical dyes started in the [11].................... .
This helped save trees.

Pau Brasil now protected [12].................... .

GRAMMAR Passives

> We form passives with the verb *be* + a past participle. We use passives if we don't know who does an action or if it's not important who did it.
>
> ⋯⋯⋯⋯⋯⋯⋯⋯⋯⋯⋯⋯⋯⋯⋯
>
> The national tree of Brazil *is called* 'Pau Brasil'. Camel skins *are* sometimes *made* into leather. It *was found* all along the Atlantic coast. Lots of trees *were cut down*.

A Work in pairs. Say the past participles of the verbs in the box.

cut down	find	eat	sell
introduce	hunt	use	protect

B Complete the sentences with the correct form of the verb *be* and the past participles of the verbs in brackets.

1 Our national plant …………………………………… for making medicine. (use)
2 The rubber tree …………………………………… into Liberia in the early 1900s. (introduce)
3 Elephants …………………………………… in both Asia and Africa. (find)
4 Kangaroo steaks ………………… sometimes ………………… in Australia. (eat)
5 For many years, tigers …………………………………… for their skins, but now they …………………………………… by law. (hunt, protect)
6 In the past, many trees …………………………………… and the wood …………………………………… for a lot of money. (cut down, sell)

▶ Need help? Read the grammar reference on page 162.

> We sometimes show who does an action, using *by*.
>
> ⋯⋯⋯⋯⋯⋯⋯⋯⋯⋯⋯⋯⋯⋯⋯
>
> Camel meat is eaten *by some people*.

C Work in pairs. Discuss who you think did each of the actions below.

1 He was arrested last night by … .
2 The new law was introduced last month by … .
3 My trip to Japan was paid for by … .
4 Paper was invented by … .
5 The *Harry Potter* books were written by ….. .

D Write three questions that you know the answer to, using the pattern below. Then ask other students.

> Who was … invented / written / sung / painted by?

PRONUNCIATION Passives

> When we say passives, we often use the contractions of *is* and *are* or weak forms of *was* and *were*. This means the forms of *be* are often difficult to hear.

A 🔊 13.3 Listen and repeat what you hear.

B Listen again. Write the sentences you hear.

SPEAKING

A Work in groups. Discuss these questions.

- Does your country have a national animal / tree / flower? Do you know what it is? How much do you know about it?
- What could you tell someone from another country about:
  - your country's national sport?
  - your country's national dish?
  - your country's national heroes?
  - people who have done great things and are loved by many people in your country?
- What do you think is the best thing about your country?
- Are there any things you don't like about it?

14 OPINIONS

In this unit, you learn how to:
- give your opinion about films, plays and musicals
- ask for descriptions and opinions
- discuss news and newspapers
- make predictions about the future
- talk about society and social issues

Grammar
- *will / won't* for predictions
- Verb patterns with adjectives

Vocabulary
- Describing films, plays and musicals
- Society

Reading
- A new life

Listening
- Opinions about films and musicals
- A news report

SPEAKING

A Work in pairs. Discuss these questions.
- What's the difference between a film and a play?
- What's the difference between a musical and a concert?
- When was the last time you went to the cinema, the theatre or to a concert? What did you see? What did you think of it?

VOCABULARY Describing films, plays and musicals

A Complete the sentences with the adjectives in the box.

predictable	brilliant	funny	strange
entertaining	sad	scary	terrible
depressing	violent		

1 It was .... It really made me laugh.
2 It was really .... I cried a lot at the ending.
3 It was very .... There was a lot of killing and a lot of blood in it.
4 It was really .... I spent half the time hiding behind the sofa.
5 It is very .... After ten minutes, you know how it's going to end.
6 It was .... – one of the best things I've ever seen in my life.
7 It was .... – one of the worst things I've seen in a long time.
8 It was very .... – very unusual.
9 It was very .... I felt sad for days afterwards.
10 It was really .... I really enjoyed it.

B Work in pairs. Which of the descriptions in exercise A do you think are positive and which are negative? Why?

LISTENING

You are going to hear two conversations. In the first, the people talk about a film. In the second, they talk about a musical.

A ⏺ 14.1 Listen and answer these questions about each conversation.
1 Have both people seen the film / musical?
2 If yes, what was each person's opinion of it?
3 If no, do you think the second speaker would like it? Why? / Why not?

B Try to complete each of the sentences below with ONE word. Compare your ideas with a partner. Then listen again and check.
1 a Have you ever seen a film .... *28 Days Later*?
  b I've heard .... it, but I've never seen it.
  c What's it .... ?
  d It .... terrible!
  e No, it's great! ....
2 a What did you think .... it?
  b It was quite entertaining in .... , I suppose.
  c The .... and the music were great.
  d But what about the .... ?
  e I .... it really sad.

LANGUAGE PATTERNS

Write the sentences in your language. Translate them back into English. Compare your English to the original.
I found it really sad.
I find grammar really difficult.
How are you finding the course?
I can't find my keys.
I found £20 on the street yesterday.
Did you find your phone?

C Work in pairs. Discuss these questions.
- Would you like to see *28 Days Later* or *Dogs*? Why? / Why not?
- Can you think of something you found: really scary? too violent? very predictable?

CONVERSATION PRACTICE

You are going to have conversations like the ones in *Listening*.

A On your own, make a list of six films, plays and musicals you have seen – and concerts you have been to – in the last few months.

B Work in pairs. Take turns asking if your partner has seen the things on your list. If they have not seen it, they should ask *What was it like?* If they have seen it, they ask *What did you think of it?* Continue the conversations.

DEVELOPING CONVERSATIONS

What's it like?

If we want someone to describe something or someone, we often ask *What is / was ... like?*

A: I've never seen it. *What's it like?*
B: It's brilliant. It's really, really scary.

A Match the questions 1–8 to the answers a–h.

1 What was the film like?
2 What was the acting like?
3 What was the band like?
4 What was the ending like?
5 What's the food like there?
6 What's your boss like?
7 What're your parents like?
8 What was your holiday like?

a Very sad. I couldn't stop crying.
b She's great. She's very easy to talk to.
c Quite good. They played their roles very well.
d It started well, but I didn't like the ending.
e Oh, it was wonderful. It was very relaxing and we were very lucky with the weather.
f They were great. They played for two hours and did all their most famous songs.
g My mum's great, but I don't get on with my dad.
h Amazing! They do a delicious garlic chicken!

B Work in pairs.
Student A: ask the questions in exercise A.
Student B: read the answers.

C Change roles.
Student B: ask the questions in exercise A.
Student A: invent your own answers.

D On your own, write three *What is / was ... like?* questions for other students in the class. Then ask them.

SPEAKING

Work in groups. Discuss these questions.
- Do you ever read newspapers? Which one / s? Why?
- Are there any newspapers you don't like? Why not?
- Do you ever watch the news on TV or listen to the news on the radio? If yes, how often?
- What are the big news stories at the moment? What do you think about them?
- What kind of news stories can you see in the photos below? Would you like to read about each story?

LISTENING

You are going to hear a news report.

A Work in pairs. Discuss in which order the different kinds of news usually appear on news reports.

sports news	international news
show business news	national news
financial news	the weather forecast

B 🔊 **14.2** Listen and put the different kinds of news in exercise A into the order you hear them. There is one you don't need.

C Compare your answers with a partner and say how you decided.

D The groups of words 1–5 come from the news stories. Listen again and take notes on how the words are connected.

1 optimistic	power	voting
2 cut	lost	close
3 peace talks	border	funding
4 engaged	two months	actor and model
5 captain	injured	competition

E Work in pairs. Say how the words in exercise D are connected, using the words in exercise A.

F Work in groups. Discuss these questions.
Have you heard any recent stories about any:
- elections?
- companies losing money?
- people losing their jobs?
- wars?
- famous people getting engaged?
- sports people getting injured?

What do you think about each story? Why?

GRAMMAR *will / won't* for predictions

A Below are five comments from the chat rooms on the radio station's website. Match each comment to one of the five stories you heard.

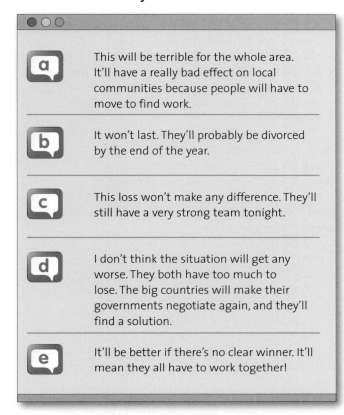

a This will be terrible for the whole area. It'll have a really bad effect on local communities because people will have to move to find work.

b It won't last. They'll probably be divorced by the end of the year.

c This loss won't make any difference. They'll still have a very strong team tonight.

d I don't think the situation will get any worse. They both have too much to lose. The big countries will make their governments negotiate again, and they'll find a solution.

e It'll be better if there's no clear winner. It'll mean they all have to work together!

NATIVE SPEAKER ENGLISH

make a difference

If something *makes a difference*, it changes a situation in a good way. If something *doesn't make any difference*, it doesn't change a situation in any way.

This loss won't make any difference.
He's made a real difference to people's lives.
The course made a big difference to the way I do my job.
It doesn't make any difference to me what you think!

B Which of the comments in exercise A are optimistic and which are pessimistic (= the opposite of optimistic)?

We can use *'ll* (= *will*) + verb to make predictions – to say what we think is certain or probable in the future. The negative form is *won't* (= *will not*).

In all the examples in exercise A, you can also use *be (not) going to* + verb instead.

C Complete the sentences with *will* or *won't*.

1 I probably .... come out with you tonight. I need to finish some work.
2 You can try and talk to her if you want, but it .... make any difference.
3 I think he .... be a very good leader.
4 They .... win the game. They're not good enough.
5 The new law might help a bit, but it .... completely solve the problem.
6 I don't think I .... pass the exam. I haven't done enough work for it.
7 We .... probably arrive sometime in the evening. It depends on the traffic.
8 The company lost a lot of money this year. I expect we .... all lose our jobs before too long!

The contraction *'ll* is pronounced /əl/. *Won't* is pronounced /wəʊnt/.

D 🔊 14.3 Listen. Repeat what you hear.

E Listen again and write the sentences you hear.

F Work in pairs. Ask and answer the questions. Use the answers below.

1 Do you think you'll ever speak perfect English?
2 Do you think you'll live to be 80?
3 Do you think your country will ever win the World Cup?
4 Do you think you'll ever live or work abroad?
5 Do you think you'll ever be really rich or famous?
6 Do you think we'll find life on other planets?
7 Do you think there'll ever be world peace?
8 Do you think we'll ever learn how to look after the environment?

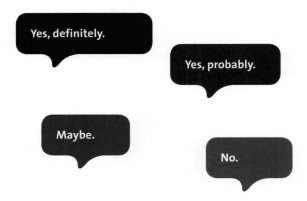

Yes, definitely.

Yes, probably.

Maybe.

No.

G Write two predictions of your own about what *will / won't* happen in the future. Explain your ideas to some other students. Do they agree with you?

▶ Need help? Read the grammar reference on page 163.

VOCABULARY Society

A Decide which ending in *italics* goes with each of the sentences a–c that follow.

1 The economy is quite *weak / strong*.
   a There's a lot of unemployment.
   b It's easy to find a job.
   c Wages are high.

2 Crime is *very bad / not a problem*.
   a There's a lot of violence and murder.
   b There's a lot of stealing.
   c You don't need to lock your door at night.

3 People are *very friendly / not very open*.
   a They don't invite you into their homes.
   b It's easy to make friends.
   c They keep themselves to themselves.

4 The climate's *good / not very nice*.
   a It's dry and warm all year round.
   b It's really cold in winter and too hot in summer.
   c It's very wet. It rains all the time.

5 Healthcare is *very good / quite poor*.
   a Treatment is expensive. Some people can't pay for it.
   b It's free for everyone.
   c It's very efficient.

6 The quality of life is *very good / not very good*.
   a Families are close and children are happy.
   b You have hardly any free time.
   c It's very relaxed.

B Spend two minutes remembering the sentences in exercise A. Then work in pairs and test each other.
Student A: keep your book open. Say sentences a–c.
Student B: close your book. Say the correct sentences 1–6.

C Work in pairs. Write one more example for each situation in exercise A. For example:
It's safe to walk at night. (2 Crime is not a problem.)

D In groups, read your examples. The other students guess the sentences 1–6.

READING

You are going to read what two immigrants say about the different countries they have moved to.

A Before you read, discuss these questions.
  • Are there many people from your country living abroad? Why? In which countries?
  • Is there immigration in your country? Where from?
  • Do you know anyone who has moved to another country or city? Why did they move?
  • What other reasons are there to move to another country?

B Work in two groups.
Group A: read the text on the opposite page.
Group B: read the text in File 5 on page 167.

Read your text and decide how the writer would answer these questions.
1 How long have you lived here?
2 Why did you move here?
3 Do you like it here?
4 What do you think of the people?
5 What do you think of the climate?
6 What do you think of the healthcare system?
7 How's the economy doing?
8 Is there much crime?
9 Do you think you'll ever go back to your country?

C Compare your answers with someone who read the same text as you. Which country do you think the writer is from and where do you think they are living?

D Now find someone from the other group. Without looking at your texts, interview each other. Use the questions in exercise B.

E With the same partner, discuss which of the two writers has a better quality of life. Why?

A NEW LIFE

I've lived here for five years now. I really like it. I came here to work. There are lots of jobs in computers and technology and wages are higher than in my country. People here are very relaxed and open. They often invite you to their homes for a barbecue.

I really don't miss anything about my country. We don't have long, dark, cold winters here – it's basically warm all year round. But if you want snow, you can go to the mountains and ski. I can also watch ice-hockey games, which I love. In fact, it's great for sport here. The only problem is I work long hours, so I don't have time to take advantage of all the opportunities.

Before I came here, I heard crime was bad and that there were problems with healthcare, but I haven't had any problems. Certainly, in the big cities, there are a lot of murders, and walking in the streets is dangerous, but I've never seen anything like that. I leave my door unlocked in my house and no-one has ever stolen anything. As for healthcare, well, it depends if you have medical insurance, because treatment's expensive. Luckily, my company pays for mine and I've found the facilities fantastic – very efficient.

GRAMMAR Verb patterns with adjectives

> These two sentences mean the same thing.
> Notice the position of the adjective *dangerous*.
> *Walking* in the streets *is dangerous*.
> *It's dangerous to walk* in the streets.
>
> If we want to make a verb the subject of a sentence, we use an *-ing* form.
>
> We can also use *it* + *be* + (*not*) adjective + (*not*) *to* + infinitive.

A Discuss whether you use similar grammar in your language.

B Rewrite the sentences using one of the patterns in the explanation box above.
1 Finding work here is easy.
2 It was difficult to meet people.
3 Learning the local language is helpful.
4 Meeting other people in the same situation was good.
5 It's nice to sit and have a coffee by the river.
6 Not criticising people is important if you want to do well.

▶ Need help? Read the grammar reference on page 163.

C Make true sentences about the place you live or work, using the patterns in the explanation box.
1 It's easy ....
2 It's important ....
3 It's nice ....
4 .... is difficult.
5 .... is quite cheap.

SPEAKING

A In groups, discuss what you think of the things in the box in your country:

crime	healthcare	politics
the climate	the quality of life	work

B Do you know any other cities or countries well? How do they compare with your country?

07 REVIEW

REVISE TOGETHER

CONVERSATION PRACTICE

Work in pairs. Do one of these *Conversation practice* activities.
Nature, Unit 13, page 101.
Opinions, Unit 14, page 107.

ACT OR DRAW

Work in pairs. One person acts or draws the words. *Don't* speak. Your partner tries to guess the words. Then change roles.

a planet	murder	vote	hunt
a band	blood	hide	a farm
breathe	windy	injured	a pool
a desert	a field	ride	rob
a barbecue	a storm	snow	crops

QUIZ

Work in groups. Answer as many questions as possible.
1 Where do you find **grass**?
2 Say the name of someone who wrote **plays**.
3 Do you see a **cottage** in a city or in a village?
4 What happens in a **general election**?
5 When might you **miss** your friends and family?
6 What's the problem if there's a lot of **unemployment**?
7 What do you get a **wage** for?
8 Why do some farmers use **chemicals**?
9 When do you get **ice** on the road?
10 What's the opposite of **noisy**?
11 Say three kinds of **entertainment**.
12 Why might a **political party** have to **share power**?
13 When do people have **nightmares**? How do they feel?
14 What might happen if there are lots of **dark clouds**?
15 Say two places that are often **crowded**.

FAST WRITER

Work in groups. See who is quickest to write each of 1–5.
1 Eight animals.
2 Eight words to describe films, plays, etc.
3 Four sentences predicting the weather – two with *might*.
4 Four sentences with a passive – one with a negative.
5 Four predictions – two with *will*, two with *won't*.

COLLOCATIONS

A One student reads a group of collocations from Unit 13 of the *Vocabulary Builder*. Where there is a '~', say 'blah'. Your partners guess the word. Who guesses the most?

> Watch *blah*, have a big *blah*, turn on the *blah*, a *blah* programme.

> TV?

> That's right.

B Now do the same with Unit 14 of the *Vocabulary Builder*.

PRONUNCIATION

/h/ is said with a little air. The other sounds in the chart are said with the voice from the throat.

/h/	/m/	/n/	/ŋ/	/l/	/r/	/w/	/j/
hide	me	rain	sing	lock	rest	wild	yet

A ♫ R 7.1 Listen and say the words and sounds.

B Practise saying these words with /h/. Breathe lightly.

hero	horse	hope	health	horrible	hand

C For /m/, /n/ and /ŋ/, you use your nose to make the sound. Hold your nose and say these words.

funding	model	training	unemployment

D Work in pairs. Try to say these words.
1 /hjuːdʒ/
2 /wʌns/
3 /jʌŋ/
4 /ˈendɪŋ/
5 /ˈprəutiːn/
6 /ʌnˈjuːʒuəl/
7 /ˈvæljubl/
8 /ekəˈnɒmɪk/

E ♫ R 7.2 Listen and check the words in the audioscript on page 181. Listen again and repeat the words.

F Work in pairs. Practise saying the sentences. Who has good pronunciation? Which sounds are difficult for you?
1 Many sports people are on huge wages.
2 I want to be a model when I grow up.
3 He hurt his arm when he went hunting.
4 Farming is an important industry here.
5 I saw a young wild horse running in the hills.
6 My health is more valuable to me than money.

LISTENING

You are going to hear four news stories.

A ✹ R 7.3 Listen and match themes a–d with stories 1–4 .
a weather
b crime
c entertainment
d famous people

B Listen again. Match e–h with stories 1–4.
e Someone got married recently.
f A business is doing badly.
g A bird was killed.
h There might be a lot of cars on the roads.

[… / 8]

GRAMMAR

A Complete with the passive form of the verbs in brackets.
1 Most of the cotton we use ………………… in India. (produce)
2 Unfortunately, there are almost no tigers now in this area because they ………………… so much. (hunt)
3 The tigers ………………… by law now. (protect)
4 There was a lovely tree opposite our house, but unfortunately it ………………… . (cut down)
5 Who ………………… that book ………………… by? (write)
6 Where ………………… this …………………? Was it here? (make)

[… / 6]

B Complete the sentences with ONE word in each gap.
A: What's the forecast for tomorrow?
B: It said it's ¹………………… to continue raining.
A: When do you think it ²………………… stop?
B: It's difficult ³………………… say. It sometimes rains for days. When are you going back home?
A: I don't know now. I ⁴………………… go back early. It's horrible to ⁵………………… sightseeing in the rain.
B: No, stay. There are things to do indoors. ⁶………………… out on Friday night is great too, even if it's raining.
A: OK – and I suppose the weather might get better.

[… / 6]

C Change into statements (+), negatives (-) or questions (?). In one sentence, use a different pronoun.
1 I'll do it before Friday. (-)
2 Is it easy to find work there? (+)
3 I might go to the party. (-)
4 I don't think they'll miss her a lot. (+)
5 It's usually served with rice. (-)
6 I think they'll win. (?)

[… / 6]

ADJECTIVES

Choose adjective that is not correct.
1 He's a *famous / popular / wild* writer.
2 The film was really *dangerous / violent / depressing*.
3 It's a *wild / economic / dangerous* animal.
4 He's a(n) *varied / intelligent / strong* leader
5 The economy's *weak / strong / optimistic*.
6 Healthcare here is quite *poor / efficient / peaceful*.
7 It's a *predictable / huge / powerful* country.
8 We had some really *windy / crowded / horrible* weather.

[… / 8]

COLLOCATIONS

Match the verbs in the box to the group of words they go with in 1–8.

solve	make	fail	steal
damage	invite	grow	vote

1 ~ me to a party / ~ you into their home / not be ~ d
2 ~ for the Peace Party / ~ in a general election / ~ against
3 ~ the problem / ~ the argument / try to ~ it
4 ~ crops / the economy ~s / ~ in the field
5 ~ my bag / ~ my car / ~ money from the company
6 peace talks ~ / ~ an exam / ~ to win
7 ~ a big difference / ~ friends / ~ him captain
8 ~ the economy / ~ your car in an accident / ~ the environment

[… / 8]

VOCABULARY

Complete the words in the text.
We live in a small ¹cot…… in the middle of the countryside. Our nearest ²nei…… is a sheep farmer. He lives around six kilometres away. Nothing much grows around here apart from grass because the ³so…… isn't very good. There are very few trees – just grass, hills and wind turbines that ⁴pro…… electricity. People ask me how I can live here, with so few people and no ⁵ent…… . But those people are only thinking of shopping or nightlife. I do lots of fun things. I ride my ⁶ho…… , I practise shooting with my gun and I sometimes go ⁷hu…… . I read a lot and watch DVDs. And it's so safe and peaceful here. No crime, no traffic – just ⁸fr…… air and the sound of the wind and the birds.

[… / 8]

  [Total … /50]

In this unit, you learn how to:
- talk about useful technology
- find out how much people know
- talk about computers and the Internet
- spell and give addresses
- talk about marketing

Grammar
- *be thinking of + -ing*
- Adverbs

Vocabulary
- Machines and technology
- Computers and the Internet

Reading
- A questionnaire about computers and technology
- Going viral!

Listening
- *I'm thinking of buying ...*
- A questionnaire about computers and technology

VOCABULARY Machines and technology

A Label the pictures with the words in the box.

washing machine	dishwasher	hairdryer
vacuum cleaner	mobile phone	laptop
digital camera	games console	

B Work in groups. Discuss these questions.
- Which of the things in the pictures do you have?
- Which brands do you have?
- Which is most useful? Why?
- What other machines or technology do you own?
- Are there any you don't have, but would like?

C Check you understand the words in bold. Then work in pairs. Look at the pictures again and point to:
1 a **cable**
2 a **screen**
3 a **plug**
4 a **keyboard**
5 where you **turn** them **on** and **turn** them **off**
6 where the **battery** goes
7 **buttons** you can **press**

LISTENING

You are going to hear three conversations about technology. In each conversation, someone makes a recommendation.

A ⊘ 15.1 Listen and complete the table.

	Kind of machine	Brand	What's good about it?
1		Bell	
2		Kotika	
3		Bonny	

B Work in pairs. Discuss these questions.
1 Do you think the things they recommend sound good or not? Why? Are they missing anything?
2 How much does each thing cost in your country?

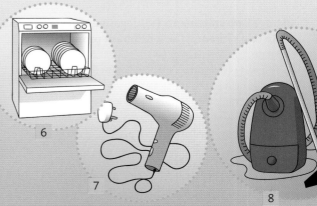

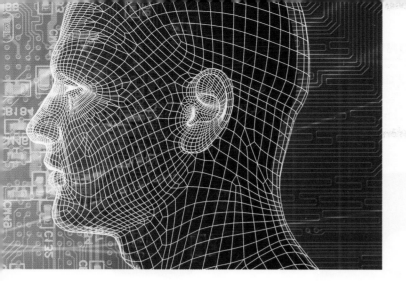

B Work in pairs.
Student A: say each sentence in exercise A. Then ask *Can you recommend anything / anywhere?*
Student B: make recommendations.

C Change roles and repeat exercise B.

D Write three sentences about things you – or people you know – are thinking of doing. Explain your ideas to a partner.

DEVELOPING CONVERSATIONS
Do you know much about ...?

> To find out how much people know about general topics, we often say *Do you know much about ...?* To answer, say *No, not really / A bit / Yeah, quite a lot.*
>
> A: *Do you know much about* computers?
> B: *A bit.* Why?

A Find people in your class who know a lot about the things in the box.

history	geography	cars	computers
Australia	the moon	tennis	cows

B Try to ask extra questions to find out how much each person really knows.

CONVERSATION PRACTICE

You are going to have conversations like the ones in *Listening.*

A Decide on two technology items you're thinking of buying. Decide how much you want to spend on them.

B Talk to some other students. Explain what you're thinking of buying and why. Ask for and make recommendations.

C Tell a partner who gave you the best advice.

NATIVE SPEAKER ENGLISH

ages
We often say *ages* instead of *a long time.*

It's taking me ages.
I haven't seen him for ages.
I waited ages for you!
My flight was delayed for ages.

GRAMMAR *be thinking of + -ing*

> To talk about plans that we are not 100% sure about, we often use *be thinking of + -ing.*
>
> I'*m thinking of* buying a laptop.
> She's *thinking of* starting her own Internet company.
> We'*re thinking of* getting a new washing machine.

A Complete the sentences with the correct form of *be thinking of* and the verbs in brackets.

1 I .... my dad some new clothes, but I don't know any good shops. (buy)
2 My brother .... an English course next year. (do)
3 We .... to the cinema later. (go)
4 I .... the mobile phone company I use. (change)
5 My parents .... a new car. (buy)
6 They .... somewhere warm for their holiday. (go)
7 I .... a pet for my younger sister. (get)
8 My sister .... Engineering at university. (study)

▶ **Need help? Read the grammar reference on page 164.**

VOCABULARY
Computers and the Internet

A Use the extra information in 1-8 to guess the meanings of the words in **bold**. Translate these words into your language.

1 A: That's a great photo.
   B: I'll send it to you, if you like. What's your **email address**?
2 A: Did you get the photo that I sent?
   B: I don't know. I haven't **checked** my emails today.
3 A: I can't find the email you sent me. I **received** it, but maybe I **deleted** it by mistake.
   B: Don't worry. I'll re-send it.
4 My school has its own **website** at www.stphil.edu.
5 There's a really funny video on YouTube. **Do a search** for 'dog + skateboard'.
6 I read an interesting article on the *Graddy* website. I'll send you the **link** if you want to read it.
7 If you don't have the software, you can **download** it free from their website.
8 My computer died last year and I lost a lot of my **documents**. I save everything on a **memory stick** or **online** now!

B Write your translations on a piece of paper. Close your book. Point at each of your partner's translations. Your partner should say the words in English.

C Work in groups. Discuss these questions.
- Which websites do you visit most?
- What was the last link you received? Did you send it to anyone else or did you delete the email?
- Do you have a memory stick? What do you keep on it?
- Do you download anything for free? What?

LANGUAGE PATTERNS

Write the sentences in your language. Translate them back into English. Compare your English to the original.
I'll send you the link if you want to read it.
I'll check if you like.
If you want the software, you can download it from their website.
You can turn the music down if you want.
If you need help, tell me.
If it's cheap, buy one for me.

PRONUNCIATION Spelling addresses

A 🔊 15.2 Listen to each group of letters and repeat them.

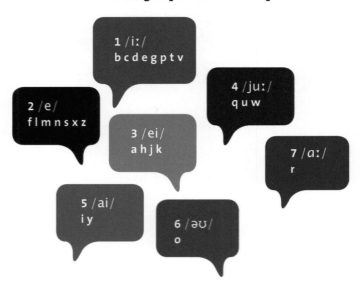

B Work in pairs. Say the alphabet in the correct order. Take turns saying the letters. Which letters are the most difficult for you to say?

When we say websites and email addresses, we say 'dot' for . and 'at' for @. We usually say 'co', 'com', 'net', 'org', etc. as one word.

C 🔊 15.3 Listen and write the three different addresses.
1 Her website: ....
2 Her email: ....
3 Her home: ....

D Write a website, an email and a home address. Then work in pairs. Say your addresses and spell them for your partner to write down.

LISTENING

You are going to listen to – and answer – a questionnaire about computers and technology.

A Before you listen, work in pairs and read the possible answers. Discuss what you think the questions are.

B 🔊 15.4 Listen and check the questions.

C 🔊 15.5 Now listen to the whole questionnaire and tick ✔ the answers that are best for you.

D Work in pairs. Compare your answers. Who do you think likes technology more?

E Change partners. Tell your new partner about two people you know – one who loves technology and one who hates it. Give examples of how they love / hate it.

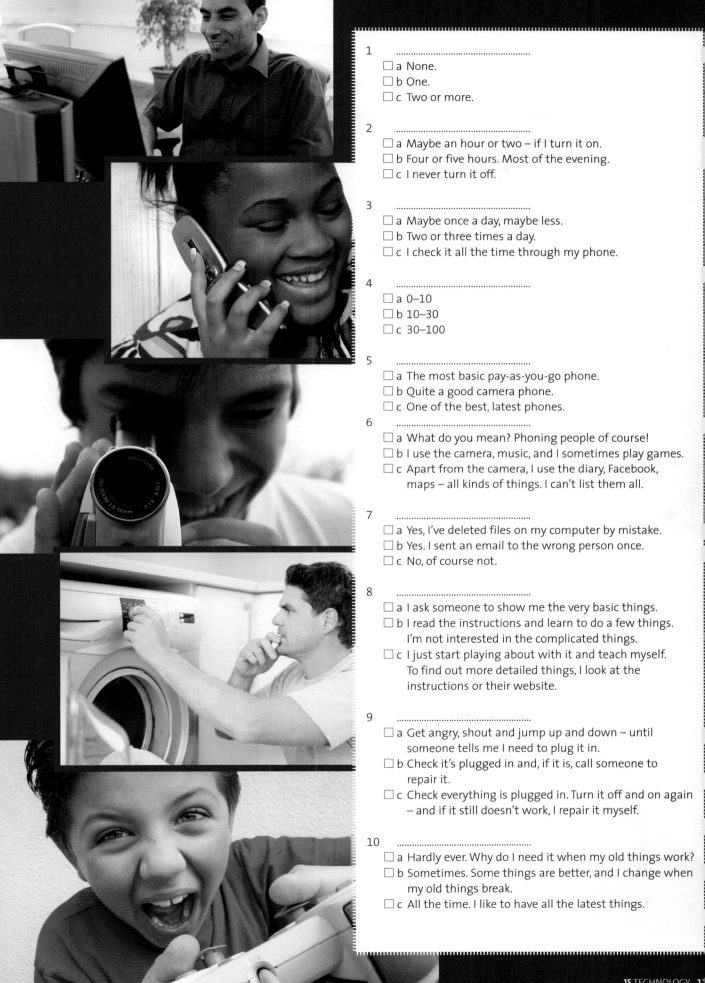

1
....
- [ ] a None.
- [ ] b One.
- [ ] c Two or more.

2
....
- [ ] a Maybe an hour or two – if I turn it on.
- [ ] b Four or five hours. Most of the evening.
- [ ] c I never turn it off.

3
....
- [ ] a Maybe once a day, maybe less.
- [ ] b Two or three times a day.
- [ ] c I check it all the time through my phone.

4
....
- [ ] a 0–10
- [ ] b 10–30
- [ ] c 30–100

5
....
- [ ] a The most basic pay-as-you-go phone.
- [ ] b Quite a good camera phone.
- [ ] c One of the best, latest phones.

6
....
- [ ] a What do you mean? Phoning people of course!
- [ ] b I use the camera, music, and I sometimes play games.
- [ ] c Apart from the camera, I use the diary, Facebook, maps – all kinds of things. I can't list them all.

7
....
- [ ] a Yes, I've deleted files on my computer by mistake.
- [ ] b Yes. I sent an email to the wrong person once.
- [ ] c No, of course not.

8
....
- [ ] a I ask someone to show me the very basic things.
- [ ] b I read the instructions and learn to do a few things. I'm not interested in the complicated things.
- [ ] c I just start playing about with it and teach myself. To find out more detailed things, I look at the instructions or their website.

9
....
- [ ] a Get angry, shout and jump up and down – until someone tells me I need to plug it in.
- [ ] b Check it's plugged in and, if it is, call someone to repair it.
- [ ] c Check everything is plugged in. Turn it off and on again – and if it still doesn't work, I repair it myself.

10
....
- [ ] a Hardly ever. Why do I need it when my old things work?
- [ ] b Sometimes. Some things are better, and I change when my old things break.
- [ ] c All the time. I like to have all the latest things.

SPEAKING

A **Look at the different ways of selling things in the photos. Then discuss these questions in groups.**
- Which ones do you like the most / least?
- What are the advantages / disadvantages of each way?
- Can you think of any other ways of selling or advertising things? What's good / bad about each one?

READING

You are going to read an article about using technology to sell things.

A Read the introduction below. Then discuss these questions in pairs.
1 Why do you think it's called 'viral marketing'?
2 How do you think viral marketing works?
3 What do you think makes it effective?
4 What kind of products do you think it might work best with?
5 Can you think of any examples of viral marketing?
6 Can you think of any possible problems with it?

Going Viral!

When most people think of viruses, they think of diseases that move quickly from person to person or of computer viruses which cause serious damage. However, in recent years, 'viral marketing' has become one of the most popular ways of selling.

Viral marketing started in the 1990s and is a development of older ways of telling people about brands. In the past, happy customers told friends about products they enjoyed. What's new, however, is that viral marketing uses the Web to tell people about new brands and increase sales. The power of the Internet allows people to spread news more quickly and more widely.

B Read the rest of the article. Did your answers to exercise A agree with the article?

Viral marketing includes videos on sites like Facebook or YouTube, text messages and advertising games. The best examples are those that give away free services or products in the first place to sell something else later; they move quickly and easily from person to person and they **target** the right people. Nowadays, everything – from chocolate bars to movies – uses these new **methods**, often very creatively.

Viral marketing works well with cheaper products that people buy without thinking too much. It works badly with high-cost products, which people think about more before buying.

Perhaps the first example of online viral marketing working successfully was Hotmail's idea of advertising itself in its own emails. Every message sent by the half a million users in 1996 ended with the line 'Get your private, free email at www.hotmail.com'. In the next year, over 12 million people **joined**!

However, there are also problems. Firstly, many people now see viral advertising messages as no different from **junk emails**, and don't want to click on **unknown** links. Secondly, as marketing gets more creative, there's more risk of people **misunderstanding** it or not realising it's connected to a product.

C Work in pairs. Look at the words in **bold** in the article. Decide if they are verbs, nouns or adjectives. Discuss what you think they mean.

GRAMMAR Adverbs

> Adverbs can tell us more about verbs: they say how we do things. They usually come after the verbs they describe.
>
> Most adverbs are formed by adding *-ly* to an adjective (e.g. slow – slow*ly*). However, there are some irregular ones.
>
> | fast – fast | early – early | hard – hard |
> | late – late | good – well | |

A Find seven adverbs in the article about viral marketing. Which verbs do they come after?

B Complete the sentences with the adverbs formed with the adjectives in the box.

| bad | early | good | hard |
| late | quick | quiet | slow |

1 I'm really tired today! I went to bed very .... last night.
2 I can't hear you. You're speaking too ....
3 I can't understand them. They talk very ....
4 I'm really tired. I need to go to bed .... tonight.
5 She's working very .... at the moment. It sounds very stressful.
6 She's very good at languages. She speaks English very ....
7 What's wrong with you? Why are you walking so .... ? Hurry up!
8 My parents are angry because I did .... in my exams.

▶ Need help? Read the grammar reference on page 164.

C Work in pairs. Ask each other these questions. Use the answers below.
1 How well do you speak English?
2 How well do you usually do in tests / exams?
3 How well do you know your country?
4 How well can you swim?
5 How well can you draw?
6 How well can you spell?

Really well.

Quite well.

Not very well.

Really badly.

D Write two similar questions to the ones in exercise C. Then ask some other students your questions.

16 LOVE

VOCABULARY Love and marriage

A **Work in pairs. Discuss these questions.**
1 What's the difference between *girlfriend*, *wife* and *partner*?
2 What's the equivalent for men?

> We often say *partner* instead of *girlfriend / boyfriend* when the couple are older or are living together. We can also use it if we don't know if the couple are married or not.

B **Discuss if the words in the box refer to a girlfriend / boyfriend, a wife / husband or either.**

married + wedding	broken up + getting on
a date + asked me out	divorced + jealous
live together + move in	in-laws + approve
anniversary + married	pregnant + baby

C **Complete the sentences with the pairs of words in exercise B.**
1 We're going to have a party for my parents' .... on Saturday. They've been .... for 25 years.
2 My daughter is six months .... She's due to have her .... on Christmas Day!
3 We're getting .... next summer. Would you like to come to the .... ?
4 Sorry I can't go with you. I have .... on Friday. This boy at school .... and I've liked him for ages.
5 I'm pleased they're going to get .... I never liked him. He was very .... and controlled what she did.
6 We've decided we're going to .... I'm going to .... to her flat. I spend so much time there already and this way we can share the cost of the rent.
7 Sorry, I'm a bit upset. I've .... with Toni! To be honest, we weren't .... very well. We argued quite a lot and now he's met someone else.
8 I get on with my .... now, although they didn't .... of our marriage at first.

D **Spend five minutes writing what you would say or any questions you would ask in response to the people in exercise C.**

E **Work in pairs. Take turns saying the sentences in exercise C. Your partner should respond, using their ideas. Try to continue each conversation together.**

LISTENING

You are going to hear four short conversations. In each one, someone gives news about a relationship.

A 🔊 **16.1 Listen. Answer the questions for each conversation.**
1 Who do the people talk about?
2 What's going to happen?

B **Choose the correct words. Then listen again to check your answers.**
1 a How long *are they / have they been* together?
   b She's very *well-looking / good-looking*.
2 a Next May *sometimes / sometime*.
   b *What's / What does* his partner like?
3 a Did I *tell / say* you Fiona and Kieran are going to get divorced?
   b What a *shame / mistake*. They're both such nice people.
4 a A *guy / boy* in my French class.
   b He's quite *high / tall* and he has lovely eyes.

C **Work in groups. Discuss these questions.**
- Do you think it's good to live together before you get married?
- Do you know anyone who moved in with a partner / got married after only being together a short time?
- Does anyone you know have a partner you don't like?
- What divorces have you heard of in the news recently? What was the cause?
- Do you think karaoke is a good thing for a first date? Why? / Why not? What might be better?

NATIVE SPEAKER ENGLISH

guy
We often use *guy* instead of *man*. There's no equivalent for *woman*.

A guy in my French class.
He's a really nice guy.
Ask the guy on the reception desk.

DEVELOPING CONVERSATIONS
How long ...?

You can find out the duration of something from the past to now by asking *How long ...?* with the present perfect. You can answer with just the time or with phrases like *not (very) long*.

A: *How long have they been* together?
B: Two or three months.

A: *How long have they been* married?
B: Not very long. Four years, I think.

A **Put the words into the correct order to make questions.**
1 you long how have together been ?
2 have married how you been long ?
3 known how have other they long each ?
4 house lived long how have you in this ?
5 long how there she worked has ?
6 car you have long how had your ?

B 🔊 **16.2 Listen and check, and write the answers you hear.**

C **Practise saying the questions and answers.**

D **Work in small groups. Take turns to ask two different *How long ...?* questions each. Your partners should give true answers.**

CONVERSATION PRACTICE

You are going to have similar conversations to the ones you heard in *Listening*.

A **Write a piece of news about a relationship starting *Did I tell you ...?* It can be true or invented. Look at the audioscript on page 182 if you need to, and underline the questions the people use to continue the conversations.**

B **Ask different students your question starting *Did I tell you ...?* Your partner should ask questions to help continue the conversation.**

SPEAKING

A Work in groups. Discuss these questions.
- What do you think *love at first sight* means?
- Have you ever heard any stories about love at first sight? Do you believe them?
- Do you think it's possible to fall in love with things or places – as well as people – at first sight?
- Can you give any examples?

LISTENING

You are going to hear three people talking about their experiences of love at first sight.

A Before you listen, look at the photos below. In pairs, discuss how each picture might be connected to the idea of love at first sight.

B 🔊 16.3 Listen and match each person to a picture. Were you right about what each person fell in love with?

C Listen again and decide which sentences below are true.
1. a They needed to move quickly because they planned to start a family.
   b They made an appointment to see the house they bought.
   c They tried to negotiate a better price.
2. a His first guitar was a present.
   b His uncle was a very important person in his life.
   c He now plays music for a living.
3. a Second Life is an online dating company.
   b She met her future husband in a nightclub.
   c She isn't actually married yet.

D Work in pairs. Discuss these questions.
- Where would your dream house be? What would it be like?
- Can you play any musical instruments? How well?
- Which people have had a big influence on you?
- Have you heard of Second Life before?
- What do you think is good / bad about it?

GRAMMAR The past continuous

> We form the past continuous with *was / were* + – *ing*. Use it to show that one action started but didn't finish before another action happened. The other action is usually in the past simple.
>
> Last year, *I was spending* a lot of time online and, one night, I met my future husband.

A Complete these sentences from *Listening* using the correct past continuous form of the verbs in brackets.
1. We .... seriously to begin with, but then I got pregnant and we had to find somewhere fast. (not / look)
2. One day, we .... home from another appointment when suddenly we saw it! (drive)
3. He .... in a band at the time and this had a big influence on me. (play)
4. I .... in a Second Life nightclub, he came in and it was love at first sight. (work)

B Read the audioscript on page 183 to check your answers.

C Complete the sentences with the correct past continuous form of the verbs in the box.

do	have	listen	open
stay	visit	walk	watch

1. We .... dinner in a restaurant in town and she was at the next table.
2. I .... in a hotel in Singapore and I shared the lift with him one day.
3. He .... a new shop in my city and I went to see him.
4. We .... some friends in Vienna and we saw her at the airport.
5. I .... some shopping in town and I saw it in one of the shops. It was love at first sight!
6. I .... through a street market one day and I saw it on a table.
7. I .... TV one night and there was an advert for it. I thought it looked amazing.
8. I .... to the radio one day and heard this song. I just fell in love with it.

▶ **Need help? Read the grammar reference on page 165.**

PRONUNCIATION
Sentence stress and weak forms

In positive past continuous sentences, *was* and *were* aren't usually stressed. Instead, we use the weak forms /wəz/ and /wə/.

In negative past continuous sentences, *was* and *were* are stressed.

A In the sentences, the stressed sounds are in **bold**. In pairs, practise saying the sentences.
1 **So**rry. I **was**n't **lis**tening.
2 She **was**n't **fee**ling **very well**, so she **went home**.
3 I **could**n't **hear** because **you** were **tal**king.
4 We **were**n't **get**ting **on** so we **bro**ke up.
5 I was **wor**king in **Greece** when we **met**.
6 I **lost** because I **was**n't **try**ing.

B 🔊 16.4 Listen and check. Repeat the sentences.

SPEAKING

A Spend three minutes deciding how to answer the questions below. Try to use the past continuous. *Grammar*, exercise C might give you some ideas.
- Have you ever fallen in love with something you saw / heard? What was it? Where were you? What were you doing?
- Have you ever seen – or met – any famous people? When? Where were you? What were you doing?
- How and when did you first meet your best friends? Where were you? What were you doing?
- Think about some couples you know. How did they first meet? Where were they? What were they doing?

B Work in groups. Discuss your answers to the questions in exercise A.

SPEAKING

A Which of these ideas do you prefer? Why?

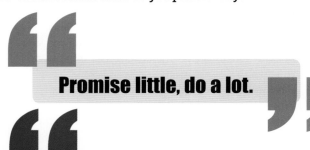

> **Promise little, do a lot.**

> **It's better to break a promise than never to make one.**

- Do you ever make promises? Who to?
- What's the last promise you made? For example:
  I promised to take my son to the cinema.

GRAMMAR *will / won't* for promises

> To make promises, we usually use *will / won't*. We sometimes add *I promise.*
> ....
> A: Dad, can we go to the cinema today?
> B: Sorry, I'm too busy. *I'll* take you next week,
> *I promise.*

A Work in pairs. Make promises using *will / won't* and these ideas.

1 promise to call later
2 promise not to tell anyone
3 promise to try harder
4 promise not to be late
5 promise not to make a mess
6 promise to tell you when I hear more news

> We often promise something by using *will / won't* as a short response:
> ....
> A: Call me later.   A: Don't be late.
> B: *I will.*   B: *I won't.*

B Work in pairs. Take turns to say and respond to the sentences. Respond using *I will. / I won't.*

1 Don't start before I get back.
2 You need to pay me back tomorrow.
3 Remember to go to the bank.
4 Don't forget to call your gran to thank her.
5 Be careful.
6 I don't want you to miss the train.

▶ Need help? Read the grammar reference on page 165.

READING

You are going to read some short poems based on promises.

A Read the poems on the opposite page and match each poem to one of these titles.
In memory
New born
Breaking up
A threat kept

B Before you discuss your choices, match the bold words in the poems with the meanings 1–9.

1 Two times.
2 Stop holding something.
3 Make someone feel confident by saying positive things.
4 Become less strong (of a colour, sound or memory).
5 Make a small mistake.
6 Look after.
7 Plants / Flowers that you don't want in your garden.
8 Stay.
9 Believe someone is honest.

C Work in pairs. Explain your choices of title and agree on the same ones. Decide who is making the promises and who to.

D Work in groups. Did you all agree in exercise C? Now discuss these questions.
- Which poem did you like most?
- Were there any lines you didn't understand? Can your partners explain them?

SPEAKING

A Work in groups. Discuss these questions.
- Can a parent love a child too much? Why? / Why not?
- Is it always better to stay married? Why? / Why not?
- What ways do you remember people who have died?
- Have you ever been threatened? What happened? How did you react?

B Work in pairs. Think of promises (or threats) that these people might make.
- a couple who are in love
- a child to a parent
- a student to a teacher
- a teacher
- a boss
- a politician

C Now choose one of the people in exercise B – or use your own ideas – and write a short poem. Follow the pattern of one of the poems you read in *Reading*.

D Read out your poems and vote for the best one.

1 ....

This I promise.
I'll try to be a person you want to love.
I'll try to **encourage** *and not to criticise –*
Try to ask, not to tell.
I'll protect you and be there to hold you,
But I promise I'll **let go** *–*
Let you grow.

2 ....

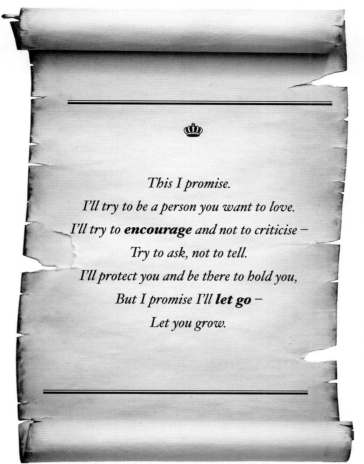

I'm sorry.
How could you?
I'll be better; I'll be stronger.
How can I know?
I'll be here; I won't **slip up** or fall.
How can I **trust** *you?*
Because I'll love you.
And you didn't before?

3 ....

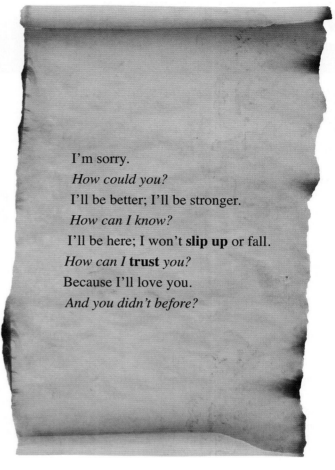

I'll **tend** *your garden.*
I'll remove the **weeds** *that may cover it.*
I'll plant new flowers when others die.
I won't let it **fade***.*
I'll keep it alive.
And you'll **remain** *-*
In my heart.

4 ....

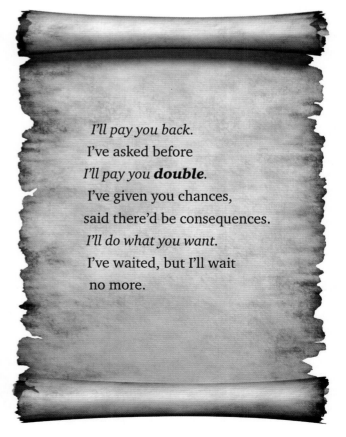

I'll pay you back.
I've asked before
I'll pay you **double***.*
I've given you chances,
said there'd be consequences.
I'll do what you want.
I've waited, but I'll wait
no more.

REVISE TOGETHER

CONVERSATION PRACTICE

Work in pairs. Do one of these *Conversation practice* activities.

Technology, Unit 15, page 115.
Love, Unit 16, page 121.

ACT OR DRAW

Work in pairs. One person acts or draws the words. *Don't* speak. Your partner tries to guess the words. Then change roles.

a wedding	a button	a screen	slip
pregnant	argue	the moon	hold
pleased	a guitar	delete	drop
a battery	a cable	click	text
damage	knock	a plug	a list

QUIZ

Work in groups. Answer as many questions as possible.
1 What's the opposite of **advantage**?
2 Say three **musical instruments**.
3 Who might you **have a date** with?
4 What kind of people do you have **appointments** with?
5 Why would you say **'What a shame'**?
6 Why do couples **break up**?
7 Who are **in-laws**?
8 What do you do in a **nightclub**?
9 What do you say if you want to **accept** an offer?
10 When do you **replace a battery**?
11 What has a **keyboard**?
12 Is something that is **complicated** easy or difficult?
13 What things do you **download**, and where from?
14 What do you say to **encourage** someone?
15 Say two things that can **fade**.

FAST WRITER

Work in groups. See who is quickest to write each of 1–5.
1 Six machines or pieces of technology.
2 Eight words connected with computers and the Internet.
3 Four sentences with an adverb.
4 Four things with *be thinking of*, using *I, he, we, they.*
5 Four promises or threats.

COLLOCATIONS

A One student reads the lists from Unit 15 of the *Vocabulary Builder*. Where there is a '~', say '*blah*'. Your partners guess the word. Who guesses the most?

> Watch *blah*, have a big *blah*, turn on the *blah*, a *blah* programme.

> TV?

> That's right.

B Now do the same with Unit 16 of the *Vocabulary Builder*.

PRONUNCIATION Word stress

If a word has more than one syllable, one syllable is stressed more than the other(s). Unstressed vowels are usually either a /ə/ or an /ɪ/ sound.
In a dictionary, the stress is marked with a ' before the stressed syllable. For example:

a**ddress** /əˈdres/   **me**ssage /ˈmesɪdʒ/

A ⏺ R 8.1 Listen and repeat the words. Make sure you use a weak /ə/ or /ɪ/ for the unstressed sounds.

for**get**	re**move**
ma**chine**	**ma**rriage
target	**pow**er
pro**tect**	**me**thod

B Work in pairs. Try to say these words.
1 /ˈθretən/
2 /rɪˈmeɪn/
3 /dɪˈveləpmənt/
4 /ɪˈfektɪv/
5 /ədˈvɑːntɪdʒ/
6 /ˈdaɪəri/
7 /ˈdɒkjʊmənt/
8 /nɪˈgəʊʃieɪt/

C ⏺ R 8.2 Listen and check the words in the audioscript on page 183. Listen again and repeat the words.

D Work in pairs. Practise saying the sentences. Who has good pronunciation? Which sounds are difficult for you?
1 My digital camera is broken.
2 The instructions were very complicated.
3 I forgot my diary, but I remembered my date.
4 It's an effective method with one disadvantage.
5 Couples should think seriously about marriage.
6 Technology and machines have developed a lot.

LISTENING

You are going to hear four conversations.

◆ R 8.3 Listen and decide if the sentences are true or false. Listen twice if you want.

1 a The hairdryer is broken.
   b The woman needs a new one.
2 a The man's laptop isn't working very well.
   b The woman suggests getting a different computer.
3 a Their friends have been married for three years.
   b Their friends want to move because of Jack's job.
4 a Rebecca and her husband are breaking up.
   b Rebecca's going to have a baby in March.

[... / 8]

GRAMMAR

A Complete the sentences with the correct form of the verb *be*.

1 I .... thinking of going to the cinema later.
2 I broke my leg when I .... playing football.
3 We met when we .... working for a local company.
4 They .... thinking of moving house.
5 What .... you thinking of doing this evening?
6 I saw Mariah Carey once when she .... coming out of a hotel.

[... / 6]

B Add the adverb form of the adjective in brackets to complete the sentences.

1 I can't run very because I have a bad leg. (quick)
2 He works too. (hard)
3 Can you swim? (good)
4 I didn't do in my exam. (bad)
5 We arrived so that we could get a seat. (early)
6 It only worked for a while. (successful)

[... / 6]

C Complete the conversation with ONE word in each gap. (*won't / weren't* etc. = one word)

A: What ¹........................ you doing last night? I called.
B: Sorry, my phone was turned off and I saw your message too ²........................ to call.
A: Don't worry. I ³........................ doing anything special. I just thought you might like to go out.
B: Actually, I was with Simon. He asked me to marry him!
A: Really! Did you say yes?
B: Of course! We're thinking of ⁴........................ married this August so don't go on holiday then.
A: I ⁵........................ ! It's great news. I promise I'll ⁶........................ there.

[... / 6]

NOUNS

Complete the sentences with the words in the box.

influence	methods	email	link
anniversary	brand	diary	sight

1 We don't usually celebrate our wedding ....
2 It was love at first ....
3 My grandad was a big .... on my life.
4 I need to check my .... and send one too.
5 I'll send you the .... to the website.
6 I wrote the appointment in my ....
7 There are many ways to target people in advertising, but one of the best ....s is viral marketing.
8 It's a .... which people like and trust.

[... / 8]

COLLOCATIONS

Match the verbs in the box to the groups of words they go with in 1–8.

join	move	receive	approve
press	plant	slip up	promise

1 ~ junk email / ~ a letter / ~ some bad news
2 ~ to do it / ~ to help / ~ her not to be late
3 ~ flowers / ~ a tree / ~ a crop
4 ~ house / ~ in to his girlfriend's flat / ~ out
5 ~ in my exam / ~ and fall / ~ badly
6 ~ the switch / ~ the start button / ~ the key
7 ~ a chat group / ~ the army / ~ a club
8 my parents don't ~ / ~ of the marriage / ~ the plan

[... / 8]

VOCABULARY

Choose the correct words.

1 The guy *promised / threatened* to shoot us if we didn't give him the money, but we persuaded him to let *go / fall* of the gun.
2 I don't *trust / honest* him. He's *broken / damaged* his promises too many times.
3 We often *argued / jumped* about who should do the washing-up, so we bought a *dishwasher / washing machine*.
4 I tried to *turn / make* on the computer, but nothing happened. Then I saw someone had pulled the *plug / keyboard* out.

[... / 8]

 [Total ... /50]

VOCABULARY
Common questions

A Complete the conversation with the questions in the box.

> what's your surname?
> do you have a middle name?
> where do you live?
> what's your first name?
> what's your telephone number?
> where are you from?
> when were you born?

A: I need to ask you some questions so we can complete this form.
B: OK.
A: Right, [1] ....
B: David.
A: And [2] ....
B: Abbott – that's a–double b–o–double t.
A: OK. I've got it. And [3] ....
B: Yes, it's Sebastian.
A: OK and [4] ....
B: Canada. I'm Canadian.
A: Oh, OK. Right. And [5] ....
B: In Dublin. 25 Cook Street.
A: And [6] ....
B: It's 07791–773–119.
A: OK – nearly finished. One more question,
  [7] ....
B: 1980. October the fourth.
A: OK. Great. That's everything. Thanks.

B Work in pairs. Take turns to ask and answer the seven questions in the conversation above.

WRITING Completing forms

Complete the form below for the person in the conversation in *Vocabulary*, exercise A. The first answer is given.

SURNAME ___*Abbott*___

FIRST NAME _____

MIDDLE NAME(S) _____

GENDER ☐ MALE
☐ FEMALE

NATIONALITY _____

DATE OF BIRTH _____

ADDRESS _____

TELEPHONE NUMBER _____

VOCABULARY Nationalities

A Complete the table.

Country	Nationality
	Canadian
the United States	
Ireland	
India	
	Scottish
England	
	Australian
China	
	Thai
	Japanese
France	
Germany	
	Italian
	Polish
Russia	
	Spanish
Brazil	
	Mexican
Turkey	
	Egyptian

> **The nationality words above are adjectives. We can also use them to describe food, people, etc.**
>
> I love *Mexican* food.
> I live with two *Australian* women and a *Polish* man.
> I watch a lot of *Italian* football.

B Work in pairs. Discuss what you can see in the photos below.

C Work in groups. Discuss these questions.
- Can you name any famous people from each of the countries in exercise A?
- Do you know any people from any of these countries? Who?
- What do you know about the different kinds of food from each country?
- Do you know any other famous things from each country?

PRACTICE

Complete the form with your own answers.

SURNAME

FIRST NAME

MIDDLE NAME(S)

GENDER   MALE ☐
                FEMALE ☐

NATIONALITY

DATE OF BIRTH

ADDRESS

TELEPHONE NUMBER

02 WRITING
PEN FRIENDS

SPEAKING

Work in groups. Discuss these questions.
- Which people in the photos like doing the same things as you?
- How often do you do these things?
- Are you good at them?
- Are there any activities in the pictures you really don't like doing? Why not?

WRITING Looking for a pen friend

A Complete this Internet advert with the words in the box.

first	brothers	foreign	full	meeting
part-time	playing	student	parents	usually

B Work in pairs. Discuss how you are similar to Tiiu and how you are different. For example:

> She likes swimming, and I do too.

> She lives with her parents, but I don't. I live on my own.

Hi,

My name's Tiiu (pronounced Tee-you). Well, that's my ¹........................... name. My ²........................... name is Tiiu Lipping, but people ³........................... just call me T! I'm from Estonia, in the north of Europe – it's next to Russia and above Latvia – and I want to write to someone in a ⁴........................... country. It's a good way to practise my English.

I live in the capital city, Tallinn. I'm a ⁵........................... at Tallinn University. I'm studying Medicine. I want to be a doctor in the future. I also work ⁶........................... in a shop. I enjoy it because I like ⁷........................... people and the money's OK.

I like swimming, ⁸........................... tennis and reading. I live with my mum and dad and my three ⁹........................... . It's OK. I really want to have my own flat, but my ¹⁰........................... say I'm too young – I'm 19.

Anyway, if you want to write to someone from Estonia, try me! Tell me about yourself.

Tiiu

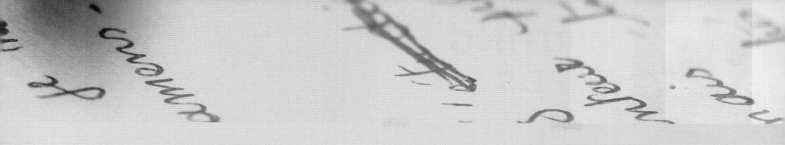

KEY WORDS FOR WRITING *and*

And **is a linking word. We use *and* to join words and phrases together.**
I live with my mum and dad. I live with my three brothers.
= I live with my mum and dad *and* I live with my three brothers.

....

Note that we don't need to repeat *I live with*.

....

When more than two words or phrases are connected, we only use *and* between the last two.
I like swimming. I like playing tennis. I like reading.
= I like swimming, I like playing tennis *and* reading.

....

Note that we don't need to repeat *I like*.

Connect these sentences using *and*.

1   I play volleyball. I play golf.
....

2   Bangkok is really crowded. It's polluted.
....

   3   I like reading. I like learning languages. I like computers.
....

4   My brother lives in Dubai. My sister lives in Istanbul.
....

5   I live with my mum and dad. I live with my sister. I live with my aunt. I live with my grandfather.
....

PRACTICE

Write a reply to Tiiu. Tell her:
*   where you are from and where you live.
*   what you do.
*   what you like doing.
*   who you live with.

Use some of these expressions.
*   My full name is .... , but people usually call me ....
*   I'm from .... and I live in ....
*   I live with .... / I live on my own.
*   I like .... , ... and ....

SPEAKING

A **Match the cards in the box to the pictures.**

a birthday card	a Valentine card
a Christmas card	a get well soon card
a Mother's Day card	a wedding card

B **Work in groups. Discuss these questions.**
- Do you ever send cards or e-cards? Who to? When? Why?
- Can you remember the last card you sent?
- Can you remember the last card you received?
- What kind of thing is good to write in the different kinds of cards in the box?

VOCABULARY
Beginning and ending cards

To show who a card is for, we usually write *Dear* + first name. For example:
Dear Yoichi,
Dear Tom and Susanna,

- -

We usually finish with one of these expressions and then our first name.
Regards,   (= for people we don't know very well)

Best wishes   (= for friends)
All the best,

Lots of love,   (= for family members and old friends)
Love,

1

2

3

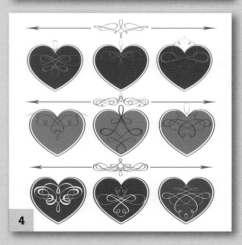

4

5

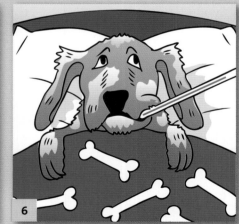

6

Cover the explanation and complete the cards with ONE word in each gap.

1........................... Sally,

Happy birthday!
I hope you have a great day.

2........................... wishes,
Trini

Dear Maria ³........................... Miguel,

Congratulations on your new baby boy.
I hope you are all well.

Lots of ⁴........................... ,

Rebecca

Dear Aaron,

Good luck with your new job.
I hope everything goes well.

All the ⁵........................... ,

Suzie

KEY WORDS FOR WRITING *hope*

We use *hope* to show what we want to be true or to happen in the future.
I *hope* you are all well. (= now / at the moment)
I *hope* everything goes well. (= in the future)

Note that when we use *hope* to talk about the future, we use a verb in the present simple form after it.

A Match the sentences with the follow-up comments.
1 Sorry to hear you were ill.
2 Sorry to hear about your computer.
3 Good luck with your exams next week.
4 Good luck with your interview.
5 Happy birthday.
6 Happy Christmas and New Year.

a I hope you have a fantastic day.
b I hope you get the job.
c I hope it isn't too expensive to replace.
d I hope you're feeling better now.
e I hope you enjoy your holiday.
f I hope you pass them all.

B Work in pairs. Discuss why people hope the things in the sentences below. For example:
I hope it doesn't rain.

> Maybe the person wants to go to the beach.

> Yes, or maybe they want to play football in the park.

1 I hope it's open tonight.
2 I hope she got home OK.
3 I hope you like it.
4 I hope they lose!
5 I hope it doesn't take too long.

C Think of two things you hope are true or that you hope happen in the future. Tell a partner your ideas.

PRACTICE

Write three cards to different people. They can be birthday cards, cards wishing someone good luck, wedding cards, etc. Use some language from these pages.

SPEAKING

Work in groups. Discuss these questions.

- Where are the most popular meeting places in your town / city?
- Where do you usually meet your friends?
- Do you usually arrive before, at or after the time you agree to meet? Why?
- What are good meeting places for these different kinds of people:
  - parents with children?
  - teenagers?
  - older people?
  - people going on a date?

WRITING Making arrangements

A Complete the email with the words in the box.

four	me	that	what	where

To   melkent@shoemail.gb

Subject   Tomorrow

Hi Mel,

Let me know ¹………………… time you want to meet tomorrow – and ²………………… . My class finishes at ³………………… , so any time after ⁴………………… is fine with ⁵………………… .

All the best,

Emma

B Complete Mel's reply to Emma with the words in the box.

can	from	on	near	easy

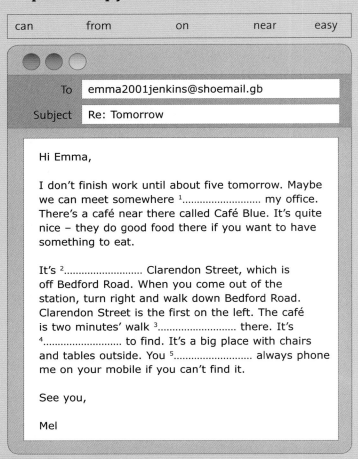

To   emma2001jenkins@shoemail.gb

Subject   Re: Tomorrow

Hi Emma,

I don't finish work until about five tomorrow. Maybe we can meet somewhere ¹………………… my office. There's a café near there called Café Blue. It's quite nice – they do good food there if you want to have something to eat.

It's ²………………… Clarendon Street, which is off Bedford Road. When you come out of the station, turn right and walk down Bedford Road. Clarendon Street is the first on the left. The café is two minutes' walk ³………………… there. It's ⁴………………… to find. It's a big place with chairs and tables outside. You ⁵………………… always phone me on your mobile if you can't find it.

See you,

Mel

C Write the names of the places from Mel's email in a–d on the map. Then compare with a partner.

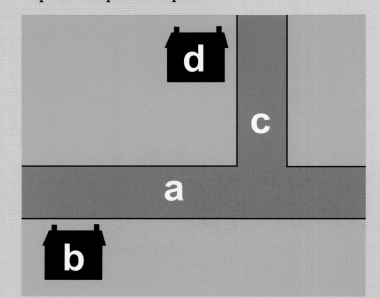

GRAMMAR The present simple to talk about the future

> We use the present simple to talk about timetables in the future – trains, planes, buses, classes, work, films, etc.
>
> My class *finishes* at four.
> I *don't finish* work until about five tomorrow.

A Complete the sentences with the present simple form of the verbs in brackets.

1 What time .... you .... work tomorrow? (finish)
2 What time .... your flight on Sunday? (be)
3 I .... work until 12 tomorrow, so we can meet in the morning. (not / start)
4 I don't want to miss the last bus. It .... at 11.30. (leave)
5 The shop .... until ten, so let's meet at around half past nine. (not / open)
6 My train .... at eight, so we can meet after that. (arrive)
7 The café .... at eight, so we need to get there before then. (close)
8 I think the film .... at about seven. (end)

B Work in pairs. Discuss these questions.

- What time does your class finish today?
- When is your next English class? What time does it start and finish?
- What time do you start work / school tomorrow?

KEY WORDS FOR WRITING *which*

> We can use *which* to add more information about a thing / place to the same sentence.
>
> It's on Clarendon Street, *which* is off Bedford Road.
> = It's on Clarendon Street. Clarendon Street is off Bedford Road.

Connect these sentences using *which*.

1 I work in Leeds. Leeds is about 30 kilometres from my house.

....

2 I come from Gabon. It is in central Africa.

....

3 The party is in Menteng. Menteng is in the centre of the city.

....

4 There's an Italian restaurant near the cinema. It does really good pizza.

....

5 I want to see a film called *Departures*. The film starts at eight.

....

PRACTICE

Write your own reply to Emma. Arrange where and what time to meet. Use Mel's email to help you.

05 WRITING
VISITING FRIENDS

SPEAKING

Work in groups. Discuss these questions.
- Do you have any friends or relatives in other towns, cities or countries?
- Where do they live? What do they do there?
- Have you ever visited them? If yes, when? How long for? Did you have a good time?
- Have they ever visited you? If yes, when? How long for? Did you take them anywhere special?

VOCABULARY Places to visit

A Match the words in the box to the pictures.

beach	church	lake	tower	castle
gallery	island	mosque	waterfall	

B Work in pairs. Discuss these questions.
- Which of the places in the box do you have near where you live?
- Do you ever visit these places? How often?
- Which places do you recommend the most? Why?

WRITING 1
Arranging to visit a friend

A Complete the email with the words in the box.

can	planning	where
like	when	while

To   jackcracker@shoemail.gb

Subject   Visiting the UK!

Hi Jack,
I'm ¹.......................... to come to the UK in the summer. I'd ².......................... to visit you in Nottingham, if possible. ³.......................... you send me an email to tell me if and ⁴.......................... I can visit? Also, ⁵.......................... else do you think I should go ⁶.......................... I'm in England? I'm going to stay for about three weeks.

Best,
Giorgio

B Look at this email. <u>Underline</u> everything that is the same as in Giorgio's email.

To   f.cremers@shoemail.gb

Subject   Visiting Germany!

Hi Frank,
I'm planning to come to Germany on holiday in April. I'd like to visit you in Frankfurt, if possible. Can you send me an email to let me know if and when I can visit? Also, where else do you think I should go while I'm in Germany? I'm only going to stay for about three weeks.

Best,
Tanya

C Write an email to a friend in another country. Use language from the two emails above.

WRITING 2
Making recommendations

A Below is a reply to one of the emails from Writing 1. Complete it with the words in the box.

it depends	really pleased
you like	OK with you
the weather's nice	you prefer

To   t.tucker@shoemail.gb

Subject   Re: Visiting Germany!

Hi Tanya,
Thanks for your email. It was really nice to hear from you again. I'm ¹.......................... to hear you're planning to come to Germany in April. If ².......................... , you can stay at my flat. I've got a spare room. I'm afraid it's not very big, but you can sleep there, if that's ³.......................... .

You asked about places to visit. Well, ⁴.......................... what you want to do. If you like cities, you should go to Berlin. It's great, and there are lots of things to do there. It's also good if you're interested in history. If ⁵.......................... the countryside, you should go to the Allgäu, in the south. It's a really lovely place to go if ⁶.......................... . There are lots of rivers and lakes, and some amazing old castles.

Anyway, write to me again when your plans are clearer. I'm really looking forward to seeing you again.

Best,
Frank

B Which place sounds better to you – Berlin or the Allgäu? Why?

KEY WORDS FOR WRITING *if*

We often make suggestions using *If you ..., you should ... .*

If you like cities, *you should* go to Berlin.
If you prefer the countryside, *you should* go to the Allgäu.

A Match 1–5 to a–e to make whole sentences.
1 If you like tennis,
2 If you like the countryside,
3 If you like the sea,
4 If you like shopping,
5 If you're interested in history,

a you should go to the Komensky Museum.
b you should go to Wangfujing Street. That's where the big department stores are.
c you should go to Albufeira. It has some great beaches.
d you should watch some games at Wimbledon.
e you should go to Brittany. It's really beautiful.

B Write three similar sentences about your country.
If you .... , you should ....
If you .... , you should ....
If you .... , you should ....

We use lots of other expressions with *if*.

If you like, you can stay at my flat.

C Complete the sentences with the words in the box.

like	necessary	OK	possible	weather

1 You can stay at our house, if you ....
2 I'd like to come and visit you when I'm in London, if ....
3 I really need some help. I can pay someone, if ....
4 Do you want to go for a picnic on Saturday if the ....'s nice?
5 I'm going to arrive at your house at around six o'clock, if that's .... with you.

D Translate the five expressions with *if* from exercise C into your language.

PRACTICE

Write to a foreign friend who is planning to visit your country. Before you write, underline any language in Frank's email that you want to use.

SPEAKING

Work in groups. Discuss these questions.
- What do you know about each of the different kinds of food in the pictures below?
- Which have you tried? What did you have? Did you like it?
- What other different kinds of food have you tried? When? Where? What did you have?

WRITING Food from my country

A Complete the email with the words in the box.

grill	heard	pork	share
healthy	pasta	red	typical

To   pshaw@shoemail.gb

Subject   Food!

Hi again,

How're you? I hope you're well. You asked me about ¹............................ Argentinean food. Well, let me tell you about it.

I love it, even though it's not very ²............................ ! In Argentina, we eat a lot of ³............................ meat – especially beef. I think we have the best beef in the world. Our cows are free to run around in the countryside! We usually ⁴............................ the beef on a barbecue, and we cook lots of other meat like this, too – lamb, ⁵............................ , chicken. We usually eat the meat with salad or chips.

We also eat a lot of pizza and ⁶............................ because there are lots of Italians living here. We have great ice cream, too!

Oh, I nearly forgot, we have a special drink called *mate*, which is very important here, too. Have you ⁷............................ of it? It's a kind of tea and we ⁸............................ it with friends. It's very nice.

Anyway, write and tell me about the food in your country.

All the best,
Héctor

B Work in pairs. Discuss these questions.
- Have you ever tried Argentinean beef – or any other Argentinean food?
- From Héctor's email, do you think Argentinean food sounds good? Why? / Why not?
- What sounds best to you?
- Have you ever heard of *mate*?
- What kinds of food / drinks do you usually share with friends?

KEY WORDS FOR WRITING
even though ...

> We use *even though* to connect ideas. It shows that something is true or happened and that this is surprising because of something else that is true or that happened.
> I love Argentinean food, *even though* it's not very healthy.
> (= It's surprising I love it, because it's not very healthy.)
>
> ....
>
> *Even though* can also come at the beginning of a sentence.
> *Even though* she eats a lot of fast food, she never puts on weight.
> (= It's surprising she never puts on weight, because she eats a lot of fast food.)

A Work in pairs. Think of a possible ending for each of the sentences.
1 Even though it's quite expensive, I love ... .
2 I eat a lot of red meat, even though ... .
3 Even though I drink a lot of coffee, I ... .
4 I like him a lot, even though ... .
5 Even though I am English, I ... .

B Connect the sentences using *even though*.
1 I got the job. I didn't have any experience.
   ....
2 I got a job in Japan. I didn't speak any Japanese.
   ....
3 I didn't study. I passed my exam.
   ....
4 I'm not very good at cooking. I love it.
   ....
5 They're going to move to Italy. They don't speak Italian and they haven't got any work there.
   ....

PRACTICE

A Choose the words that are true for you and your country.
1 We *eat a lot of / don't eat much* red meat.
2 We usually *grill / fry / roast* meat.
3 We *eat a lot of / don't eat much* fish and seafood.
4 We *eat a lot of / don't eat much* fresh fruit and vegetables.
5 We eat quite a lot of *potatoes / pasta / rice*.
6 The food here *is quite / isn't very* spicy.
7 *I think / I don't think* we eat very healthily.
8 *I think / I don't think* our food is the best food in the world!

B Now write an email to Héctor in Argentina. Tell him about the food in your country. Use language from exercise A and from Héctor's email. Start like this:

Dear Héctor,
Hi, how're you? Thanks for your last email. It was really interesting. So let me tell you about the food in … .

SPEAKING

Work in groups. Discuss these questions.
- Do you like taking photos? Are you good at it?
- What do you take photos of?
- Do you share photos on the Internet? On which websites?
- Do you often look at other people's photos?
- Do you like seeing photos of yourself? Why? / Why not?
- Have you got any photos on your mobile phone? What of?

WRITING Describing photos

You are going to read two descriptions of the photos on this page.

A **Before you read, which words in the box do you think go with each photo on the right?**

her tail	protected	forest
cheer up	wolves	cute

B **Now read the texts and see if you were right.**

C **Discuss these questions.**
- Which photo do you like best? Why?
- Do the pictures and text
  - make you want to have a cat? Why? / Why not?
  - make you want to go to Great Bear Forest? Why? / Why not?
- Has anyone ever bought you something to cheer you up? What? Why were you sad in the first place?
- Have you ever been for a walk in the rain? Where? Why did you go?

1   This is a picture of me with my new cat, Twinky. It's a she. I've been ill, so my parents bought her to cheer me up. And it worked! She looks so cute and she's really funny – especially when she chases her tail! She makes me laugh. She's seven months old now and she runs around and plays all the time. I love her. I'm feeling a lot better now so I might go back to school next week or the week after.

2   This is a picture of me and my friends walking in Great Bear Forest. It's near where I live in Vancouver, so we often go there – sometimes just for the day and sometimes longer. As you can see, the scenery is amazing with the mountains and rivers and trees. The area is protected because some of the trees are 1,000 years old and there are animals like bears and wolves – oh, and there are salmon too. It's sunny sometimes, but the day we took this photo, it rained all day. We decided to walk across the river because we were already so wet! Luckily, it was also a warm day, so we didn't get cold. I know I don't look happy, but we really had a good time!

KEY WORDS FOR WRITING *so*

> We use *so* to link a reason to an action.
> ....
> reason   action
> <u>I've been ill</u>, *so* <u>my parents bought her to cheer me up</u>.
>
> We also use *so* to mean *very*.
> She looks *so* cute.

A Find an example of each use of *so* in text 2 in *Writing*.

B Add *so* in the correct place in the sentences.
1 I look strange in this photo.
2 It was his birthday I made him a cake.
3 It rained a lot we spent most of the holiday indoors.
4 I was happy when I opened the present.
5 You can't see her very well in the photo because it was dark.
6 We missed our plane we had to wait in the airport for six hours.

C Rewrite these sentences with *so*.
1 You look very young there!
2 We didn't go because it snowed.
3 I took a photo because I wanted to show you my dog.
4 You look very bored. Were you?

GRAMMAR Linking verbs

> *Look* can be followed by an adjective, like the verb *be*.
> She *looks so cute*.
> I know I don't *look happy*, but we had a good time.
> ....
> *Get, feel, seem, sound* and *taste* can be used in the same way.

Complete the sentences with the correct form of the verb and the adjective in brackets.
1 The man who .... in this photo is my brother. (look / bored)
2 This is a photo of me when I was trying the local tea – it .... (taste / horrible)
3 I didn't have a jersey with me so I .... (get / really cold)
4 I didn't speak to her very much, but she .... (seem / nice).
5 I hate this photo. I .... in it. (look / stupid)
6 This is a photo of the band I went to see. It's a shame you can't hear their music – they .... (sound / great)

PRACTICE

You are going to write about a photo.

A Work in pairs. Choose one of the photos on this page or one of your own. Talk about:
- where the photo was taken.
- who the people are.
- what they are doing.
- the weather.
- how they look, feel, etc.
- anything that happened before or after the photo was taken.

B Write a short description of between 40 and 100 words.

SPEAKING

Work in groups. Discuss these questions.
- Do you send text messages much?
- Do you use abbreviations? Which ones?
- Have you ever texted in English?
- Do you answer the phone in your house / at work?
- Do you write down notes for people? What was the last note you wrote? Who for?

VOCABULARY Texting

These numbers and letters are short forms that people use for texting.

1	= one
2	= to, too or to-
4	= for or sound /fɔː/
8	= the sound /eɪt/
b	= be or sound /biː/
c	= see
r	= are
u	= you
ne	= any
thx	= thanks
asap	= as soon as possible

People also often miss out letters if the word is clear without them, and sometimes they change them.
Hapy New Yr
Luv u

A Write these in normal words.
1. I'm l8.
2. c u l8r 2day.
3. ruok?
4. ne1 there yet?
5. thx 4 ur help.
6. Just arrived. gr8 2 b here!

B Work in pairs. Write these sentences as text messages.
1. I'll see you tomorrow.
2. Are you free now?
3. Can you be here as soon as possible?
4. I'm on my way. Do you need anything?

WRITING Messages and notes

Look at the text messages and notes. They tell a story of a love affair between Dominic (Dom) and Lily (L).

A Put the messages and notes a–j in order. Here is the first one.

Hpy Bday!
Sent smthng
in post. Hope
u got it.
Luv u. L x

gd idea. c u at 12.

a

u wan 2
meet 4 lnch?

b

Gone to
lunch

c

Dom phoned.
Said it was urgent.
Sounded upset

d

e — hope ur ok!

f — Sorry, Lily. It's over. Not u, me! I'll try and xplain 1 day. Sorry

g — where r u?

h — prblm! Don't w8 4 me.

i — tried 2 ring. No answr! v worried. Luv u. L xx

j — Thx 4 presnt. Its gr8, but 2 much!

The order is:

1 ☐ 2 ☐ 3 ☐ 4 ☐ 5 ☐

6 ☐ 7 [e] 8 ☐ 9 [i] 10 ☐

B Compare your ideas. Did you have the same order?

C Work in pairs. Discuss the questions.
- What do you think the present was?
- What do you think happened to Dom?
- What do you think of him?
- Have you heard of anyone else ending a relationship? How did they do it? Is there a good / bad way to do it?

GRAMMAR Notes and missing words

> **When we write notes and messages, we often leave out some grammar words.**
> *You OK?* = Are you OK?
> *Gone to bank.* = I have gone to the bank.
> *Ian called. Can't come to meeting.* = Ian called. He can't come to the meeting.
> ....
> **We often use imperatives.**
> *Call her.* = Can you call her?

A In full sentences, write the first four messages of the story – j, b, a and c.

B Write these as notes.
1 Melissa phoned. She's going to be late.
2 Can you go to the shops? We need some milk and a packet of pasta.
3 I had to go out. Your dinner is in the fridge. You can heat it up in the microwave.

PRACTICE

You are going to have short conversations with text messages.

A Work in pairs. Write a text message for your partner.

B Give your message to your partner and write a reply to theirs. Continue for two or three turns.

01 STARTER UNIT

PLURALS

For regular nouns, add -s or -es or change -y to -ies.

car	→	cars	baby	→	babies
pen	→	pens	factory	→	factories
class	→	classes			

Irregular nouns

child	→	children	person	→	people
man	→	men	woman	→	women

Uncountable nouns

Some nouns are uncountable. They are not usually in the plural.

money   cheese   water

Exercise 1

Correct the sentences by making the nouns plural.

1 Do you have any pen?
2 We have three child.
3 There are three big factory near here.
4 I want three bottle of water, please.
5 Man don't talk about how they feel.
6 He is six year old.

A / AN / SOME

Use a with a singular noun or an when it starts with a vowel.

a hamburger	a man	an apple
a bottle	a person	an orange

Use some with a plural noun.

some bottles	some people	some apples

With uncountable nouns, don't use a / an. Use some or nothing.

I want some cheese.	I like cheese.
Do you need some money?	He has money.
Put some music on.	I don't listen to music.

Exercise 1

Complete the sentences with a / an / some.

1 We need to buy .... oranges.
2 I have two brothers and .... sister.
3 Give him .... money.
4 Have .... apple, if you want.
5 There are .... people outside.
6 He's .... very nice person.
7 My mum has .... older brother.
8 .... hamburger and .... chips, please.

02 STARTER UNIT

DON'T / DO

Make negatives with don't + verb. Use doesn't with he / she / it. Don't = Do not. Doesn't = Does not.
I don't like coffee.
Don't talk!
She doesn't speak English.

Make questions with do you / they / we + verb or does he / she / it.

Do you like coffee?	Does he like football?
Do they work?	How long does it take?

Exercise 1

Make the sentences negative.

1 Talk to him.
2 She likes me.
3 I like her.
4 We go to the cinema a lot.
5 He works.

Make questions.

6 you / like / tea?
7 where / you / work?
8 which one / they / want?
9 she / play / tennis?
10 when / the class / finish?

PRONOUNS AND POSSESSIVE ADJECTIVES

A pronoun replaces a noun before a verb (subject) or after a verb (object).
My dad likes coffee.
He likes it.

A possessive adjective before a noun shows who owns it.
I think you have my book!

subject	object	possessive
I	me	my book
you	you	your book
he	him	his book
she	her	her book
it	it	its food
we	us	our book
they	them	their book

Exercise 1

Choose the correct words.

1 I / Me / My want to take a photo.
2 Are you hungry? Eat I / me / my sandwich!
3 She / Her is 13.
4 Say it / its again. I didn't hear.
5 Listen to he / him / his.
6 Where's they / them / their house?
7 We / Us / Our like tennis.
8 Phone I / me / my tonight.

BE

The verb *be* is special. Look at how it changes. It also has a short form.

I am	I'm 17.
You are	You're late.
He is	He's a nurse.
She is	She's married.
It is	It's 12 o'clock.
We are	We're tired.
They are	They're hungry.

Change the word order to make questions.
Sorry, *am I* late?
Are you hungry?
What time *is it*?
Are they married?

NOT ~~I am late?, You are hungry?, What time it is?~~ etc.

Add *not* to make negatives.
I'm *not* cold.
He's *not* married.
It's *not* a problem.
They're *not* here yet.

Exercise 1
Write sentences and questions using the notes.
1 I / be / cold.
    I'm cold.
2 He / be / 16.
3 My sister / be / a doctor.
4 My children / be / both girls.
5 They / be / late.
6 It / be / six o'clock.
7 I / be / not / hungry.
8 We / be / not / married.
9 It / be / not / very expensive.
10 be / you / very tired?
11 be / it / nice?
12 how old / be / they?

GRAMMAR WORDS

Remember these useful grammar words:

Words	Examples
Verb	want, go, have, look
Noun	brother, coffee, tennis, problem
Adjective	good, big, red, expensive
Preposition	in, on, of, from, at

Sentences are usually subject–verb–object (SVO)
S   V   O
I learn English at school.

        S   V   O
My teacher helps us a lot.

Exercise 1
Write the plural form.
1 parent ....
2 house ....
3 woman ....
4 child ....
5 baby ....
6 factory ....
7 person ....
8 car ....
9 man ....
10 apple ....

Exercise 2
Choose the correct words.
1 She has *a / an / some* baby.
2 *His / He / Some* house is very big.
3 I *am / is / are* 25.
4 I live with *their / them / they*.
5 Do you want *a / an / some* apple?
6 *His / She / Yours* sisters are at my school.
7 Write it on *an / some / me* paper.
8 Where is *she / you / her*?
9 *Do / Are / Is* you like chocolate?
10 There are *a / an / some* men in my class, but not many.

Exercise 3
Put the words in the correct order.
1 you how are?
2 him ask .
3 I you like .
4 coffee wants she some .
5 when class does your start ?
6 sport I watch don't .
7 brother a my has car nice .
8 her to he doesn't talk .

Exercise 4
Complete the questions with *do, does, is* or *are*.
1 .... you like chocolate?
2 Where .... she work?
3 .... you OK?
4 Which one .... you prefer?
5 Where .... she from?
6 What time .... it?
7 .... you hungry?
8 What .... you want?

Exercise 5
Complete the text with ONE word in each gap.

Hi. I [1]........................ Alex and this is [2]........................ family. We [3]........................ from the UK. We [4]........................ in a big house in Bristol. I have [5]........................ older brother and [6]........................ younger sister. My sister and I are students. My brother [7]........................ married. He's a doctor. [8]........................ wife is called Poppy and [9]........................ is a teacher. We see [10]........................ a lot because they live very near us.

01 PEOPLE AND PLACES

THE VERB *BE*

The verb *be* is followed by adjectives (*cold, hungry,* etc.) or nouns (*Bruce, Germany,* etc.).

Hello. *I'm* Bruce. (= I am)
You're late! (= You are)
He's a doctor. (= He is)
She's 21. (= She is)
It's cold today. (= It is)
We're from Venezuela. (= We are)
They're our friends. (= They are)

Negatives

I'm not hungry. (= I am not)
You're not in the right class. (= You are not)
He's not French. (= He is not)
She's not very interesting. (= She is not)
It's not cheap. (= It is not)
We're not happy about it. (= We are not)
They're not married. (= They are not)

You can also say: *You aren't ... , My dad isn't ... , My mum isn't ... , The book isn't ... , We aren't ...* and *Things aren't... .*

In normal spoken English, we use short forms.

Questions

Am I next?
Are you OK?
Is he happy here?
Is she ill today?
Is it cold outside?
Where *are we*?
Where *are they*?

Exercise 1

Re-write the sentences with the short forms of *be*.

1 I am cold.   ....
2 You are in Class 1.   ....
3 He is not here today.   ....
4 She is my sister.   ....
5 It is not very nice.   ....
6 We are on holiday.   ....
7 They are late!   ....

Exercise 2

Complete the sentences with the correct forms of *be*.

1 A: Hi. How ...... you?
   B: I ...... OK, thanks.
2 A: Where ...... you from? ...... you English?
   B: No, I ...... not. I ...... Irish, actually.
3 A: How ...... your parents? ...... they OK?
   B: Yes, they ...... fine, thank you.
4 A: Where ...... your boyfriend from? ...... he
      French, too?
   B: No, he ...... not. He ...... English.
5 A: What ...... your friend's name?
   B: Oh, I ...... sorry. This ...... Rachel.

THERE IS ... / THERE ARE ...

Use *there is / there's* with singular nouns.
Use *there are* with plural nouns.

There's a nice café near here.
There's some food in the kitchen.
There's a lot of traffic today.

There are a few cheap hotels in town.
There are some great beaches in that area.
There are lots of people outside.

Negatives

There isn't any / much milk.
There's no milk.
There aren't any / many glasses in here.
There are no glasses.

Questions

Is there a bus stop near here?
Are there any good cafés in town?

Some nouns are uncountable singular nouns.
traffic crime countryside.

Exercise 1

Complete the sentences with *there's, there isn't, there are* or *there aren't*.

1 .... lots of nice shops near my
   house.
2 .... any coffee in here.
3 .... some great countryside in
   the north.
4 .... any hospitals in the area.
5 .... a lot of crime in the town.
   It's awful!
6 .... any schools in the village!
7 .... no traffic on the roads
   today. It's great!
8 .... two or three little bars
   near the beach.

Exercise 2

Correct the mistake in each sentence.

1 There is no cheap hotels.
2 Not there are any jobs here.
3 It have a lovely river in the town.
4 There are lots of noise!
5 There is a lot of traffics in my hometown.

> ### Glossary
>
> **awful:** if something is awful, it's very bad
> **a bar:** you can buy alcoholic drinks in a bar
> **boring:** something boring is not fun or interesting

THE PRESENT SIMPLE

We use the present simple to talk about facts that are always true and habits.

I *live* in Madrid.
You *drink* a lot of coffee!
She *wants* to be a doctor.
He *goes* swimming every day.
It *rains* a lot in the winter.
We *live* in the north of the country.
They *live* in the south.

Notice that with *he / she / it*, we add *-s* at the end of the verb. However, we write *he goes, she does, it has* – not *he gos, she dos, it haves*.

Negatives

I *don't like* the town very much. (= do not)
You *don't know* my town, I'm sure.
He *doesn't have* any brothers or sisters. (= does not)
She *doesn't feel* safe.
It *doesn't snow* very often.
We *don't go* there very often.
They *don't visit* us very often.

Notice that with *he / she / it*, we use *doesn't* – not *don't*.

Questions

Where *do I go* now?
Where *do you live*?
What *does he do*?
Where *does she work*?
How much *does it cost*?
How *do we know*?
Do they have any children?

Notice that with *he / she / it*, we use *does* – not *do*.

Exercise 1

Choose the correct words.

1 My brother *have / has* three children.
2 Does he *like / likes* his job?
3 Where *do / does* your grandparents live?
4 I *doesn't / don't* like football.
5 It *don't / doesn't* rain much.
6 She *has / have / haves* a boyfriend.

Exercise 2

Complete the questions.

1 Where .... your parents live?
2 When .... she finish work?
3 How many hours .... your mum work every day?
4 How much .... this bag cost?
5 What music .... you like?
6 What .... your father do?
7 Why .... they like him? He's awful!
8 How .... it feel?

REVISION

Exercise 1

Make the sentences negative.

1 I like French food.
....
2 I'm hungry.
....
3 She works here.
....
4 They're from this country.
....
5 I work at the weekends.
....
6 He's in the office today.
....
7 They live together.
....
8 It's cold today.
....
9 There are some shops in the village.
....
10 There's some sugar in the kitchen.
....

Exercise 2

Complete the sentences in the present simple. Use short forms where possible.

1 She .... sport. (not / like)
2 There .... any nice shops near there. (not / be)
3 When .... you usually .... your house in the morning? (leave)
4 There .... a bank in the village. (not / be)
5 We .... English. We .... Scottish. (not / be, be)
6 .... there a post office near here? (be)
7 My father .... a new job. (have)
8 .... they open today? (be)
9 I'm sorry. I .... (not / understand)
10 Where .... she .... ? (live)

Exercise 3

Complete the sentences with ONE word in each gap.

1 Where .... you from?
2 Where .... you work?
3 My sister .... two children.
4 I .... 26 and my sister .... 33.
5 It's a nice house, but it .... have a garden.
6 I .... like shopping, but my wife loves it!
7 My boyfriend .... a teacher. He .... in a school in Seville.
8 .... you speak English?
9 He .... a sister, but I ....
10 .... your mother work?

02 FREE TIME

VERB FORMS

Look at these sentences with -*ing* forms.

I like *watching* TV.
I love *teaching* English.
I hate *living* in the city.
I enjoy *working* on my own.

Notice spelling changes:

live	→	living	swim	→	swimming
have	→	having	run	→	running
dance	→	dancing	chat	→	chatting

Look at these sentences with *to* + verb.

I don't want *to live* in an old building.
I need *to go* now.
Try *to use* the words you learn.
Decide what *to do*.

Remember that we form questions using *do / does* + verb (without *to*).

Do you to *have* any free time?
Where *does* she to *live*?

Exercise 1

Complete the sentences with the correct form of the verbs in brackets.

1 I don't like *swimming* much. (swim)
2 Do you want .... later? (go out)
3 I try .... running every day. (go)
4 I hate .... and I'm very bad at it. (dance)
5 Does your friend .... it here? (like)
6 I need .... tonight. (study)
7 My dad loves .... tennis. (play)
8 We need .... where .... lunch. (decide, have)

Exercise 2

Correct the mistake in each sentence.

1 My brother likes read a lot.
2 Does she to speak English?
3 My parents say that they want have more free time.
4 I don't really enjoy to work in an office.
5 I always try go to bed before 11.
6 I need finishing my homework before I go out.

> ### Glossary
>
> **on my own:** me only
> **run:** go fast
> **history books:** books about facts in the past
> **cook:** make food

ADVERBS OF FREQUENCY

I We They	always usually / normally often sometimes	have a coffee after lunch.
He She	occasionally hardly ever never	has a coffee after lunch.

Negatives

I *don't* go out *very often*.
She *doesn't* visit us *very often*.

Questions

usually / normally

A: Where do you *usually* go out at night?
B: *Normally* into town, but we sometimes go to the beach area.

A: What do you *normally* do at the weekend?
B: I *usually* go to the countryside with my family.

ever (= sometimes / occasionally)

A: Do you *ever* go to the theatre?
B: No, never.

A: Do you *ever* go swimming?
B: Occasionally, but not very often.

Exercise 1

Choose the best adverb.

1 I usually read novels, but I *sometimes / normally* read history books.
2 I don't earn much money, so I *hardly ever / sometimes* go out for dinner.
3 I really like football, but I *never / often* go and watch the matches at the stadium.
4 My mum *usually / always* finishes at six, but she sometimes works late – until eight or nine.
5 I *never / occasionally* drink coffee. I hate the taste and I think it's bad for your health.
6 I love cooking. I *always / occasionally* make dinner for my family.

Exercise 2

Put the adverb in the correct place in each sentence.

1 I sleep until 12 on Sunday mornings. (often)
2 My parents do sport. (hardly ever)
3 I don't go shopping. (very often)
4 I decide what to do in my family. (never)
5 A: Do you go out dancing? (ever)
   B: Sometimes, yes. With friends.
6 A: What time do you get up? (usually)
   B: At seven o'clock during the week.

A / ANY AND ONE / SOME

Do you have Do you want Do you need Have you got	a	bag pen dictionary car tissue watch alarm clock	?
	an	egg idea	
	any	clean clothes ideas scissors	

We can use *any* with some singular nouns. These are uncountable nouns. For example:

work	water	paper
money	milk	fruit
time	tea	salt
help	juice	sugar

In answers, we often replace singular nouns with *one*.

A: Do you have *a car*?
B: No, but I sometimes rent *one*.

We can replace plural / uncountable nouns with *some*.

A: Do you have *any coloured pens*?
B: Yes, there are *some* in my bag. Help yourself.

A: Is there *any milk*?
B: I think there's *some* in the fridge.

Exercise 1
Complete the sentences with ONE word in each gap.
1 Do you have .... ruler?
2 Do you need .... seat?
3 Do you have .... sugar?
4 Do you have .... clothes that you want me to wash?
5 A: Do you want .... fruit?
  B: Yes, please. Have you got .... orange?

Exercise 2
Complete the answers with *one* or *some*.
1 A: Have you got a pen?
  B: I think there's .... on the table.
2 A: Do you have any money with you?
  B: I have .... How much do you need?
3 A: Does Jessica want a cup of coffee?
  B: No, she has .... already.
4 A: Have you got any water?
  B: No, sorry. I think Gary has ....
5 A: Do you have any tissues?
  B: No, but you can get .... from the bathroom.

REVISION

Exercise 1
Complete the sentences with the pairs of words. You might need to change the order.

want + very often	often + like
love + usually	hate + always
hate + never	hardly ever + need

1 I .... doing sport. I .... do something – swimming or running or tennis – every day.
2 I'm not very fit because I .... do any exercise. I .... to start going to a gym or something.
3 I .... to have more free time. I don't go out ....
4 I .... cook dinner for my parents. I .... doing it.
5 I .... getting up early. I .... get up before 11 at the weekends.
6 I .... being late. I .... get to school early.

Exercise 2
Put the words in the correct order.
1 new like I meeting people .
2 I to game buy a want computer .
3 to do you music listening like ?
4 go I cinema to the hardly ever .
5 chat sometimes on I Internet the .
6 I Wednesdays play on tennis usually .
7 get usually what time you home do ?
8 you dancing go do out ever ?

Exercise 3
Write questions with *a / an / any*.
1 A: you / have / white paper?
  B: Yes. Here you are.
2 A: he / have / job / at the moment?
  B: No, he's unemployed.
3 A: you / want / tissue?
  B: Thanks.
4 A: you / need / alarm clock?
  B: No, it's OK. I've got one on my phone.
5 A: you / have / scissors?
  B: Yes. There are some on the kitchen table.
6 A: you / need / help?
  B: No, thanks. I'm OK

Glossary

rent: pay money to use something for a time
fridge: cold place for food.
wash: clean with water
alarm clock: a clock that wakes you up

03 HOME

PREPOSITIONS OF PLACE

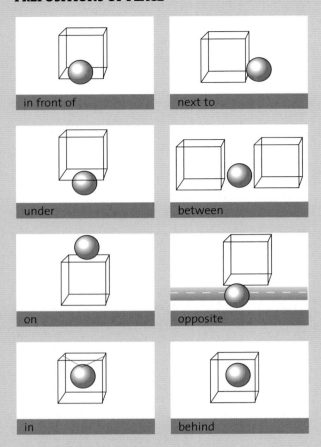

in front of

next to

under

between

on

opposite

in

behind

Notice these expressions we use to describe places.
at the end of the road
on the left / right / corner
in the next street / my street

Exercise 1
Complete the sentences with ONE word in each gap.
1 There's a big car park .... the end of this road.
2 He spends a lot of time .... his room.
3 My house is number 53. It's .... the left.
4 There's a new supermarket .... the corner of Station Road and Queens Road.
5 My sister lives .... the next street to me.
6 I work .... to the big bank in town.
7 There's a good café just .... this road.
8 There are lots of places to eat .... the area.
9 It's small. It's .... two restaurants – a fast food place on one side and a French place on the other.
10 There's a cash machine .... Blackstock Road – .... the right.

> ### Glossary
>
> **car park:** a place to leave your car
> **fast food:** hamburgers, French fries, fried chicken, etc.
> **cash machine:** a place where you can use your cash card to get money

POSSESSIVE ADJECTIVES AND PRONOUNS

subject	object	adjective	pronoun
I	me	my	mine
you	you	your	yours
he	him	his	his
she	her	her	hers
we	us	our	ours
they	them	their	theirs

Possessive adjectives (*my*, *your*, etc.) go before nouns.
Do you like *my jacket?* It's new.
Our house is very near here.

Possessive pronouns (*mine*, *yours*, etc.) can replace a possessive adjective + noun.
I've got my book. That's *yours*.
If you think my room is messy, then look at *hers!*

John's / my parents'
To make clear who or what has the thing, use a noun + *'s*.
her family   his car   their problem
Maria's family   my dad's car   the school's problem

We don't normally say *the family of Maria, the car of my dad* or *the mistake of the school*.

With plurals ending in *s*, use *s'*.
my friends' houses   my parents' wedding

Instead of *his / hers / theirs*, we can just use noun + *'s / s'*.
It's not my car, it's John's / my parents'.

Exercise 1
Choose the correct words.
1 He works for his *parent's / parents'* company.
2 Do you like *Melanie's brothers / brother's Melanie*?
3 I sometimes borrow my *dad's car / car's dad*.
4 That's my *mother's / mothers'* sister.
5 No. That's *your / yours* seat. This one is *Simon's / the seat of Simon*.
6 Hi. *My / Mine* name's Hugh. What's *your / yours*?
7 I sometimes stay in a *friend's flat / flat's friend*.
8 That's *my / mine* sister and this is *her / hers* husband. *Their / Theirs* flat is in Ginza.

Exercise 2
Correct the mistakes in the underlined parts.
1 I like <u>hers room</u>, but I prefer mine.
2 Where do <u>yours parents</u> live?
3 <u>My mums' part of the family</u> are from Malta.
4 What's <u>theirs address</u>?
5 <u>The sister of my boyfriend</u> lives with us.
6 It's not her flat; it's <u>her friends'</u>.
7 I don't like <u>the government ideas</u>.
8 We visit <u>my grandparents house</u> a lot because our house is five minutes away from <u>their</u>.

CAN / CAN'T

To ask (someone) to do something, use *Can*.

| Can | I | stay? |
| | you | open the window? |

Look at these common answers to the questions.

+	–
Of course.	Sorry, no.
Sure.	I'm afraid not.
Go ahead.	Sorry, *you / I can't*.

If something is not possible, use *can't*.

I		do the exercise.
He / She	can't	hear it.
We / They		come to the class.

If something is possible, use *can*.
You can sit where you want.
I can drive.

Exercise 1

Write questions with *can* and explanations with *can't*. The question sometimes comes before and sometimes after the explanations.

I / hear you   you / speak louder
I can't hear you. Can you speak louder?

1 you / move   I / see the board
2 I / do this exercise   you / help me
3 you / turn it up   I / hear the CD
4 I / come to the class   you / tell me the homework
5 I / read the board   I / sit nearer
6 I / go to the toilet   I / wait

Exercise 2

Complete 1–6 with *can* or *can't*. Use the pictures below.

1 You .... watch it. You're only 16.
2 You .... smoke in here.
3 Go ahead. Anyone .... use it.
4 You .... pay here. You need to go over there.
5 You .... go in with me because I'm a member.
6 You .... pay with a cheque, but you .... by card.

Information   4

Members and guests only   5

REVISION

Exercise 1

Complete the sentences with ONE word in each gap.

1 A: Is .... a post office near here?
  B: Yes, there's .... at the end of the road, ... the church.
2 A: Is there a restaurant .... the village?
  B: No, but there's a pub .... this road, ... to the shop.
3 A: Where's the bus stop to go to town?
  B: ....'s just there – in .... of the café .... the right.

Exercise 2

Complete the second sentences using *'s, s'* or a pronoun. For example:

It belongs to me.   →   It's *mine*.
My parents own it.   →   It's *my parents'*.

1 It belongs to him. It's ....
2 They belong to Steve. They're ....
3 They belong to them. They're ....
4 It belongs to the school. It's ....
5 My brothers own the flat. It's ....
6 Doesn't it belong to you? Isn't it .... ?
7 We don't own our house. The house isn't ....
8 It belongs to her. It's ....

Exercise 3

Choose the correct words.

1 A: I *can / can't* find my notebook.
  B: It's *on / in* the shelf, *between / opposite* the dictionary and the black book. I put it there.
  A: Oh right. *Can / Do* you pass it to me?
  B: Sure.
2 A: Who are the two boys in the photo?
  B: The one *on / in* the left is *my / mine* son, and the other boy is a friend of *his / hers*.
  A: Is that your *son's / sons'* guitar?
  B: Yes, but he *can / can't* play it.

> **Glossary**
>
> **go ahead:** do it!
> **pay:** give money for something
> **belong:** if something belongs to you, it's yours
> **own:** if you own something, it's yours
> **shelf:** a place where you put things, e.g. books, cups

04 HOLIDAYS

THE PAST SIMPLE

be

I / He / She / It	was	late.
You / We / They	were	here.

There	was	a cinema here before. a lot of traffic.
	were	lots of people. ten students here yesterday.

Regular verbs
Add -*ed* to the base form of the verb, or -*d* when the base form ends in -*e*.
I played tennis and really loved it.

Notice these spellings.

try – tried	study – studied
chat – chatted	stop – stopped

Irregular verbs
See the full list in the *Vocabulary Builder*.

Past time expressions

yesterday	yesterday morning	last night
two days ago	last week	a few weeks ago
last year	five years ago	when I was 16

Exercise 1
Underline the irregular past forms and write the base verbs at the end of the sentence.
I <u>felt</u> ill, so I <u>went</u> home. *feel, go*

1 I went shopping and got some new boots.
2 I was lucky. I found €20 on the pavement.
3 I slept badly because I drank too much coffee.
4 We met at school. I sat next to her in class.
5 I spent three years in Japan. I taught English there.
6 I saw her yesterday and she said hello to you.

Exercise 2
Complete the story with the past simple form of the verbs in brackets.
This summer, I ¹.......................... (go) to the beach with some friends and we ².......................... (make) a fire. We ³.......................... (sit) round the fire all night and ⁴.......................... (eat) lots of food, ⁵.......................... (talk), ⁶.......................... (tell) jokes and ⁷.......................... (laugh) a lot. At six in the morning, we ⁸.......................... (watch) the sun coming up. It ⁹.......................... (be) beautiful. We really ¹⁰.......................... (love) it. Then we ¹¹.......................... (swim) in the sea. We ¹².......................... (be) very cold afterwards! I ¹³.......................... (get) home at nine o'clock in the morning. I ¹⁴.......................... (have) breakfast and then I ¹⁵.......................... (sleep) till five in the afternoon!

PAST SIMPLE NEGATIVES

wasn't / weren't

I / He / She / It	wasn't	here before
You / We / They	weren't	

There	wasn't	one person on the beach. time to do it.
	weren't	many people. enough seats for everyone.

didn't

I You He / She We They	didn't	hear you. try very hard. come yesterday. go. want anything.

Other negatives
***Couldn't* is the past of *can't*.**
I couldn't go to the class. I was busy.

Other words can also show a negative with the past simple. For example: *never, no-one, nothing, hardly (ever)*, etc.
I never played computer games when I was young.
No-one went to the class last week.
There was nothing to see in Bolton.

Notice we only use one negative word!
He knew nothing about it.
He didn't know anything about it.
NOT *He ~~didn't know nothing~~ about it.*

Exercise 1
Complete the sentences with *didn't / wasn't* or *weren't*.
1 Sorry, I .... hear you. Can you say it again?
2 Sorry I .... clear. It was my mistake.
3 Sorry I .... buy you a present.
4 Sorry there .... more people at the party.
5 Sorry I .... there. I had to work.
6 Sorry I .... see you on Friday. I left early.
7 Sorry I .... do my homework. I was busy.
8 Sorry there .... someone to meet you at the airport.
9 Sorry to hear you .... well last week.
10 Sorry I .... call you yesterday. I forgot.

Exercise 2
Correct the mistake in the verb in each sentence.
1 I don't go to school last week because I was ill.
2 The weather didn't be very nice yesterday.
3 I didn't had a coffee this morning.
4 There weren't time to finish.
5 I didn't do nothing at the weekend.
6 I can't swim when I was at school.

PAST SIMPLE QUESTIONS

Was	it / he / she	OK?
Were	you / they	

	I	tell you it's my birthday?
	you	go out yesterday?
Did	it	rain?
	he / she	go?
	we	see you last?
	they	arrive?

We usually just say *Yes* or *No* to answer questions like these, but sometimes we add *was / wasn't* or *did / didn't*.

A: Did you go out yesterday?
B: *Yes (I did).* I went to the park with some friends.
A: Was it sunny?
B: *No (it wasn't).*
A: Did it rain?
B: *No (it didn't).* It was just quite cloudy.

Question words

Put question words at the beginning of the questions.

How	was your holiday?
Where	was the hotel?
What	did you do?
Who	did you see?
How	long did you stay?
When	did you get back?

Exercise 1

Put the words in the correct order to make questions.
1 did what last do you night ?
2 see you what did film ?
3 it good was ?
4 did go who with you ?
5 where you your buy shoes did ?
6 they very were expensive ?
7 get did you else anything ?
8 you in Jenson's usually do shop ?

Exercise 2

Match the answers a–h to the questions in exercise 1.
a *Four Seasons.* It's a love story.
b No, not really. They were €50.
c No, I didn't. I didn't have any more money.
d Yes, it was really good.
e No, I don't. That was the first time.
f I went to the cinema.
g I went on my own, actually.
h In Jenson's, the department store in town.

Glossary

flight: journey by plane
by (a lake): next to

REVISION

Exercise 1

Write the past forms of the verbs.
1 work ....
2 meet ....
3 make ....
4 move ....
5 want ....
6 stay ....
7 put ....
8 sit ....
9 stop ....
10 try ....
11 see ....
12 walk ....
13 play ....
14 study ....
15 can ....

Exercise 2

Complete the pairs of sentences with a past and a present form of the verbs in the box.

be	have	get	know
go	leave	feel	sleep

1 a They usually .... to the cinema at the weekend.
  b We .... walking in the mountains yesterday.
2 a I'm sure I .... my mobile phone here a moment ago.
  b .... your things there on the table.
3 a Can I go? I .... ill.
  b She .... ill in the class and went home.
4 a We .... a party for my son last night.
  b .... a nice day!
5 a It .... really wet when we were on holiday.
  b It .... lovely weather today!
6 a I normally .... home at seven.
  b I .... home at five this morning.
7 a Put your hand up if you .... the answer.
  b I .... him well at school, but that was ten years ago.
8 a He usually .... very well, but last night he didn't.
  b She was really tired, so she .... during the flight.

Exercise 3

Write the full conversation using the notes.
1 A: Where / you / go / on holiday?
2 B: We / go / to the Czech Republic.
3 A: you / stay / in Prague?
4 B: No / we / not. We / rent / an apartment / by a lake in the mountains.
5 A: it / nice?
6 B: Yes, it / be. We / have / a great time.
7 A: What / you / do?
8 B: We / not do / much. We / read, / we / swim / in the lake / – just relax.
9 A: you / like / the food?
10 B: Yes / we / love / it! We / eat out / a lot.
11 A: How long / you / be / there?
12 B: Two weeks. We / arrive / back yesterday.

05 SHOPS

THIS / THAT / THESE / THOSE

Use *this / these* with singular and uncountable nouns that you can reach or touch.

Use *that / those* with plural nouns that you can't reach.

this	is nice	these	are nice
that	one	those	ones
	book		books
	cheese (uncountable)		people (plural)

This / That / These / Those can replace a noun.
What's this?
Whose are those?

Exercise 1
Correct the mistake in each sentence.
1 Can you give me this book over there?
2 Where are that pens you gave me for my birthday?
3 Whose is these? It's not mine.
4 That jeans are nice. Where did you get them?
5 Which do you prefer? This boots or those ones?
6 This cheeses is really nice. Can I have some more?

PRESENT CONTINUOUS

Use the present continuous to talk about things happening around now which are temporary and not finished.

I	am		improving.
She / He / It	is	(not)	trying.
You / We / They	are		working.

Are	you / they	
Is	she / he	getting tired?

When speaking, we usually use contractions (*I'm / she's / they're / who's / what're*, etc.).
I'm working.
What're you studying?

Notice the spelling changes.
have → *having*   move → *moving*
get   → *getting*   stop → *stopping*

Exercise 1
Make present continuous sentences using the notes.
1 Can you come back later? I / talk / to someone.
2 Where / he / go?
3 They / build / some flats opposite my house.
4 you / look for / something?
5 I / not go / outside now. It / rain.
6 She / chat / to her mother on the phone.
7 Shhh! The baby / sleep.
8 He's not ready. He / get / dressed.

REVISION

Exercise 1
Complete the sentences with *this* or *these*.
1 .... cake's delicious. Do you want some?
2 I can't open the top of .... bottle. Can you do it?
3 I need some new shoes. .... ones are really old.
4 .... book's really interesting. You can read it after I finish it, if you like.
5 Where do you want me to put .... things?

Complete the sentences with *that* or *those*.
6 Where did you get .... shoes? They're really nice.
7 What's .... over there?
8 The fruit in .... shop isn't very good.
9 We went to .... restaurant last week.
10 Can you move .... papers? I want to set the table.

Exercise 2
Add the correct form of *be* in the sentences. For example:

are
What you trying to do?
1 Who Tamara talking to?
2 I looking for a job at the moment.
3 I not feeling very well.
4 you waiting for someone?
5 You making a mess. Clean the table when you finish.
6 He went into town. He doing some shopping.
7 Henry and Terry not coming, so we can start the meeting now.

Exercise 3
Correct the mistake in each sentence.
1 We're stay in the Grand Hotel.
2 I not am working at the moment.
3 What she's doing in Australia?
4 Is you staying here a long time?
5 He's runing in a marathon today.
6 They're haveing a meeting.

> ### Glossary
>
> **build:** if you build a flat or house, you make / construct it
> **rain:** if it's raining, the weather is wet
> **ready:** if you are ready, you're prepared to start something
> **marathon:** 49 km race

06 STUDYING

MODIFIERS

Modifiers go before an adjective.

It's They're	very / really good. good. quite good. not very good.	(= great) ↑ (= bad)

Use *a bit* instead of *quite*, but only with 'negative' meanings.

It's *a bit / quite* expensive.   It's *a bit quite* good.

Exercise 1

Add the modifier in brackets in the correct place.

1 It's cold in here. Can we turn on the heating? (quite)
2 Thanks for inviting us. We had a great time. (really)
3 It isn't varied. We always do the same things. (very)
4 He's nice, but he's strange! (a bit)
5 He's good at sciences. He gets A grades. (really)
6 My teachers were helpful, so that made the course easier. (quite)

COMPARATIVES

To compare two things, use a comparative adjective + *than*.

I think History is *better than* Geography.
He's *taller than* his brother.

Some comparative adjectives are irregular.

good → *better*   bad → *worse*   far → *further*

For short adjectives, add *-(e)r*.
If they end in *-y*, change to *-ier*.

hard – *harder*   nice – *nicer*   easy – *easier*
cheap – *cheaper*   big – *bigger*   lazy – *lazier*
strange – *stranger* hot – *hotter*   friendly – *friendlier*

For longer adjectives, use *more*.

more interesting   *more popular*   *more varied*

We use *much* (= a lot) or *a bit* (= a little).

It's *much* better.   It's *a bit* easier.

Exercise 1

Complete the sentences with the comparative form of the adjectives in brackets.

1 I think English is .... to learn than German. (easy)
2 My brother's a bit .... than me. (big)
3 Basketball is .... than football in my country. (popular)
4 I think the people in the south are .... than the people in the north. (friendly)
5 The weather is .... in my country than here. It's .... (bad, cold)
6 The TV is .... here. It's much .... (good, varied)
7 It's .... to pass exams now. (difficult)

REVISION

Exercise 1

Re-write the sentences with an adjective in the box + *not very*.

interesting	warm	big	good

1 The film's quite bad.
2 The class was a bit boring.
3 The school's quite small.
4 I'm quite cold.

Re-write 5–8 with an adjective in the box + *quite*.

cheap	difficult	low	near

5 The exam wasn't very easy.
6 The rent for my flat isn't very expensive.
7 The school I work for isn't very far from here.
8 He didn't get very high grades.

Exercise 2

Complete the sentences with the comparative form of the adjective in brackets.

1 My English is getting .... (good)
2 The climate is getting .... (warm)
3 The situation is getting .... (bad)
4 Housing is becoming .... (expensive)
5 The population is getting .... (big)

Exercise 3

Make comparisons using the verb *be* and a comparative form. For example:

He / messy / me   *He's messier than me.*

1 Your class / a high level / mine
2 You / good at sciences / me
3 Chinese / useful / French
4 My daughter / tall / my son
5 My dad / tidy / my mum
6 This year / difficult / last year
7 My exam results / bad / yours

Exercise 4

Complete the conversation with ONE word in each gap.

A: How's your course going? You said you found it
   ¹..................... hard last year.
B: It ²..................... getting easier. It's still a
   ³..................... difficult, but my teachers are much
   better ⁴..................... last year. Last year, the teachers
   weren't ⁵..................... patient, but this year, they are
   ⁶..................... helpful.

07 FAMILY AND FRIENDS

AUXILIARY VERBS

Use auxiliary verbs (e.g. *be, do, have, can*) to avoid repeating the main verb and / or words that follow it. For example, in short answers:

Are you over 18?	Yes , I *am.* / No, I'*m not*
Is he staying with you?	Yes, he *is.* / No, he *isn't.*
Do you live near here?	Yes , I *do.* / No, I *don't*
Did you get the tickets?	Yes, I *did.* / No, I *didn't*
Can you see the board?	Yes, I *can.* / No, I *can't.*

We can also use them when comparing things using *but* and *so / too.*

My brother *went* to the party, *but I didn't.*
I *can drive,* but my husband *can't.*
I'*m* quite tall, *and* my sister *is too.*
I *speak* French and *so does* my son, but my husband *doesn't.*

Exercise 1
Choose the correct words.
1 A: Can you take me to the airport?
   B: Sorry, I *can / can't.* I'm busy.
2 A: Did you see the film on Channel Six last night?
   B: Yes, *I saw the film / I did.* It was really good.
3 A: Do either of you like football?
   B: I *did / do,* but Jack doesn't.
4 A: Are you feeling OK?
   B: No, *I aren't / I'm not.* I've got a bad headache.
5 I stayed till the end of the party, but Tom *don't / didn't.*
6 Thanks for the gift. I love it and the kids *do / love* too.
7 If he can become President, then so *can / do* I.

HAVE TO / DON'T HAVE TO

Have to shows a thing is necessary (= you need to do it).
Don't have to shows a thing is not necessary (= you can choose).

I *have to go.* I'm late.
He's very ill. He *has to go* to hospital.
You *don't have to do* it if you don't want to.
He's lucky. He *doesn't have to* start work until ten.

Make questions like this:
Do you / I / we have to do it?
Does she / he have to go?

Exercise 1
Complete the sentences with the correct form of *(don't) have to.*
1 I .... do some shopping. We have no food.
2 He can't come. He .... look after his sister.
3 I .... work today, so we can go out for the day.
4 She can't play today. She .... finish her homework.
5 We have lots of time. We .... rush.
6 .... I .... go to bed now?
7 The exam's easy. You .... study hard to pass it.
8 What time .... he .... be there?

REVISION

Exercise 1
Complete the replies with the correct form of *be, do* or *can.*
1 A: I'm sure Russell Crowe isn't from New Zealand.
   B: Yes, he .... He was born there.
2 A: I'm sure she doesn't know what she's doing.
   B: She .... ! Be patient.
3 A: I'm sure we saw that film together before.
   B: No, we .... – I don't remember anything about it!
4 A: I'm sure we can't sit here.
   B: We .... I mean, there's nothing to say we .... !
5 A: That's stupid!
   B: No it .... ! It's a good idea.
6 A: You didn't put the milk back in the fridge.
   B: Yes, I .... Maybe someone else took it out after me.
7 A: Can you help me carry these things?
   B: Sorry, I .... I have a bad back.

Exercise 2
Replace the words in *italics* with *do, does* or *did.*
1 I studied marketing at university and my brother
        did
   ~~studied marketing~~ too.
2 My father doesn't like sweet things, but I *like sweet things.*
3 We don't usually eat together during the week, but we always *eat together* on Sunday.
4 I didn't write any notes in the lesson, but Juan *wrote some notes.*
5 I don't have any money, but my sister *has some money.*
6 You went to Camp Hill School! I *went to Camp Hill School* too! When exactly?

Exercise 3
Write the second sentences with the correct form of *(don't) have to.*
1 Sorry, I can't talk now. I / go.
2 Johan says sorry he can't come. He / work late.
3 Is it an important exam? you / pass it?
4 She's lucky. She / travel far to get to work.
5 I'm bored. we / stay?
6 You don't need to go to bed now. We / get up very early tomorrow.

> ### Glossary
>
> **rush:** if you rush, you go fast, especially when you're late or something is very important
> **hard:** if you study or work hard, you do it a lot
> **sweet:** if something is sweet, it has sugar in it
> **bored:** how you feel if something is boring

08 PLANS

BE GOING TO + VERB

We use *be going to* + verb to talk about definite plans and decisions for the future. We often use a future time expression with *be going to*, for example: *tonight, this weekend, next month, next year.*

I	am		start work this week.
You	are		work with me.
He	is		finish school this year.
She	is	*(not) going to*	study Fashion.
It	is		take a very long time.
We	are		stay in a hotel.
They	are		arrive tomorrow night.

Make questions like this.
Are you going to see Ian later?
Is he going to get a taxi to his hotel?

Notice that we often say *I'm going* instead of *I'm going to go.* Both are correct and mean the same thing.

Exercise 1
Correct each sentence by adding one word.
1 I'm not to do anything special tonight.
2 How are you going get home?
3 Where they going on holiday this year?
4 What your sister going to study?
5 How much it going to cost?
6 I going to have dinner with my parents tonight.

WOULD LIKE TO + VERB

We use *would like (or love) to* + verb to talk about things we want – or hope – to do in the future. We often use time expressions with *would like to one day, sometime in the future, sometime in the next few years,* etc.
He'd like to / love to spend less time working.
We'd like to move to a bigger house.
I wouldn't like to be him!
Would you like to have dinner with me tomorrow night?

Exercise 1
Write sentences using *would / wouldn't like (to).*
1 I / really / spend a year in South America.
2 you / have children?
3 She / change jobs sometime soon.
4 I / not / be famous!
5 My brother / learn how to cook.
6 you / something to eat?
7 you / come shopping with me?
8 you / a drink?

REVISION

Exercise 1
Complete the sentences with ONE word in each gap.
1 Where .... your brother going to study?
2 I'd really like .... learn Spanish.
3 It's an OK city, but I wouldn't .... to live there.
4 We .... going to have a party on Friday.
5 What .... you like to eat tonight?
6 I'm just going .... go home and sleep.
7 When .... your parents going to arrive?
8 I'm .... going to tell you again!

Exercise 2
Complete the sentences with the correct form of the verbs in the box.

finish	fly	get	invite	move
retire	start	travel	work	

1 Does your brother like .... for Sony?
2 We're going .... married in June and we'd like .... you to the wedding.
3 I'm going .... university next year, and then I'd like .... my own business.
4 I'd love .... around the world, but I don't really like ....
5 My parents are going .... next year. They'd like .... to a warmer country.

Exercise 3
Choose the correct words.
1 *I wouldn't like to / I'm not going to* come to the meeting tomorrow. I have to be somewhere else.
2 *I'd like to / I'm going to* go to the concert, but the tickets are really expensive!
3 *I'd like to / I'm going to* learn to drive, but I don't have enough money.
4 *I wouldn't like to / I'm not going to* be her!
5 *Would you like to / Are you going to* see my holiday photos?
6 Sorry. I can't come to the class tomorrow. *I'd like to / I'm going to* go to the dentist.

Exercise 4
Put the words into the correct order to make time expressions.
1 weekend this
2 afternoon later this
3 the sometime in future
4 summer this
5 next weeks in sometime few the
6 this later evening
7 years the next sometime in few
8 three the months in sometime next or four

09 EXPERIENCES

PRESENT PERFECT 1

To find out if someone has a particular experience or not, use the present perfect (*have* + past participle). We sometimes add *ever* to mean 'once in your life'.

Have	you / they	(ever)	been to Germany?
Has	she / he		seen *Manchild*?

Answer with *Yes (I have) / No (never / I haven't)*. To add or ask about details, use the past simple. For example:

A: *Have you seen the new Bond film?*
B: *Yeah, I saw it at the weekend.*
A: *What did you think of it?*
B: *It was quite good. I don't normally like action films.*

Make statements like this:

I / You / We / They	have (not / never)	been there.
He / She	has (not / never)	seen it.

Don't use the present perfect with past time expressions.
~~Have you seen~~ Did you see the film <u>yesterday</u>?
~~I've been~~ I went to the supermarket <u>a few days ago</u>.

Exercise 1
Choose the correct form of the verb.
1 A: *Have you seen / Did you see* the new So! video?
   B: No, I haven't. Is it good?
2 A: *Have you seen / Did you see* John yesterday?
   B: No. Sorry.
3 A: *Have you been / Did you go* to Africa?
   B: Yes. *I went / have been* there a few years ago.
4 A: *I've never been / I didn't go* to a Thai restaurant.
   B: No? *Have you tried / did you try* other Asian food?
   A: Once. *I've been / I went* to an Indonesian restaurant when I was in Holland, but *I haven't liked / I didn't like* it.

PRESENT PERFECT 2

The present perfect is *have* + past participle. Past participles are usually the same as the past simple form, but some are different.

*Have you ever **failed** an exam?*   (fail–failed–failed)
*Have you **read** 'War and Peace'?*   (read–read–read)
*I've **broken** my leg twice.*   (break–broke–broken)

Check the table on page 70–71 of the *Vocabulary Builder* for more irregular verbs.

Exercise 1
Make present perfect questions and statements.
1 you / ever / try Mexican food?
2 she / be here before.
3 he / ever / have an accident?
4 I / lose my mobile several times.
5 you / book your flight?
6 we / never / ask for anything before.

REVISION

Exercise 1
Complete the lists with the correct form of the verbs.
1 buy – bought – ....
2 .... – chose – chosen
3 come – came – ....
4 cut – .... – cut
5 do – did – ....
6 drive – .... – driven
7 .... – felt – felt
8 get – got – ....
9 know – knew – ....
10 .... – left – left
11 put – put – ....
12 .... – sold – sold
13 steal – stole – stolen
14 take – .... – taken

Exercise 2
Match questions 1–8 with the answers a–h.
1 Have you ever been to the King Hotel restaurant?
2 Have you ever read *War and Peace*?
3 Have you ever met anyone famous?
4 Have you ever eaten oysters?
5 Have you ever lived abroad?
6 Have you ever seen a dead body?
7 Have you done kung fu before?
8 Have you played this game before?

a No, but I've played something similar.
b Yes, I have. I worked in Dubai for two years.
c No, I've never read anything by Tolstoy.
d Yes. I had some once, but I didn't really like them.
e No, but I saw Al Pacino in a pizza place in New York.
f No, never, but I did karate when I was little.
g I studied Medicine, so we had to see them.
h Yes. I took my wife there once. It was very romantic.

Exercise 3
Write questions using the present perfect or past simple.
A: [1]........................... London before? (visit)
B: No, this is our first time.
A: When [2]........................... ? (arrive)
B: Two days ago. We're really enjoying it.
A: Where [3]........................... ? (be)
B: Well, on Sunday we went to Buckingham Palace and Hyde Park, and yesterday we went on the London Eye.
A: [4]........................... it? (enjoy)
B: Yeah, it was great. You get a great view from the top.
A: Yes. [5]........................... round any of the museums? (look)
B: No, but we're going to the British Museum tomorrow.

> ### Glossary
>
> **oysters:** a kind of shellfish
> **abroad:** any country which is not your own
> **dead:** adjective to describe something that has died

10 TRAVEL

TOO, TOO MUCH, TOO MANY

Too shows something is bad = 'it's more than we want'.

adjective	uncountable noun	plural noun
too busy	too *much* crime	too *many* people
too expensive	too *much* traffic	too *many* cars
too early	too *much* noise	too *many* flights

If you feel happy / OK about something, use *very / lots of*:

The train is ~~too~~ *very fast. It only takes ten minutes.*
There are ~~too many~~ *lots of trains. It's good.*

Exercise 1

Complete the sentences with *too, too much* or *too many*.

1 There are .... trucks on the motorways.
2 The council is going to cut the service because it costs .... money.
3 I don't drive into town. It's .... difficult to park.
4 The government wants to expand the airport. They say it's .... small.
5 People are protesting because they say they're paying .... tax.
6 Taxi drivers find it difficult to make money. There are .... other taxis in the city, so there's .... competition.

SUPERLATIVES

To compare more than two things, use *the* + a superlative adjective.
It's *the fastest* way to get there.

For short adjectives, add *-(e)st*. If they end in *-y*, change to *- iest*.

hard – *hardest*	nice – *nicest*	easy – *easiest*
cheap – *cheapest*	hot – *hottest*	lazy – *laziest*
strange – *strangest*	big – *biggest*	busy – *busiest*

For longer adjectives, use *the most* + adjective.
the most interesting   the most popular

Some superlative adjectives are irregular.

good – *best*	bad – *worst*	far – *furthest*

We often use superlatives with *ever* + the present perfect.
It's *the best* holiday I've (*ever*) had.

Exercise 1

Find the five mistakes and correct them.

1 It was the loudest band I've ever heard!
2 I live in one of the busyiest streets in town.
3 It was the most bad day of my life.
4 The easiest way to get around is on foot.
5 Yesterday was hotest day of the year.
6 That was the difficultest exam I've ever taken!
7 I'm the more taller person in the class.
8 They were the nicest people I've ever met.

REVISION

Exercise 1

Correct the mistake in each sentence.

1 There are toos cars parked on my road.
2 There were too much people on the train.
3 They knocked down the house because it was too much dangerous.
4 The service they provide is great – it's too fast.
5 There is too many rubbish on public transport.
6 It's good because there are too many buses at night.

Exercise 2

Complete the sentences with the superlative form of the adjective in brackets.

1 It's the .... restaurant in the area. (cheap)
2 The .... way to get here is on the motorway. (quick)
3 What's the .... film you've ever seen? (funny)
4 The .... chapter in the book was the one about the war. (interesting)
5 Where's the .... metro station? (near)
6 That was the .... day of my life! (exciting)
7 The .... time of the year is July. (hot)
8 The .... way to travel is by bicycle. (nice)

Exercise 3

Complete the text with ONE word in each gap.

I love New York. I think it's [1]........................ greatest city in the world. It has every kind of shop and museum and restaurant. There's almost too [2]........................ choice – I can't decide what to do.

The transport system is really good. I don't drive or have a car because it's [3]........................ expensive to park, but I really don't need one. The subway is quite cheap and reliable and there are [4]........................ of buses and taxis, but the [5]........................ way get around is on foot. That way, you can see all the fantastic buildings and feel the great atmosphere. It's [6]........................ nice.

There aren't many things I don't like here, but the [7]........................ thing for me is the weather in the summer. It's terrible. It's [8]........................ hot. It's often over 35°C in August and I have to work then.

Glossary

truck: a truck is very big 'car' to transport things
motorway: a motorway is a very big road – usually between cities – where you can drive fast
competition: if there's a lot of competition, it's difficult, because lots of companies / people want the same thing
on foot: if you go somewhere on foot, you walk
chapter: books often have different parts or chapters

11 FOOD

A LOT OF, SOME, ANY, MUCH, MANY AND A BIT OF

A lot of, some and any can go with both uncountable (singular) nouns and plural nouns.

Use much / a bit of with uncountable (singular) nouns.
Use many / a few with plural nouns.

	uncountable nouns	plural nouns
Do you eat	much / a lot of salt? any fruit?	many / a lot of chips? any vegetables?
I eat	a lot of ice-cream. quite a lot of sugar. some / a bit of fish.	a lot of biscuits. quite a lot of sweets. some / a few spices.
I don't eat	much / a lot of rice. any cheese.	many / a lot of cakes. any vegetables.

Exercise 1
Complete the sentences with ONE word in each gap.
1 I'm a vegetarian. I don't eat .... meat or fish.
2 I don't read .... books – maybe two novels a year.
3 A: Did you add .... salt to this? I can't taste it.
   B: Oh, no! I forgot.
4 I've had a .... biscuits so I'm not very hungry.
5 I put .... sugar in it, so it wasn't too bitter.
6 A: Do you eat a .... of rice?
   B: .... a lot, but I sometimes have pasta instead.

INVITATIONS AND OFFERS

For invitations, ask Would you like to ...?
Would you like to come to my house for dinner tonight?

To offer to do something, ask Would you like me to ...?
Would you like me to move my car?
Would you like me to get you anything from the shops?

To offer people things, you can ask Would you like ...?
Would you like any ... help / food / wine?
Would you like a ... drink / banana / cup of tea?

We can use want instead of would like.
Do you want ... to come / me to move / a drink?

Exercise 1
Write questions with Would like ... . For example:
Invite someone for dinner.
Would you like to go out for dinner?
1 Offer someone something to eat.
2 Offer to set the table.
3 Invite someone for a game of tennis next week.
4 Offer to do the washing-up.
5 Offer someone some chocolate.
6 Invite someone to your birthday party.

REVISION

Exercise 1
Choose the correct words.
1 I ate a lot of / a few chocolate and I feel a bit sick now.
2 I only have tea. I don't have any / much coffee.
3 I used quite a lot of / quite much chilli, so it's spicy.
4 Have you seen much / any good films recently?
5 I watch a lot of / any comedies, but not many / some dramas.
6 A: What vegetables would you like?
   B: Just some / any potatoes and a bit of / a few carrots.

Exercise 2
Write offers and invitations using the notes.
1 like / go to that restaurant?
2 like / cake?
3 like / me / cook dinner?
4 want / fish or meat for dinner?
5 want / us / phone him?
6 like / us / bring something to drink?
7 like / me / drive you to the airport?
8 want / stay with us while you're visiting.

Exercise 3
Complete the text with ONE word in each gap.

I love cooking. I started when I was eight or nine. I made
¹........................... chocolate biscuits with my mum. I really
enjoyed it. After that, we made a ²........................... of cakes
together. My poor dad had to eat them all and he put on
³........................... lot of weight!

Now I cook other kinds of food – I make the dinner a
⁴........................... times a week. Tonight I'm going to do steak
with ⁵........................... bit of sauce and some chips. I actually
don't cook ⁶........................... meat – I prefer doing fish – but
my dad bought the steak.

I'm 16 this year, so I can leave school. I'd ⁷........................... to
go to cookery school and become a chef, but my parents
want ⁸........................... to continue my school studies.

Glossary

novel: a novel is a book with one long story
biscuits: biscuits are thin, dry cakes
bitter: if something is bitter, it's not sweet, like black coffee
comedies: a comedy is a film which is funny
drama: a drama is a film which is serious

12 FEELINGS

SHOULD / SHOULDN'T

We use should(n't) + verb to suggest actions. *Should* shows we think it's a good idea to do the action. *Shouldn't* shows we think it's a bad idea to do the action.

| I
You
He / She
We
They | should | have a holiday.
go to the doctor.
do more exercise. |
| | shouldn't | smoke.
work so hard.
spend so much money. |

We often add *maybe*. It makes the advice sound less strong.
Maybe you should lose some weight.

Exercise 1

Complete the sentences with a pronoun + *should / shouldn't*.

1 A: I feel a bit sick.
   B: .... lie down.
2 A: My stomach hurts and I've got diarrhoea.
   B: .... have any more to eat today.
3 A: He says he's really stressed and has no energy.
   B: .... take some time off work.
4 A: Hurry up! We're late.
   B: .... take a taxi.
5 A: The kids are always tired in the morning.
   B: .... stay up so late.
6 A: My back's stiff and it often hurts.
   B: .... go and see someone about it.

PRESENT PERFECT 3

Use the present perfect to talk about actions that happened sometime before now, but have a present result. Don't use it with a past time expression (e.g. *yesterday, a few days ago*).
He's broken his leg, so he can't drive at the moment.
I've never seen him, so I can't tell you what he looks like.

We often use *already* and *yet* with the present perfect. *Yet* goes with negatives and questions.
He *has already had* two holidays this year.
We *haven't been* to the castle *yet*, but we want to go.
Have you *asked* her *yet*?

Exercise 1

Correct the mistake in each sentence.

1 I broken my arm, so I can't write.
2 I'm sorry, but I have forget your name.
3 I was to Spain eight or nine times in my life.
4 I already do my homework, so can I watch TV?
5 I've seen that film last year.
6 I haven't been to that restaurant already. Is it good?

REVISION

Exercise 1

Complete each sentence with *should* or *shouldn't* and a verb in the box.

| be | carry | drive | eat | see | take |

1 A: That's a bad cough.
   B: I know. I've had it for a week. Maybe I
      .... a doctor about it.
2 A: I feel really strange.
   B: Well, you .... home. Would you like me to call a taxi instead?
3 A: I cut my finger cooking dinner.
   B: That was stupid! You ....
      more careful in future.
4 A: I've got a really bad headache.
   B: Really? Maybe you .... a couple of aspirin.
5 A: The doctor said I need to lose weight.
   B: Well, maybe you .... so many sweets!
6 A: My back hurts.
   B: Really? Well, you .... those boxes.

Exercise 2

Complete the sentences with the present perfect form of the verbs in brackets.

1 I started it last week, but I ....
   it yet. (not finish)
2 How many times .... you ....
   there? (be)
3 Prices .... a lot this year. (rise)
4 .... you .... any good books recently? (read)
5 You .... a lot of food! (cook)
6 We .... time to make a decision yet. (not have)

Exercise 3

Choose the correct words.

1 He's really nice. *We went / We've been* out together a few times recently.
2 I can't play tennis tomorrow. *I've hurt / I hurt* my leg.
3 *I've been / I have ever been* to Paris twice.
4 I've never *spoken / spoke* to him before.
5 *Have you tried / Did you try* Lebanese food before?
6 *We've been / We haven't been* to the museum yet.
7 *I've seen / I saw* Nicole yesterday.
8 She *travelled / has travelled* a lot. She's been all round Asia and South America and last year she *visited / has visited* Nigeria and Ghana.

13 NATURE

MIGHT AND *BE GOING TO*

Make predictions with *might* + verb or *be going to* + verb. *Might (not)* shows possibility. *Be (not) going to* shows certainty.
I *might not go to the party. I might stay at home instead.*

A: *I need to give this book back to Dan.*
B: *I can give it to him, if you like. I'm going to see him later.*

We can use *may* instead of *might*.
I *may* be a bit late. It depends what time my meeting ends.

We often see these expressions with *might*:

possibly	I'm not sure	I haven't decided
it depends	I don't know	

Exercise 1
Choose the correct words.
1 *We might / We're going to* have a barbecue on Sunday.
2 I might *possibly / definitely* get a new car soon.
3 *We might / We're going to* be free at the weekend, but I need to speak to my wife first and check.
4 Look at those clouds! *It might / It's going to* rain soon.
5 *She may / She's going to* come with us. It depends if she can get time off work.

PASSIVES

We can use many verbs in two ways.
Farmers *use a lot of chemicals* on the crops. (active)
A lot of chemicals are used on the crops. (passive)

Passives are formed with the verb *be* + the past participle.
We usually use the passive if we don't know who does the action or if it's not important.

It	is	made in France.
My bike	was	locked to the fence.
They	are	sold on the Internet.
	were	found near here.

Exercise 1
Complete the passive sentences with the correct form of the verb *be*.
1 Around 60 million litres of wine .... produced in Turkey each year.
2 Our cat .... killed by a car.
3 Vampire bats .... only found in South America.
4 The herb .... often taken to cure colds.
5 A: I like that painting.
   B: Yes, it's nice. We .... given it at our wedding.
6 A: Do you want to go out tonight?
   B: I've got no money. I .... not paid until Friday.

REVISION

Exercise 1
Rewrite the sentences using *might* to show possibility.
1 They said it's going to rain later.
2 I'm definitely not going to be in the office tomorrow.
3 She's going to call you this afternoon.

Re-write the sentences using *be going to* to show certainty.
4 It said there might be a storm tonight.
5 We might go to Bulgaria for our holiday this year.
6 My dad might drive us to the station.

Exercise 2
Make passive sentences with the past participles of the verbs in brackets.
1 Rice isn't .... in our country. (grow)
2 It's all .... here. (import)
3 Wild cats are .... all over this part of the country. (find)
4 Curry is usually .... with rice. (serve)
5 Our car was .... last weekend. (steal)
6 We were .... by the police. (stop)
7 He was .... in the war. (kill)
8 The cottage was .... in the 17th century. (build)

Exercise 3
Correct the mistake in each sentence.
1 I don't might see you tomorrow.
2 We is going to finish the work by Tuesday.
3 Most of the wine here are imported.
4 It is maked in Vietnam.
5 They might probably move to the country next year.
6 We are climbed that mountain last year.

> ### Glossary
> **vampire bats:** vampire bats are animals that fly at night and eat blood
> **cure:** if you cure a cold or illness, you make it better
> **import:** if you import products, you bring them into your country from abroad
> **wild:** if an animal is wild, it lives free in nature

14 OPINIONS

WILL / WON'T FOR PREDICTIONS

We use *'ll* (= *will*) / *won't* (= *will not*) + verb to make predictions about the future in the same way as we use *be (not) going to* + verb. We often use *will* (but not *won't*) with *I think ... / don't think ...* .

It *won't* be a problem. I'm sure of it.
I think he*'ll* get the job.
I *don't think* I*'ll* go.

We usually ask questions using *do you think* + *will* + verb.

Do you think you*'ll see* her tonight?
Who *do you think will win*?

We can add *probably* to show we're not 100% sure. Note the different position with *will / won't*.

We*'ll probably go* somewhere in Greece.
It *probably won't make* any difference.

Exercise 1

Choose the correct words.

1   I think *they'll / they'll to* finish it next year.
2   They said *there'll be / there be will* snow tonight.
3   When *will the meeting start / will start the meeting*?
4   She *won't / won't not* be happy about it.
5   I'm sure they *don't will / won't* be late.
6   I don't think *you'll / you won't* pass the exam.
7   I *probably won't / won't probably* see you before then.
8   What *will / will be* your parents do about it?

VERB PATTERNS WITH ADJECTIVES

If we want to make a verb the subject of a sentence, we use an *-ing* form.

We also use *it* + *be* + *(not)* adjective + *(not) to* + infinitive.
Renting a flat here *is* quite *expensive*.
It's quite *expensive to rent* a flat here.
Not seeing my family for so long *was hard*.
It was hard not to see my family for so long.

Exercise 1

Complete the sentences with the correct form of the verb in the box.

read	park	vote	notice
find	walk	offer	worry

1   It was quite difficult .... accommodation.
2   .... in the streets at night is perfectly safe.
3   It's almost impossible .... the car in town.
4   .... children's books was helpful when I was learning Spanish.
5   Not .... a drink to a visitor is very rude.
6   It's interesting .... the differences between the two countries.
7   I think it's important not .... about making mistakes.
8   I think .... in any election is useless.

REVISION

Exercise 1

Change the sentences into negatives (–) or questions (?).

1   They'll win. (–)
2   He'll get the job. (?)
3   It was difficult to laugh in that situation. (–)
4   I'll probably see you before Christmas. (–)
5   I think the economy will improve this year. (–)
6   It's easy to find work. (?)

Exercise 2

Complete the sentences with the correct form of the verb in brackets (in the *-ing* form, *to* + infinitive or *will / won't* + infinitive).

1   It's important .... the contract carefully. (read)
2   .... is quite cheap in our area. (eat out)
3   Do you think the Social Democrats .... the election next year? (lose)
4   I think it's good .... and meet new people. (travel)
5   Do you think .... abroad is easy? (move)
6   It definitely .... soon. You'll have to wait. (not happen)
7   It's not easy .... the right person. (find)
8   I don't think it .... any difference to the result. (make)

Exercise 3

Correct the mistake in each sentence.

1   It was lovely see you again.
2   It don't will cost too much.
3   Watch the news can be very depressing sometimes.
4   What you will do with the money you won?
5   It was difficult for you to learn Russian?
6   It's easy don't remember people's names.
7   It's easy make mistakes. Everyone does it.
8   It's no rude to talk about money in my country.
9   To live in the city is really stressful.
10 Is not difficult to do this exercise.

Glossary

accommodation: accommodation is a flat, house, hotel room, etc. where you stay or live
perfectly safe: if a place or thing is perfectly safe, it is 100% safe
useless: if something is useless, it isn't good
rude: if someone is rude, they aren't polite. People can get upset if you are rude

15 TECHNOLOGY

BE THINKING OF + -ING

We use *be thinking of + -ing* to talk about plans we are not 100% sure of, but have already thought about.
I'*m thinking of* doing a Web design course next year.
We'*re not thinking of* buying a new one yet.
Where *are you thinking of* going?

Exercise 1
Write present continuous sentences using the notes.
1 I / think / join a gym.
2 What brand / you / think / buy?
3 They / think / move sometime next year.
4 I hope he / not / think / leave the company.
5 Who / you / think / ask?
6 They said on TV that they / not / think / change the price.
7 Which university she / think / apply to?
8 I / think / try to make my own computer.
9 Why / he / think / retire? He's only 48.
10 Please tell me you / not / think / marry him!

ADVERBS

Adverbs are usually formed by adding -ly to an adjective (e.g. *quick – quickly*). We can use adverbs to give more information about how we do things. Adverbs usually come after the verb they give extra information about.
You can *eat quite cheaply* there.
She *answered* all the questions *very confidently*.
He's *acting really strangely* at the moment.

Notice that we often use *quite / very / really* before adverbs.

Don't forget these common irregular adverbs.
fast – fast   early – early   hard – hard
late – late   good – well

Exercise 1
Complete the second sentences with the correct adverb.
1 a He has a quiet voice.
   b He speaks very ....
2 a She's very hard-working.
   b She works really ....
3 a He's a very good cook.
   b He cooks really ....
4 a She's quite a creative person.
   b She solved that problem very ....
5 a I had a bad night's sleep.
   b I slept quite .... last night.
6 a We had a late night.
   b We stayed out ....

REVISION

Exercise 1
Change the sentences into positive statements (+), negative statements (–) or questions (?), with the pronouns in brackets.
1 I'm thinking of changing jobs. (? / she)
2 Is he thinking of making his own website? (– / we)
3 They're not thinking of having children yet. (+ / I)
4 Are you thinking of buying a new one? (+ / he)
5 She's thinking of applying for a Master's. (– / I)
6 We're not thinking of selling the company. (? / they)

Exercise 2
Choose the correct words.
1 He's a very *confident / confidently* speaker.
2 It's a really old car. It's really *slow / slowly*.
3 I got home really *late / lately* last night.
4 My gran drives really *slow / slowly*.
5 I'm not very *well / good* at Maths.
6 You speak Italian very *good / well*.
7 He's quite *bad / badly* at tennis, but he tries really *hardly / hard*.
8 I understand Chinese quite *good / well*, but my pronunciation is *awful / awfully*.

Exercise 3
Correct the mistake in each sentence.
1 He really quickly speaks!
2 Where you thinking of moving to?
3 I'm thinking to complain to the company about it.
4 You look really nicely in that suit.
5 He's studying hardly for his exams at the moment.
6 The camera works perfect now.
7 We're thinking get married next year.
8 You drive too fastly.

> **Glossary**
>
> **apply:** if you *apply to* university, you write and try to enter. You can also *apply for* a degree course or a Master's – and *apply for* a job
> **marry:** if you marry someone, you have a wedding and get married
> **complain:** if you complain to someone about something, you tell them you are not happy about something and that you want them to do something

16 LOVE

THE PAST CONTINUOUS

We form the past continuous with *was / were + -ing*.
Use it to show that one action started but didn't finish before another action happened. It is often used with the past simple. The other action is usually in the past simple.

I *was shopping* in town when I saw one on sale.
I *wasn't enjoying* my job, so I decided to leave.
Where *were you living* when you two met?

Exercise 1

Write past continuous sentences using the notes.

1 Sorry I didn't answer your call. I / talk / to someone on another line.
2 What / you / do when you heard the news?
3 It not / work very well, so I took it back to the shop.
4 We / have dinner when my sister suddenly told us she was pregnant!
5 They not / get on very well, so they decided to break up.
6 We / sit / in the cinema when he suddenly tried to kiss me. It was horrible!

WILL / WON'T FOR PROMISES

To make promises, we usually use *will / won't*.
We sometimes add *I promise*.

A: Dad, can we go to the cinema today?
B: Sorry, I'm too busy. *I'll take* you next week, *I promise*.

We can also use *will / won't* in short answers.

A: You need to be careful.   A: Don't forget.
B: I will.   B: I won't.

Exercise 1

Choose the correct words.

1 I promise *I'll / I won't* tell anyone.
2 I'll wait . *You'll / You won't* have to go on your own.
3 Don't worry, *I'll / I won't* be there on time.
4 *I'll / I won't* bring you back a nice present, I promise.
5 A: Have you spoken to the bank yet?
    B: *I'll / I won't* do it as soon as possible.
6 A: I hope you're not going to do that again.
    B: Don't worry, *I will / I won't*.
7 A: Take care.
    B: *I will / I won't*.

Glossary

line: you can *be on another line* when someone calls. If *it's a really bad line*, you can't hear very well
kiss: if you kiss someone, you put your mouth somewhere on their face
pay attention: if you pay attention, you listen and / or watch carefully to show you're interested
crash: if you crash a car, you hit something with it
earthquake: an earthquake is when an area of land / city, etc. moves a lot

REVISION

Exercise 1

Change the sentences into statements (+), negatives (–) or questions (?), with the pronouns in brackets.

1 I was working yesterday. (– / he)
2 I was living there when you two met. (? / you)
3 I will tell him. (– / I)
4 She was paying attention. (– / they)
5 Will you do it for me? (+ / I)
6 We were waiting a long time. (? / you)
7 She wasn't listening when he said the address. (+ / we)
8 Was he driving too fast when he crashed? (+ / I)

Exercise 2

Complete the sentences with one of the verbs in brackets in the past simple and the other in the past continuous.

1 I .... in the park and .... my leg. (play, hurt)
2 I .... 20 euros when I .... home. (find, walk)
3 We .... when we .... for a train. (meet, wait)
4 She .... in a band and I .... to one of her concerts. (play, go)
5 We .... a lot when I .... (move, grow up)
6 He .... down a quiet road when a car .... him. (cycle, hit)
7 She .... the course so she .... to stop. (not / enjoy, decide)
8 They .... friends in Peru when the earthquake .... (visit, happen)

Exercise 3

Correct the mistake in each sentence or pairs of sentences

1 I call you tonight, I promise.
2 A: Don't be late.
    B: I don't.
3 A: What did he say?
    B: I don't know. I wasn't listen. Sorry.
4 I will always to love you.
5 What you were doing?
6 I was runing down the street and I fell.
7 When I went into the classroom, the children was all studying quietly.
8 Someone was stealing my bike when I was buying a newspaper in the shop.

FILE 1

Starter Unit 1 page 9 Vocabulary

Student A
Ask your partner *How much is ...*
Write down the answer.
• a coffee?
• an orange juice?
• a bottle of water?
• a cheese sandwich?
• an ice cream?
• a portion of chips?

Tell your partner the answers to their questions.
Use this information:
a tea – £1.20 (one pound twenty)
a cola – £1.95
a green salad – £3.54
a chicken sandwich – £3.19
a hamburger – £3.36
an apple – 47p

FILE 2

Unit 10 page 80 Reading

The story about the Ferrari Enzo isn't true.
A photo of it appeared on the Internet, but it wasn't real. Someone created it with a computer.

All the other information was true at the time of writing.

FILE 3

Unit 3 page 31 Conversation practice
Student A

You want to go to a supermarket, a restaurant, a church, a language school and a bookshop.

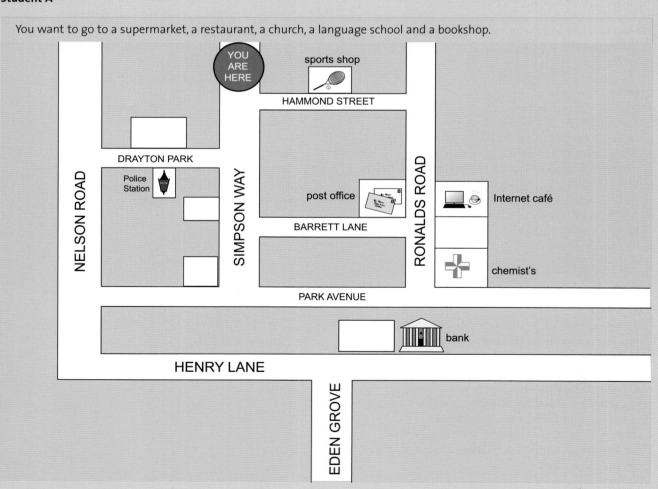

FILE 4

Unit 4 page 38 Vocabulary

> **Student A**
>
> **A** **Ask Student B when these days are. Write the dates.**
>
> Immaculate Conception, Italy
>
> ....
>
> Teacher's Day, China
>
> ....
>
> Human Rights Day, South Africa
>
> ....
>
> Independence Day, India
>
> ....
>
> Student B's birthday
>
> ....
>
> The next public holiday
>
> ....
>
> **B** **Complete the dates below. Then answer B's questions.**
>
> | | |
> |---|---|
> | Greenery Day, Japan | *4th May* |
> | Unity Day, Germany | *3rd October* |
> | Throne Day, Morocco | *30th July* |
> | Father's Day | *The first Sunday in June* |
> | My birthday | .... |
> | The next public holiday | .... |
>
> **C** **Check with B that you wrote the correct dates.**

FILE 5

Unit 14 page 110 Reading
Group B

A NEW LIFE

I came here a few years ago because of the war in my country. Of course, there is crime here – my house was robbed once – but it's not dangerous to walk in the streets. Before I came here, I was shot! When I got here, I had treatment in hospital for my injury. I heard complaints about the health service, but I thought it was good. The doctors were kind and efficient, and it was free.

When you talk to people here, they're nice and polite, but it's difficult to really know them. I also don't think families are very close here. Most of my friends here are other foreigners. We play football in the park every Sunday. In my country, our house is always open to visitors. I really miss my own family and I speak to them every day and send money home.

I've always found work doing cleaning or in construction. It's not what I want to do. I was the manager of a company back home, but you do what you have to do and, compared to my country, wages here are very high.

What do I think of the weather? I like it! I know it rains quite a lot, but actually, in my country, it's often too hot.

FILE 6

Unit 11 page 88 Vocabulary
Student A

pistachios

pear

salmon

noodles

prawns

broccoli

chickpeas

chilli

FILE 7

Unit 13 page 104 Vocabulary

dog

cat

cow

horse

pig

rabbit

sheep

lion

bear

FILE 8

Unit 11 page 88 Vocabulary
Student B

squid

lentils

yam

lettuce

almonds

strawberry

sardines

cumin

FILE 9

Unit 3 page 31 Conversation practice
Student B

You want to go to a sports shop, a bank, a post office, an Internet café and a chemist's.

FILE 10

Starter Unit 1 page 9 Vocabulary

Tell your partner the answer to their questions.
Use this information:
a coffee – £2.15 (two pounds fifteen)
an orange juice – £2.37
a bottle of water – £1.50
a cheese sandwich – £3.05
an ice cream – £1.89
a portion of chips – £2.01

Student B
Ask your partner *How much is ...*
Write down the answer.
• a tea?
• a cola?
• a green salad?
• a chicken sandwich?
• a hamburger?
• an apple?

FILE 11

Unit 4 page 38 Vocabulary

Student B

A Complete the dates below. Then answer Student A's questions.

Immaculate Conception, Italy	*8th December*
Teacher's Day, China	*10th September*
Human Rights Day, South Africa	*21st March*
Independence Day, India	*15th August*
My birthday	....
The next public holiday	....

B Ask A when these days are. Write the dates.

Greenery Day, Japan	....
Unity Day, Germany	....
Throne Day, Morocco	....
Father's Day	....
Your birthday	....
The next public holiday	....

C Check with A that you wrote the correct dates.

Starter unit 01

S 1.1
zero one two three four five six seven eight nine ten
eleven twelve twenty thirty fifty a hundred

S1.2
A: Do you have any brothers and sisters?
B: Yes. One brother and two sisters.
A: How old is your brother?
B: 39.
A: Are you married?
B: Yes.
A: Do you have any children?
B: Yes. One boy and one girl.
A: How old are they?
B: The boy's 12 and the girl is eight. Do you have any brothers and sisters?
A: No.
B: How old are you?
A: 25.

S1.3
A: Next!
B: Yes!
A: Yes, sir?
B: Umm, it's a big order.
A: OK.
B: To drink ... one coffee, three teas, an orange juice, four colas and two bottles of water.
A: OK. One coffee, three teas, an orange juice, four colas and two bottles of water.
B: Yes.
A: Anything else?
B: Yes, I want two green salads, seven hamburgers, one cheese sandwich, one chicken sandwich and five portions of chips.
A: Yep.
B: And five apples.
A: Sure. So that's seven hamburgers, one cheese sandwich and one chicken sandwich, five portions of chips, two salads and five apples.
B: That's it.
A: That's £69.64 altogether.

S1.4
1 Listen to the CD.
2 Go there.
3 Read the article.
4 Talk to a partner.
5 Open the window, please.
6 Write the answers.
7 Put your book on the table.
8 Work in groups, please.
9 The class finishes at eight.
10 What do you think?

Starter unit 02

S2.1
78 15 12,000 44 211 16 1,000 33 17 100 97 20 1,300 18 65
22 14 109 50 21 13 5,260 86 19

S2.2
A: What do you do?
B: I'm a teacher.
A: Where do you work?
B: In a school near here.
A: Which one?

B: Northpark High.
A: I know it. How do you get there?
B: I walk.
A: How long does it take?
B: 35 minutes.
A: That's good. What time do you leave home?
B: Seven. We start at 8.30.
A: How old are the children you teach?
B: 14 to 18.

S2.3
I'm you're he's she's it's we're they're

Unit 01

1.1
A: Hello. I'm Miguel. What's your name?
B: Dasha. Hi. Nice to meet you.

1.2
I = Ivy; M = Miguel
I: Hi. Come in. Sit down. My name's Ivy. I'm a teacher here. What's your name?
M: Miguel.
I: Right. Hi. Nice to meet you. And what's your surname, Miguel?
M: Sorry?
I: Your surname. Your family name.
M: Oh, sorry. It's Hernandez. That's H-E-R-N-A-N-D-E-Z.
I: OK. And where are you from, Miguel? Spain?
M: No, I'm not. I'm from Mexico.
I: Oh, OK. Which part?
M: Chihuahua. It's in the north.

1.3
Argentina Brazil China Germany Italy Japan Jordan Kenya Mexico
Morocco Oman Panama Poland Thailand

1.4
1 There's a cinema in the town.
2 It's nice. There are lots of trees and parks.
3 There are lots of hotels near the station.
4 It's not very safe. There's a lot of crime.
5 It's not a bad place, but there are too many people!
6 It's a nice city, but there's a lot of traffic!
7 There are some nice shops and restaurants near here.
8 It's OK. There's a nice beach and there are a few cafés.

1.5
Conversation 1
A: Hello.
B: Hi. It's Jan, isn't it?
A: Yes.
B: What do you do, Jan?
A: I'm a doctor.
B: Really? Where do you work?
A: In a hospital in Warsaw.

Conversation 2
C: So, Lara, what do you do?
D: I'm a teacher.
C: Oh, really? Where do you work?
D: In a secondary school in Bristol.
C: Do you enjoy it?
D: Yes, it's great.
C: What do you teach?
D: French.
C: That's good. Sorry, I don't speak French!

Conversation 3

E: Marta, what do you do?
F: I'm a civil servant.
E: Where do you work?
F: In a local government office in Brazil.
E: Oh, yes. What part of Brazil?
F: Rio Branco – in the north.
E: So do you enjoy it?
F: Yes, it's OK.

Conversation 4

G: What do you do, Filippo?
H: I'm a waiter.
G: Where do you work?
H: In a café in the centre of town – near the cathedral.
G: OK. Do you enjoy it?
H: Not really. I want a different job.
G: Oh? What do you want to do?
H: I don't know – maybe become a police officer.

UNIT 02

2.1

A: Do you like doing sport?
B: No. I'm very bad at sport. What about you?
A: Yeah, it's great. I love playing tennis and basketball. Do you like walking?
B: No – it's boring. What about you?
A: It's OK. I like going to the park.
B: Do you like playing computer games?
A: No, not really. What about you?
B: I love it. It's really good fun. Do you like going to the cinema?
A: Yes. It's great.
B: I love it too. Do you want to see *Love Train*?
A: No. I don't like 'love films'. I like horror films.
B: Oh.

2.2

Conversation 1

A: Do you like watching football?
B: Yeah. It's OK.
A: Do you want to watch the match on Saturday?
B: Where?
A: In a café in town. It's on TV.
B: OK. What time does the match start?
A: Five.
B: So what time do you want meet?
A: Is four OK? We want to get a seat.
B: OK. Where do you want meet?
A: Outside the Green Street train station.
B: That sounds good. So four o'clock outside Green Street station.
A: Yes.

Conversation 2

C: Do you like Italian food?
D: Yeah, I love it.
C: Do you want to go for lunch on Sunday? There's a really nice Italian restaurant near here.
D: Yeah. That sounds good. What time do you want to meet?
C: Is one OK?
D: Yes. Where?
C: Outside the cathedral.
D: OK.

2.3

T = teacher; S1 = student 1; S2 = student 2; S3 = student 3; S4 = student 4

T: OK. Stop there! Now compare your answers with a partner.
S1: Sorry. Can I go to the toilet?
T: There's only five more minutes till the end of class.
S1: I need to go now.
T: Oh, OK.
S1: Thanks.
T: OK. Let's check the answers. Number one – match the words and pictures?
S2: Teacher.
T: Yes. And two?
S3: Student.
T: Yes. Three?
S2: Teacher.
T: That's right. What does 'turn off' mean?
S4: 'Close'.
S3: Sorry, I don't understand.
T: Close, stop a machine. Do you have a dictionary?
S3: No, but Pepe has one.
S2: Here.
T: So it's *apagar* in Spanish.
S3: OK.
T: OK, we need to finish. Here are the other answers: four, teacher; five, both; six, teacher; seven, both; eight, both; nine, teacher; ten, both.
S2: Ten is both?
T: Yes.
S3: Sorry, how do you say this word? 'ANSWEAR'?
T: No. 'Answer'.
S3: Answer. Thanks.
T: OK. So for homework do exercise 1, page 11 in your Workbooks. Any questions?
S1: Oh, we finish?!

2.4

scissors homework tissue mobile pronunciation social cathedral interesting manager strange

REVIEW 01

R1.1

south	/θ/	free	/f/	pen	/p/	take	/t/
chat	/tʃ/	sit	/s/	she	/ʃ/	car	/k/
the	/ð/	live	/v/	big	/b/	bed	/d/
job	/dʒ/	trees	/z/	Asia	/ʒ/	go	/g/
he	/h/	man	/m/	nice	/n/	like	/l/
long	/ŋ/	**read**	/r/	**walk**	/w/	yes	/j/

R1.2

eat	/iː/	fit	/ɪ/	good	/ʊ/	food	/uː/
bed	/e/	river	/ə/	work	/ɜː/	sport	/ɔː/
bad	/æ/	fun	/ʌ/	art	/ɑː/	boss	/ɒ/
great	/eɪ/	write	/aɪ/	here	/ɪə/	where	/eə/
town	/aʊ/	boy	/ɔɪ/	go	/əʊ/	pure	/ʊə/

R1.3

1 park		2 shop		3 meet		4 wife	
5 board		6 lunch		7 news		8 breakfast	
9 mother		10 busy		11 relax		12 stations	

R1.4

Conversation 1

A: So, what do you do, Harriet?
B: I'm a business manager.
A: Oh really? Where do you work?
B: For a company in France. We make and sell pens.

A: OK. Do you enjoy it?
B: Yes, it's good.

Conversation 2
C: Where is it?
D: In the north – between Switzerland and Milan.
C: Is it a nice place?
D: It's OK. It's very small. There are only a few shops and one or two bars. The countryside is nice. It's really beautiful.
C: OK. And do you work there?
D: No. I work in Milan.

Conversation 3
E: What's the answer to question 6?
F: 'To go'.
E: Oh. Do you have a rubber? This is wrong.
F: Yes, here.
E: Thanks.

Conversation 4
G: What's your name?
H: Ling. Hi.
G: Hi, I'm Pat.
H: Hi.
G: Where are you from, Ling?
H: China.
G: Which part?
H: Harbin – it's a big city in the north.

Unit 03

🎧 3.1
Conversation 1
A: I really need to get some shampoo. Is there a chemist's near here?
B: Yes, there's one on New Street. There's a big bookshop on the right, and it's next to that.
A: OK. Thank you.

Conversation 2
C: I really need to get something to eat. Are there any restaurants near here?
D: There aren't really many places in this area, but there is a nice café on Dixon Road. They do good sandwiches and salads.
C: Dixon Road?
D: Yeah. Do you know it?
C: Yes, I think so.
D: Well, it's on the left – opposite a shoe shop.
C: Great. Thanks for that.

Conversation 3
E: Is there a bookshop near here? I need to buy a dictionary for my English course.
F: Yes, there's one just near here.
E: Oh, good.
F: It's on the corner of Chester Street and Hale Road.
E: OK. Sorry. Can you show me on the map?
F: Yes, sure. Look. We're here – on Simpson Lane and there's Hale Road and that's Chester Street there. It's on the left. It's next to a big supermarket.
E: OK. Great. Thank you.

🎧 3.2
Conversation 1
A: Simon!
B: What?
A: Look at this room!
B: What?
A: It's a mess!

B: What?
A: I can't walk across it and not break something!
B: It's not bad.
A: Can you tidy it, please?
B: Later.
A: Now, please!
B: But, mum!
A: Now!
B: OK, OK.

Conversation 2
C: Wh ... what te ... temperature is the air conditioning on?
D: 17.
C: Ca ... can you turn it down? I'm co ... cold.
D: It's not cold.
C: P ... please.
D: OK.
C: Thanks.

Conversation 3
E: What did he say?
F: 'It's not you, it's me'.
E: Oh ... and what was that?
F: 'I don't love you anymore.'
E: OK ... What? Can you turn it up? I can't hear it.
F: It's old age, Dad. Is that OK for you?
E: Yes, thanks.
G: Can you turn the TV down? I need to study and I can't concentrate.

🎧 3.3
1 I can't sleep.
2 Can you help me?
3 Can I use your bathroom?
4 Can you turn up the music?
5 I can't find my book.
6 Can I wash some clothes?
7 We can't come next week.
8 He can't drive at the moment.

Unit 04

🎧 4.1
Conversation 1
A: Hi, Helga. How are you?
B: OK, but tired!
A: Oh. What did you do at the weekend?
B: We went to a rock festival. It was fantastic.
A: Really? Who did you see?
B: Oh, lots of bands! The Killers, The Stones. Who else now? Oh, yes. I saw The Specials on Saturday night. They were good.
A: Sounds great.
B: Yeah, it was great, but I didn't sleep much.

Conversation 2
C: Hello.
D: Hi, how are you? Did you have a nice weekend?
C: Yes, it was OK.
D: What did you do?
C: Nothing much really. I did some shopping on Saturday morning. I played tennis, watched TV, the usual things.
D: It sounds OK.
C: Yeah, I needed to relax.

Conversation 3
E: Did you have a good weekend?
F: Not really.
E: Oh! That sounds bad. What did you do?
F: Nothing! I was ill. I had a bad cold. I stayed in bed all weekend.

E: Oh, no! Are you OK now?
F: Yes, but I have to work now!

Conversation 4
G: Detlev! Hi! How are you?
H: Good.
G: Did you have a nice weekend?
H: Yes, it was great.
G: What did you do?
H: Well, some friends came to visit, so I showed them the city.
G: That sounds nice. Where did you go?
H: Well, on Saturday, we went to the cathedral and for a picnic in the park, and in the evening we went into the old town. Then on Sunday, we went to the market in the morning, and then I cooked lunch for everyone.
G: That sounds great.
H: It was. It was lovely.

4.2
1　My friends visit me a lot.
2　Last time, we visited the cathedral.
3　I played a game of tennis with a friend.
4　I tried to phone you yesterday to arrange to play tennis.
5　I wanted to go out last night, but it rained.
6　I met a friend and we chatted all night.
7　We often walk together and chat.
8　We walked along the river and had a picnic.

4.3
1　January the first
2　October the nineteenth
3　March the eighth
4　November the second
5　June the twenty-fourth
6　the third Monday in January

4.4
1　The night before, we made a fire on the beach with some friends. We sat round the fire all night and we drank and ate and sang songs and laughed. We had a great time. Some of my friends swam in the sea, but I didn't. The sea wasn't very warm. Then on the 24th, I slept till four in the afternoon.
2　In March, I was in London for work so I missed the holiday. They don't have this holiday in the UK. It was sad. On Women's Day, men usually treat us very well. They do nice things and give us presents. But I didn't go out for dinner. I didn't get any flowers. Nobody said nice things to me. I sat in my hotel room and watched TV! It wasn't very nice.
3　On the holiday, we went to Snowshoe Mountain in West Virginia. The snow's good in January. We left on Saturday at three in the morning and we drove to the mountains. We got there at eight and spent the weekend skiing. It was very clear and sunny. There wasn't a cloud in the sky. We had great views. We left on Monday afternoon, but the traffic was bad. We didn't get back home to Washington till two in the morning.

REVIEW 02

R2.1

| bath | /θ/ | fun | /f/ | past | /p/ | turn | /t/ |
| change | /tʃ/ | miss | /s/ | wash | /ʃ/ | key | /k/ |

R2.2

| /p/ | /f/ | /t/ | /tʃ/ | /k/ |

R2.3

| 1 | put | 2 | cut | 3 | sofa | 4 | show |
| 5 | match | 6 | think | 7 | photo | 8 | plates |

R2.4

Conversation 1
A: Did you have a nice weekend?
B: Yes, it was OK.
A: What did you do?
B: Well, on Saturday I went shopping with my friend, Denise.
A: Oh yes? Did you buy anything nice?
B: I didn't. I didn't see any clothes I liked, but Denise bought a jacket and some shoes.

Conversation 2
C: We need to buy some things to make sandwiches for tomorrow. Is there a supermarket near here?
D: Not really. There's a fruit and vegetable shop opposite the station. It's a ten-minute walk.
C: Oh, OK. Can you show me on the map?
D: Sure. We're here and this is Amwell Road. The shop is on the corner opposite the station, here.
C: OK. Thanks.

Conversation 3
E: You're tall, Pete. Can you reach that big plate?
F: Sorry, I can't.
E: Don't worry. Pass me that chair, I can stand on that.
F: Here.
E: Thanks. Can you hold it?
F: Sure.

Conversation 4
G: Did you go anywhere in the holidays?
H: Yes, we got a cheap flight and flew to Copenhagen.
G: Really? That sounds nice.
H: It was.
G: What did you do?
H: We walked round and did some sightseeing and had some nice meals.
G: Was the weather OK?
H: Yes, it was sunny but very cold. There was snow on the ground. Here, I have some photos on my phone.

UNIT 05

5.1
Conversation 1
A: Who's next?
B: Me.
A: What would you like?
B: Can I have some apples?
A: These ones?
B: No, those red ones.
A: How many would you like?
B: Six.
A: OK. Anything else, my love?
B: Yes. Those things there. What do you call them?
A: These?
B: Yes.
A: Peaches. Do you want the yellow or the orange ones?
B: Three yellow ones.
A: There you go. That's £3.10 altogether. Thank you. Next?

Conversation 2
C: Those look nice.
D: Mmm. That yellow one especially.
C: Hello. Do you speak English?
E: A little.
C: Can we have some of that yellow cake?
E: How much? Like this?
D: A bit more. That's fine.

C: And the brown one above it? With ... is that orange on top? What's that cake made of?

E: Coffee, and yes, it's orange on top.

C: OK. I'll have a piece of that.

E: Like this?

C: That's great.

E: Five euros 46.

Conversation 3

F: English?

G: Yes. How much are those?

F: Depends. Five dollars, seven dollars fifty, ten dollars. Which do you like?

G: How much is that red one?

F: This one?

G: No, the other one, there at the top. With 'Egypt' on it.

F: This one.

G: Yes.

F: Ten dollars.

G: What size is it?

F: Any size. What do you want?

G: Can I have one in medium? Thanks.

F: There. Medium.

5.2

thirteen	fourteen	sixteen
thirty	forty	sixty

5.3

fifty	seventy	eighteen
ninety	thirteen	nineteen thousand
two hundred and fifteen	fifty thousand	

5.4

1 They're having a sale at a shop in town.

2 I'm not working very hard at the moment.

3 My mother's not here. She's doing the shopping.

4 The economy's growing fast at the moment.

5 My football team's doing very well now.

6 I hope you're enjoying this class.

7 Some friends are staying with me at the moment.

8 My brother's studying at university.

5.5

Conversation 1

A: Excuse me. Do you sell radios?

B: Yes madam. They're over there, by the till.

A: Really? I didn't see them there.

B: No? Well, come with me. Let's see. Yes, look. There they are. On the bottom shelf.

A: Oh, that was stupid! I walked past them a minute ago.

B: Don't worry. It's no problem.

A: Well, thanks for your help.

B: You're welcome.

Conversation 2

C: Excuse me. Do you sell shirts?

D: Yes, of course, sir. In the Menswear department.

C: Right. OK. And where is that?

D: On the second floor. If you go up the escalator here and turn right at the top, it's there. Next to Gaming and Computing.

C: Great. Thanks for your help.

D: You're welcome.

Conversation 3

E: Excuse me. Can you help me?

F: Yes, of course.

E: I'm looking for some sun cream. I looked in the Beauty and Make-up department, but I couldn't see any. Do you sell it anywhere?

F: Yes, we do, but it's in the Sports department.

E: Oh, that's strange.

F: Well, people use it when they go swimming, I suppose.

E: OK. So, where is the Sports department?

F: On the fourth floor. You can take the lifts from over there.

E: OK.

F: And when you get out of the lift, it's on the left.

E: Left. OK. Great. Thanks for your help.

F: My pleasure. Have a nice day now.

UNIT 06

6.1

Conversation 1

A: So what do you do, Imke?

B: I'm a student.

A: Oh, OK. What're you studying?

B: I'm doing a degree in Marketing.

A: Right. And what year are you in?

B: My first. I only started this year.

A: How's the course going?

B: Really well. It's great. I'm really enjoying it.

Conversation 2

C: So what do you do, Tom? Are you working?

D: I'm a student at university.

C: Oh, right. What're you studying?

D: Geography.

C: Really? What year are you in?

D: My second.

C: And how's it going?

D: Not very well. It's quite boring!

Conversation 3

E: What do you do? Are you working?

F: No, I'm not, actually. I'm at the polytechnic.

E: Oh, right. What're you studying?

F: Engineering.

E: Wow! OK. What year are you in?

F: My third. I finish next year.

E: And how's it going?

F: OK, but it's quite difficult. It's a lot of work!

E: I'm sure. Well, good luck with it.

6.2

1 What are you studying?

2 What year are you in?

3 Are you enjoying it?

4 How are you?

5 Are you hungry?

6 Are you good at English?

7 Where are you from?

8 Where are you staying?

6.3

A: What age do you start school?

B: Seven, but most children attend some kind of pre-school classes for a year before that.

A: And when can you leave school?

B: At 16 if you want to. You can then get a job or go to a special college to learn a trade, but lots of people stay until 18.

A: And when does the school day begin?

B: We start at half past eight in the morning.

A: And how long each day do you study at school?

B: We usually have six – sometimes seven – lessons a day. Each class lasts 45 minutes.

A: How many breaks do you get?

B: Five – between the six lessons. They last between 15 and 25 minutes.

A: How much homework do you get?

B: Quite a lot! It depends on the age of the student, but usually between an hour and a half and three hours – and possibly more! We do a lot of writing and a lot of preparation for class.

A: What kind of subjects do you study?

B: We do lots of different things – ten or more. We do Russian language, of course, as well as Russian Literature. We do English and maybe one other foreign language as well – usually French or German. Then there's History, and plenty of science subjects too: Biology, Chemistry and Physics as well as Geography and lots of Maths. We do IT and, finally, we do PE as well.

A: What's your favourite subject?

B: I like foreign languages because I find them easy and I like my teachers! I'm doing two – English and French.

REVIEW 03

🔊 R3.1

seat	/iː/	fish	/ɪ/	put	/ʊ/
true	/uː/	bread	/e/	agree	/ə/
first	/ɜː/	store	/ɔː/	match	/æ/
luck	/ʌ/	half	/ɑː/	wrong	/ɒ/

🔊 R3.2

/iː/   /ɪ/   /ʊ/   /uː/   /iː/   /e/   /æ/

🔊 R3.3

1 please   2 art   3 good   4 lose
5 important   6 exam   7 worry   8 college

🔊 R3.4
Conversation 1

A: What do you call that yellow fruit in English?

B: What, these things?

A: Yes.

B: They're plums.

A: OK. Can I have a kilo and also some apples?

B: How many?

A: Six.

B: Anything else?

A: No, thanks.

B: That's £3.30, please.

Conversation 2

C: What do you do?

D: I'm a manager in a bookshop.

C: Do you enjoy it?

D: Yes, it's great.

C: Do you like reading?

D: Yes, I love it, and I get free books.

C: That's good.

D: Yes, the only problem is, I hardly ever read them because I work very long hours!

C: Oh.

Conversation 3

E: What do you do?

F: I'm a student.

E: What're you studying?

F: I'm studying to become a primary school teacher.

E: OK. How's it going?

F: Great. I'm really enjoying it.

E: What year are you in?

F: My third year. I have my final exams in June.

Conversation 4

G: You speak English very well.

H: Yes, I go to a bilingual school in Italy.

G: Oh, really? Is your mum or dad English?

H: No, they're both Italian. They just want me to speak English well.

G: So, are all the classes in English?

H: No. Some are in Italian.

G: So, what subjects did you study in English?

H: It changes. One year we did Science in English, and the next year in Italian.

G: So, do you want to go to university in Britain?

H: No, I want to study Engineering in Rome.

UNIT 07

🔊 7.1
Conversation 1

A: Do you have any brothers or sisters, Zoe?

B: Yes, I do. I have two brothers.

A: How old are they?

B: My older brother's 28 and my younger one is 19.

A: What do they do?

B: Neil's a teacher and my younger brother, Tim, is at university.

A: What's he studying?

B: Chemistry.

Conversation 2

C: Did you go out yesterday?

D: Yeah, I did. I met my cousin and his girlfriend for a drink.

C: Oh, OK. Is he visiting?

D: No, he lives here. He is English.

C: Really?

D: Yes. My uncle Giorgio met my aunt Ruth in London and they stayed in England.

C: So, how old is your cousin?

D: 18. He's a year younger than me.

C: Do you have any other cousins here?

D: No, I don't, but I have 12 back in Italy.

C: Really? How many aunts and uncles have you got?

D: Nine. My dad has eight brothers and sisters!

Conversation 3

E: So, are you married, Ted?

F: Yes, I am. 30 years next year.

E: Really?

F: Yep.

E: So, what does your wife do?

F: She's a nurse.

E: And do you have any children?

F: Yeah, just one son – Ted Junior. He's finishing college this year.

🔊 7.2

Really? Really? Really?

🔊 7.3

1 My dad has ten brothers and sisters.
2 My brother's 15 years older than me.
3 My wife is a nurse.
4 It's my birthday today.
5 My grandma's 98.
6 My sister's in her last year at school.

🔊 7.4

1 Johan and I grew up together. We first met at school and later we shared a house together in Malmö. He's very creative. He's a photographer and he lives in New York now, but we're still very close. We talk all the time. We're friends for life, I'm sure.

2 I only know Miguel because my husband works with him. I don't really get on with him very well, but what can I do? They were already friends when we met and I respect that. He likes going out a lot. He goes to parties all night. I think he's a bit stupid. He's 38, but he thinks he's still 21! He also sometimes says stupid things about women.

3 In some ways, Claire and I don't know each other at all. She lives in Wisconsin and I live in Leeds. We never meet face-to-face. We only meet in chat rooms and we talk through Messenger. She's very sensitive and she really understands me. My friends think I'm crazy, but when I leave college, I want to go to the US and meet her in person!

4 Liu Bing – or Auntie Liu as I call her – isn't really my aunt. She's an old friend of my mum's. They went to school together and she came to our house a lot when I was a kid. She's a strong and confident woman, and she made me feel good about myself. When I moved to Shanghai, she helped me find a place to live and a job, so now she's not only my mother's friend, she's mine as well!

UNIT 08

🔊 8.1

Conversation 1

A: What're you doing now? Do you have time for a coffee?
B: No, sorry, I don't. I'm going to study in the library and do some reading for my Literature course.
A: Oh, OK. Maybe later?
B: I can't. I'm going to go home and study. I have my exams next week.
A: Oh, right. Well, good luck with them. What about after your exams? Do you want to go out somewhere? Maybe dinner one night?
B: I'm really sorry, but I can't. I … I have to work that night. Bye.
A: But I didn't say which night!

Conversation 2

C: What're you doing now?
D: I'm going to look for an Internet café. I have to check the details of my flight for next week. I need to write a few emails too. What about you? What're you doing?
C: I'm going to go running by the river. I need to do some exercise!
D: Me too! What're you doing later? Are you busy?
C: No. Why? Do you want to meet somewhere?
D: Yes, OK. Where?
C: How about in the main square at eight?
D: OK. Great.
C: Then I can show you some nice places where there aren't too many tourists.

Conversation 3

E: What're you doing now? Are you going to the meeting?
F: No, I'm not. I'm going to meet some clients and have lunch with them.
E: Oh, right. Where are you going to eat?
F: A new French place in Harajuku.
E: Oh, that sounds good.
F: Yeah. What about you? What're you doing now?
E: I have to give a presentation at the meeting, but after that I'm going to go out somewhere. Do you want to come?
F: Maybe, yeah. Call me later, OK?
E: OK.
F: Great. See you.

🔊 8.2

1 I'm going to go now.
2 He's going to cook for me tonight.
3 I'm not going to see you tomorrow.
4 I'm not going to answer that question!

5 Where are you going to stay?
6 When are you going to leave?

🔊 8.3

A: What're you doing later? Are you busy?
B: No. Why? Do you want to meet somewhere?
A: Yes. Great. Where?
B: How about in the main square, under the big clock?
A: Yes, fine. What time?
B: Is six OK?
A: It's quite early.
B: Oh, sorry. Well, how about 7.30?
A: Perfect! See you later. Bye.

🔊 8.4

Speaker 1

I'm from the Czech Republic, but at the moment, I'm living in Manchester. I'm doing a degree here. I also work part-time and I'm saving money because, after university, I'd really like to go to China to study kung fu. I practise three times a week here, and I'd like to take it to the next level.

Speaker 2

I work for a big design company in São Paulo, but I'd like to leave and start my own business sometime in the next two or three years. I don't like having a boss. I'd like to work for myself. I'd also like to start a family, have children, but maybe that has to wait!

Speaker 3

I retire next year, after working for 38 years. It's going to be strange, but I'm looking forward to it. I'd like to spend more time gardening. I have a small piece of land and I'd like to grow my own fruit and vegetables. I'd also like to spend more time with my wife and children.

Speaker 4

I'd like to be really famous. I'd like to have my own TV show and I'd like to have lots and lots of money. I'd like someone to drive me round in a big car and I'd like to eat in expensive restaurants – and I'd like everyone in the world to know my name!

REVIEW 04

🔊 R4.1

date	/eɪ/	driver	/aɪ/	career	/ɪe/
area	/eə/	noise	/ɔɪ/	cloudy	/aʊ/
soul	/əʊ/	tourist	/ʊə/		

🔊 R4.2

1 /e/ /ɪ/ /eɪ/
2 /æ/ /ɪ/ /aɪ/
3 /ɪ/ /ə/ /ɪə/
4 /e/ /ə/ /eə/
5 /æ/ /ʊ/ /aʊ/
6 /ɒ/ /ɪ/ /ɔɪ/
7 /ə/ /ʊ/ /əʊ/
8 /uː/ /ə/ /ʊə/

🔊 R4.3

1 loud	2 fair	3 tour	4 clear
5 enjoy	6 notice	7 arrange	8 client

🔊 R4.4

Conversation 1

A: What do you do?
B: Well, at the moment, I'm looking after my daughter Laura, but I worked for a car company before.
A: Oh right. How old is your daughter?
B: A year and a half.

A: Lovely – so she's walking and talking now.
B: Yes. It's nice.
A: Are you going to go back to work?
B: Yes, I'd like to continue my career, but I'm happy at home with Laura.

Conversation 2

C: What are you doing now?
D: I'm going to meet my brother for a drink.
C: You have a brother? Is he older or younger?
D: He's a year older than me. We're quite close.
C: That's nice.
D: Do you want to come and meet him?
C: I'd love to. Where are you going to go?
D: The bar opposite here.
C: OK. Can I meet you there in 20 minutes? I have to finish some work.
D: Sure.

Conversation 3

E: Who are the other two people in the photo?
F: The guy is my cousin, James, and that's his girlfriend, Amanda.
E: She looks nice.
F: Yes, she is. She's quiet, but she's very friendly. I like her.
E: When is the photo from?
F: From when we left school. We were all in the same class.

Conversation 4

G: Did you know the government is going to expand the airport?
H: Really? That's great.
G: I don't agree. It's going to be bad for the environment and it's going to cause a lot of noise.
H: Maybe, but it's going to help local business.
G: Well, I think it's a stupid idea.

UNIT 09

9.1

A: Have you been to Istanbul before?
B: Well, it's my first time, but Harry's been here before.
C: Yeah, once – but I didn't see much then.
A: When did you arrive?
B: Friday. We're really enjoying it.
A: Where have you been?
B: Well, today we went round the Bazaar. That was great. Then we went over to Galata and walked round there.
A: Did you go up the Galata Tower?
C: No. There was a long line of people and we didn't want to wait.
A: Really? You get a great view from the top.
C: Yeah, I heard. Another time maybe.
A: Have you been to Topkapi Palace?
B: Yes, we went there at the weekend. It's amazing, and it's so big!
A: I know. How long did you spend there?
B: All day! We were tired at the end.
C: Yeah, really tired!
A: I'm sure.
B: We also went to the Hagia Sophia.
A: Did you? I've never been in there.
B: But you live here!
A: I know, but sometimes you don't think about visiting places when they're near.
B: That's true. We live in London and I've never been to Buckingham Palace.
A: So, what are you doing later?
C: We want to do something that's not sightseeing. Are there any films in English here?
A: Sure. Have you seen that film *Berlin*?
B: No, we haven't, but we'd like to.
A: Me too. They say it's good.

9.2

1 One weekend last year, I rented a house in the countryside with some old friends from university for a few days. We had a really lovely time. I really needed it because of all the stress at work. We got up late every day, we had nice long breakfasts, we went for walks in the hills near the house and then we went swimming in the sea. It was lovely. We were very lucky with the weather: it was nice and sunny and the evenings were warm, so we sat outside and chatted until late. It was wonderful to see everyone again.

2 One day last year, I left work late, about nine o'clock. It was dark and I was very tired. It was summer and it was very hot so, I opened my car window. I stopped at a traffic light and suddenly two men jumped into my car. One of them had a gun, and they told me to drive. I didn't want them to shoot me, so I drove! They took me to a poor part of town, and then they stole my car, all my cash and my credit cards, and my jeans. It was awful, but, hey, I'm still alive!

9.3

1 I stopped at a traffic light
2 a poor part of town
3 It was awful, but I'm still alive
4 I rented a house
5 We sat outside and chatted until late
6 I can speak a few words of Italian.
7 It was about a week ago.
8 He had an awful accident.
9 It was a really stressful experience.
10 She fell out of a window.

UNIT 10

10.1

A Hello. I'm sorry. Do you speak English?
B Of course. How can I help?
A Hi. We'd like two tickets to Groningen, please.
B Groningen. Certainly. Travelling today?
A If possible, please, yes.
B No problem. The next train is at 12.25, so you have lots of time.
A Good.
B A single or return?
A Return, I think, but we're not sure when we're going to come back.
B Ah, so it's probably best to buy two singles. Return tickets only last one day.
A Oh, OK. How much are the single tickets?
B First class is fifty-two euros fifty and second class is twenty-seven euros ten.
A Two second class is fine, thank you.
B That's fifty-four euros and twenty cents, please. How would you like to pay?
A Is Visa OK?
B Yes, of course. Please enter your pin. Great. Thank you.
A Thank you. What platform does the train leave from?
B You need platform six, and you have to change at Hilversum.
A Oh, really? It's not direct?
B No, there are no direct trains to Groningen from here.
A I see. How long does the journey take?
B It's about two and a half hours in total. You have to wait thirty minutes in Hilversum. You arrive around three o'clock.
A OK. And it's platform six, yes.
B Yes, platform six at 12.25.
A OK. Thanks for your help.
C Did you get the tickets OK?
A Yes, it's at twenty-five past twelve. What time is it now? Do we have time for a coffee?
C Yeah – plenty of time. It's quarter to twelve.

10.2

1 Quarter to seven.
2 Five to twelve.
3 Twenty-five to three.
4 Ten to ten.
5 Talk to me.
6 I'd love to go to Thailand.
7 We have to change here.
8 I don't have to go to work today.

10.3

A: Good evening, sir, madam. How can I help you?
B: Hi. We'd like to go out for dinner. Where's the best place to eat?
A: Try Captain Nemo's. It's a lovely little restaurant by the sea. It's not the cheapest place in town, but the fish there is really excellent.
C: Oh, that sounds great. Do we need to book?
A: I can do that for you, if you like. What time would you like your table?
B: About half past eight?
C: Yes, that sounds fine. What's the easiest way to get there? Can we walk?
A: Not really. It takes about half an hour to walk there. It's probably best to take a taxi. Would you like me to book one for you?
C: Yes, please. That's great.
B: Oh, there's one other thing, before I forget. We'd like to buy some presents. Where's the best place to go shopping?
A: There's a nice market in the main square tomorrow. They have some nice things. Try there. It starts at around eight and goes on until about two.
B: It sounds perfect. Thanks for your help.
A: No problem. It's my pleasure.

REVIEW 05

R5.1

bath	/θ/	off	/f/	trip	/p/	let	/t/
catch	/tʃ/	bus	/s/	cash	/ʃ/	lock	/k/
the	/ð/	alive	/v/	bike	/b/	died	/d/
edge	/dʒ/	bars	/z/	Asia	/ʒ/	gun	/g/

R5.2

pay   bath   fat   very   map   boss   laugh   arrive

R5.3

1 born   2 cause   3 course   4 guard
5 jump   6 visitor   7 further   8 divorced

R5.4

Conversation 1
A: When did you arrive?
B: Three days ago.
A: Are you enjoying it?
B: Yes, it's been great.
A: Where have you been? Have you done any sightseeing?
B: No, we've been nowhere! We've sat by the pool and eaten some nice food, and we've read a lot. We were both really stressed before we came here and we needed to do nothing for a few days.

Conversation 2
C: Can I have a single to Handford?
D: When are you going?
C: Now. The train's going to leave in two minutes.
D: Oh, sorry. There's a delay with that train. It's going to be 35 minutes late.
C: No! There isn't a train before that?
D: There is, but it's not a direct train. It's very slow. It arrives at 12.38.
C: I'm going to be late for my meeting.
D: I'm sorry, sir. How would you like to pay?

C: Cash.
D: That's £32.45.
C: That's awful.

Conversation 3
E: What time's your flight?
F: A quarter to eight, so I need to get there at about six. How long does the train take to the airport?
E: Oh, it's quite quick. It only takes half an hour.
F: That's good.
E: So, what do you want to do today?
F: Well, I haven't been to the city museum. How about going there?
E: OK.

Conversation 4
G: Have you been to the old part of town?
H: Yes, and I don't want to go there again!
G: Really? Why not?
H: When I went there, someone jumped out in the street and stole my bag. I fell down and broke my arm.
G: No!
H: Yes. It was awful!

UNIT 11

11.1

A: Hello. I'm sorry. Do you speak English?
B: A little, yes.
A: Great. Can we have a table for two, please?
B: Have you booked?
A: No, I'm afraid we haven't.
B: Ah. We are very busy tonight. Can you wait ten minutes?
A: Yes.

C: Can we see the menu, please?
B: Of course.
C: Ah. You don't have English menus?
B: We don't. I'm sorry, but I can help you. This is chicken, this is fish – but I don't know the name of the fish in English – this is steak, this is soup and this is a bird – I don't know the name – it is similar to a chicken, but smaller. It's very, very good. I recommend this.
C: Oh. I'd like to try that, please.
B: Certainly, madam. And for you, sir?
A: The fish, please.

B: I'm sorry, sir, but the fish is finished. We don't have any more.
A: Oh, right. Well, can I get a steak, please? Well cooked. No blood.
B: As you prefer.

B: Can I take your plates?
C: Thank you. That was delicious.
B: Would you like any dessert?
A: No, I'm fine. I'm really full. Can we have the bill, please?
B: Of course. One moment.

B: Here you are.
A: Thanks. Does this include service?
B: Yes, we add 15 per cent.
C: OK. Thank you.

11.2

1 A: I'm a vegetarian.
   B: Oh, really? You don't eat meat?
   A: No. No meat, no fish. Nothing that moves!
2 A: It's cash only, I'm afraid.
   B: You don't take cards?
   A: No, I'm afraid not. We don't have a machine.

3　A: I'm really full.
　　B: Yeah? You don't want any dessert?
　　A: No, I'm fine. Really. I can't eat anything else.
4　A: We're very, very busy tonight.
　　B: So you don't have any free tables?
　　A: Not at the moment. Can you wait ten minutes?
5　A: I'd just like something non-alcoholic.
　　B: OK. So you don't drink alcohol?
　　A: No. I don't like the taste.

⏺ 11.3
N = Nicoletta; D = Domi; F = Frank
N: Would you like any more, Domi? Frank?
D: No, thanks. I'm really full.
F: Me too, but it was lovely, Nicoletta. Really delicious. Would you like me to put the plates in the kitchen?
N: Thanks. Just put them in the sink. I can do the washing-up later.
D: So, how did you cook the potatoes? They were really, really good.
N: They're very easy to do. You just wash them, and then slice each one into five or six pieces. Put them on a plate and put some olive oil and some salt and pepper on them. Chop some garlic and add that and then roast everything in the oven for about 45 minutes.
F: And how about the lamb?
N: Well, you chop some onions and fry them for ten or 15 minutes – in butter. Then chop the lamb and some tomatoes and fry them for five more minutes. Add some salt and pepper – and it's ready to eat.
F: You make it sound easy.
N: It is easy. Would you like me to email you the recipe?
F: Please.
N: Oh, by the way, I'm going to have a little party next Saturday for my birthday. Would you two like to come?
D: It depends. Are you going to cook?

⏺ 11.4
1　A: Would you like to try a piece of this cake?
　　B: Yes, please. It looks delicious. Did you make it yourself?
2　A: Would you like me to do the washing-up?
　　B: No, it's OK. Don't worry. I can do it later.
3　A: Would you like to go out for dinner sometime?
　　B: Yes, OK. Where do you want to go?
4　A: Would you like a starter?
　　B: No, thanks. I'm just going to have a main course.
5　A: Would you like me to cook for you one evening?
　　B: Oh, yes, please. I've never tried Iranian food before.
6　A: Would you like a cup of coffee?
　　B: No, thank you. It stops me sleeping!

UNIT 12

⏺ 12.1
Conversation 1
A: Are you OK?
B: Yeah, I'm OK. My stomach hurts a bit.
A: Maybe you should lie down.
B: No, it's OK. I think I'm just hungry.
A: Are you sure?
B: Honestly, I'll be fine after I have something to eat.

Conversation 2
C: Hi, it's Johnny.
D: Johnny! How are you?
C: Basically, I'm OK, but I fell off my bike and I've broken my arm!
D: Oh dear. Maybe we should cancel the meeting for tomorrow.
C: No, it's OK. It's my left arm, so I can write.
D: Are you sure?
C: Yeah, honestly, it's fine. It doesn't really hurt.

Conversation 3
E: Are you OK?
F: No, I feel a bit sick.
E: Maybe you should go out and get some fresh air.
F: Yes, I think I will. I'll be back in a moment.
E: OK. Take your time. There's no rush.

Conversation 4
H: [coughs]
G: Are you OK?
H: Yeah, yeah.
G: Have you been to the doctor?
H: No. It's just a cold.
G: Are you sure? You have a very bad cough. I really think you should see someone. Maybe it's a chest infection.
H: Honestly, it'll be fine in a couple of days.

Conversation 5
I: Are you OK?
J: Yeah, I'm fine. My back hurts a bit, that's all.
I: Maybe you shouldn't play tennis then.
J: It's OK. I told Kevin I'm going to.
I: Yeah, but are you sure you can play?
J: Yeah, my back's just stiff. I'll be fine after I warm up.

⏺ 12.2
1　I got the bus to work. I was lucky because there was a seat. I sat and read my book. It was quite a nice journey.
2　When I got to work, we had a meeting. The boss was quite angry. He shouted a bit and told us we need to work harder. I was a bit upset, but I tried not to cry.
3　After the meeting, I sat and thought about everything I had to do. I got a headache. I sent a few emails and tried to concentrate.
4　I had lunch with my aunt. She lives near work. She always makes me smile. I felt better after seeing her.
5　In the afternoon, I went to see some clients. It was a successful afternoon. I sold a few things, and it's always nice meeting people.
6　Back in the office, I had to answer about 30 emails. It was slow and not very interesting.
7　After work, I had to wait for the bus for half an hour and then it was full, so I couldn't sit and read.
8　When I got home, I went for a run with my friend, Viv. We're going to go on holiday together so we talked about that. It was a lovely warm evening.
9　After dinner, I watched the news on TV. I wanted to watch a film as well, but I fell asleep on the sofa.

REVIEW 06

⏺ R6.1
meat	/iː/	youth	/uː/	hurt	/ɜː/
warm	/ɔː/	arm	/ɑː/		

⏺ R6.2
/i/	/iː/	/bill/	/bean/
/ʊ/	/uː/	/cook/	/soup/
/e/	/ɜː/	/bed/	/bird/
/ʌ/	/ɑː/	/cut/	/heart/
/o/	/ɔː/	/chop/	/course/

⏺ R6.3
1	stir	2	pork	3	asleep	4	farming
5	interview	6	seafood	7	statue	8	approve

⏺ R6.4
Conversation 1
A: Are you ready to order?
B: I think so. What's the 'mussel chowder'?
A: It's a kind of potato soup with seafood.

B: OK. I'll have that.
A: Anything else?
B: Just a glass of water, please.

Conversation 2
C: This is nice. What's in it?
D: Potatoes, a bit of onion, some cheese, and the outside is bits of bread.
C: OK. How do you make it?
D: You boil the potatoes and, when they're soft, you mix them with the onion and cheese, and then you cover it all with small bits of bread and fry it. It's quite easy.
C: Well, it's delicious.

Conversation 3
E: Are you OK?
F: No, I feel a bit sick and my stomach hurts.
E: Oh dear. Why don't you lie down?
F: I think I will. I had some seafood today. Maybe that's the problem.
E: Maybe you should go to the doctor.
F: I'll be OK. I just need to lie down.

Conversation 4
G: You look happy.
H: I am. I passed my exams and I got good grades.
G: Really? Well done!
H: I can do the degree I want now.
G: That's great. What are you going to study?
H: Law.

Unit 13

13.1
Conversation 1
A: What do you want to do tomorrow?
B: I don't know. What's the forecast?
A: It's going to be quite hot. They said it might reach 35 degrees.
B: Really? Why don't we go to the swimming pool?
A: We could do. Which one?
B: The open-air one – and we can have lunch at the café.
A: OK. Let's do that.

Conversation 2
C: What do you want to do today?
D: I don't know. What's the forecast? It looks a bit cloudy.
C: It said it might rain this morning, but it's going to be dry this afternoon.
D: OK. Well, why don't we relax this morning and then go for a walk this afternoon?
C: Could do. Where?
D: How about taking the car and going to the hills?
C: OK. Let's do that. We haven't been to the hills recently.

Conversation 3
E: Do you want to go away at the weekend?
F: I'm not sure. What's the forecast?
E: I think it's going to be cold. They said it might snow.
F: Really? Why don't we just stay here? I don't want to drive if there's snow or ice on the roads.
E: That's true. Maybe we should do some shopping for Christmas.
F: We could do. When exactly?
E: Early on Saturday morning. We can take the train.
F: Can we be back before the football starts?
E: Maybe. What time?
F: It starts at three.
E: I guess – if we go early.
F: OK. Let's do that. We have to do it sometime.

13.2
Rachid
Camels are found across north and east Africa, and the Middle East. In Kuwait, the camel is our national animal. Camels are very important for us: they can travel for days across the desert without food or water; they can carry more than horses can, and they are quieter and more intelligent as well.

Camels also provide milk. We believe the milk is very good for you and stops you getting ill. Camel meat is eaten by some people too. It's high in protein and low in fat. Camel skins are sometimes made into leather as well.

Camels also provide entertainment. Camel racing is very popular here, though people are now asking if it is right to use foreign children to ride them.

One problem with camels is that they can really damage your car if you hit them! That's why many cars now have camel radar – machines to tell you if camels are nearby!

Morena
The national tree of Brazil is called Pau Brasil. It is often said that we took the name of our country from this tree. It grows up to 15 metres high and has lovely yellow flowers.

In the past, it was found all along the Atlantic coast, but there was quite a big problem because lots of trees were cut down. The wood from the trees is very beautiful – it's a lovely orange-red colour – and it's very valuable. It's used to make bows – to play instruments like violins with.

A red dye was also produced from the tree and sold, but in the nineteenth century they started using chemicals to make these dyes in factories. That probably saved the tree!

Pau Brasil has strong cultural, economic and historical importance for us Brazilians. It's protected by law now and we really don't want to lose it.

13.3
1 The towels are changed every day.
   The towels are changed every day.
2 We were met at the airport by a friend.
   We were met at the airport by a friend.
3 The tree's mainly found in the mountains.
   The tree's mainly found in the mountains.
4 The game was won by Canada.
   The game was won by Canada.
5 The skins are sold for leather.
   The skins are sold for leather.
6 Most of the work was done by my dad.
   Most of the work was done by my dad.
7 My bank card details were stolen.
   My bank card details were stolen.
8 The meat's usually eaten with rice.
   The meat's usually eaten with rice.

Unit 14

14.1
Conversation 1
A: Have you ever seen a film called *28 Days Later*?
B: No, I haven't. I've heard of it, but I've never seen it. What's it like?
  A: It's brilliant. It's really, really scary. It's about a terrible disease that makes people hungry for blood, and they want to kill.
B: Really? It sounds very violent!
A: Yeah, it is, but it's great! It's a very clever film. It's not a normal horror movie. It's also about the environment and politics and everything.
B: It sounds terrible – definitely not my kind of film!
A: No, it's great! Honestly!

Conversation 2

C: Have you seen that new musical *Dogs* yet?

D: Yes, I have. I saw it last week, actually.

C: Oh really? We went to see it last night. What did you think of it?

D: It was OK. Nothing special. It was quite entertaining in places, I suppose, but the story was stupid.

C: Really? Do you think so? I thought it was brilliant – one of the best things I've seen in a long time.

D: Yeah? OK.

C: The dancing and the music were great and it was very funny. I couldn't stop laughing!

D: But what about the ending? It was so predictable!

C: Not for me! I found it really sad. I started crying!

D: Really? Oh well. I suppose we just don't share the same tastes.

🔊 14.2

1 Tomorrow's general election is expected to be the closest in many years. Both the People's Party and the Popular Front are optimistic and say they expect to win, but most people think that they will probably have to share power. Voting starts at seven in the morning and closes at ten, with the final result expected early on Monday morning.

2 The country's largest chemical company, NBE, has announced that it is going to cut five thousand jobs. The company lost 385 million dollars last year and now plans to close its two biggest factories in the north of the country.

3 Abroad, peace talks between Adjikistan and Kamistan have failed and there are worries that war will now follow. The two countries disagree about where the border between them should be. Both countries receive funding and military help from their powerful local neighbours.

4 Next, pop music. Last year's TV Idol winner, Shaneez, has got engaged. The singer is planning to marry her boyfriend of two months, actor and model Kevin Smith.

5 And finally, France go into their important World Cup match against Brazil tonight without their captain and star player, Florian Mendy. Mendy injured himself in training yesterday and may now miss the rest of the competition.

🔊 14.3

1 It'll be fine.
It'll be fine.

2 I probably won't vote this year.
I probably won't vote this year.

3 It won't be easy.
It won't be easy.

4 It won't cost much.
It won't cost much.

5 I think he'll have a few problems.
I think he'll have a few problems.

6 We'll probably be a bit late.
We'll probably be a bit late.

7 We won't win.
We won't win.

8 It won't kill you. You'll live.
It won't kill you. You'll live.

REVIEW 07

🔊 R7.1

hide	/h/	me	/m/	rain	/n/	sing	/ŋ/
lock	/l/	rest	/r/	wild	/w/	yet	/j/

🔊 R7.2

1 huge	2 once	3 young	4 ending
5 protein	6 unusual	7 valuable	8 economic

🔊 R7.3

1 A man has appeared in court for shooting an eagle. The man, a farmer, said the bird was killing chickens on his farm. The eagle is protected by law and the farmer might go to prison.

2 A new musical called *The Field* has closed after just three weeks. The theatre was almost empty after reports said the story was strange and depressing and the songs were terrible. The theatre says it has lost five million dollars.

3 Temperatures for the holiday weekend may reach 40 degrees. The police are expecting a lot of traffic as people try to escape the city and go to the beaches and countryside. The Department of Health has said people should not stay in the sun too long and should use sun cream.

4 The pop singer, Shaneez, is going to divorce her husband, the actor and model Kevin Smith. The couple got married in Las Vegas four months ago. Shaneez was recently seen with the French football star, Florian Mendy.

UNIT 15

🔊 15.1

Conversation 1

A: Do you know much about computers?

B: A bit. Why?

A: I'm thinking of buying a laptop. Can you recommend anything?

B: Well, it depends. How much do you want to spend?

A: I'm not sure – about five or six hundred pounds.

B: OK. Well, for that price, try a Bell. They have quite a lot of memory, they're not too heavy and the battery lasts quite a long time.

A: That sounds perfect. Thanks.

Conversation 2

C: What happened to your phone?

D: Oh, I dropped it last night and broke the screen.

C: Oh no! How annoying!

D: I know. I'll need to replace it, but I'm actually thinking of getting one of those smart phones.

C: Oh, OK.

D: Do you know much about them?

C: Yeah, a bit. The new Kotika one is great. It's amazing. It can do everything that a small laptop does. It's very easy to use and it has a full keyboard, so it's good if you send a lot of emails.

D: Wow. OK. I'll try to have a look at that one.

Conversation 3

E: Hi. How're you?

F: Oh hi. What're you doing here?

E: I'm trying to find a birthday present for my brother. It's taking me ages.

F: What kind of thing are you looking for?

E: Well, I'm thinking of buying him a games console, but I don't know anything about them!

F: Well, Bonny does a really good one. You can use lots of online games with it, the sound is great, it looks great on the screen and it's not too expensive either.

E: OK. Well, that sounds good.

🔊 15.2

1 b c d e g p t v

2 f l m n s x z

3 a h j k

4 q u w

5 i y

6 o

7 r

🔊 15.3

1 A: www.peiterzx.co.gu. That's p–e–i–t–e–r–z–x dot co dot g–u.
 B: OK, p–e–i–t–e–r–z–x dot co dot g u.
 A: Yes.
2 A: My email's nomashy@jmal.com. That's n–o–m–a–s–h–y at
  j–m–a–l dot com.
 B: OK, n–o–m–a–s–h–y, that's all one word, right?
 A: Yes. At jmal dot com.
3 A: Flat four, 65 Farquhar Drive. That's f–a–r–q–u–h–a–r and
  d–r–i–v–e.
 B: OK. Flat four, 65 Farquhar Drive – f–a–r–q–u–h–a–r.
 A: That's right

🔊 15.4

1 How many computers do you have in your home?
2 How long is your computer on every day?
3 How often do you check your email?
4 How many emails do you get every day?
5 What kind of mobile phone do you have?
6 What do you use your phone for?
7 Have you ever done anything stupid on your computer?
8 If you buy a new piece of technology, like a digital camera, how
 do you learn to use it?
9 What do you do if you have a problem with a machine or piece
 of technology?
10 How often do you buy a new piece of technology?

🔊 15.5

1 How many computers do you have in your home?
 a None.
 b One.
 c Two or more.
2 How long is your computer on every day?
 a Maybe an hour or two – if I turn it on.
 b Four or five hours. Most of the evening.
 c I never turn it off.
3 How often do you check your email?
 a Maybe once a day, maybe less.
 b Two or three times a day.
 c I check it all the time through my phone.
4 How many emails do you get every day?
 a nought to ten
 b ten to thirty
 c thirty to a hundred.
5 What kind of mobile phone do you have?
 a The most basic pay-as-you-go phone.
 b Quite a good camera phone.
 c One of the best, latest phones.
6 What do you use your phone for?
 a What do you mean? Phoning people of course!
 b I use the camera, music, and I sometimes play games.
 c Apart from the camera, I use the diary, Facebook, maps – all
  kinds of things. I can't list them all.
7 Have you ever done anything stupid on your computer?
 a Yes. I've deleted files on my computer by mistake.
 b Yes. I sent an email to the wrong person once.
 c No, of course not.
8 If you buy a new piece of technology, like a digital camera, how
 do you learn to use it?
 a I ask someone to show me the very basic things.
 b I read the instructions and learn to do a few things. I'm not
  interested in the complicated things.
 c I just start playing about with it and teach myself. To find out
  more detailed things, I look at the instructions or their
  website.

9 What do you do if you have a problem with a machine or piece of
 technology?
 a Get angry, shout and jump up and down – until someone
  tells me I need to plug it in.
 b Check it's plugged in and, if it is, call someone to repair it.
 c Check everything is plugged in. Turn it off and on again – and
  if it still doesn't work, I repair it myself.
10 How often do you buy a new piece of technology?
 a Hardly ever. Why do I need it when my old things work?
 b Sometimes. Some things are better, and I change when my
  old things break.
 c All the time. I like to have all the latest things.

UNIT 16

🔊 16.1
Conversation 1
A: Did I tell you Owen's going to move in with his girlfriend?
B: I didn't know he had a girlfriend! How long have they been
 together?
A: Two or three months, I think.
B: That's not long! What's she like?
A: She's nice, and she's very good-looking!
B: Lucky him. So, where are they going to live?
A: Pickwick somewhere.

Conversation 2
C: Did I tell you my brother Gerrard is going to get married?
D: No. When's the wedding?
C: Next May sometime.
D: That'll be nice. So what's his partner like?
C: She's quite annoying, actually. We don't really get on.
D: Oh dear.

Conversation 3
E: Did I tell you Fiona and Kieran are going to get divorced?
F: No! Why's that?
E: I think she wanted kids, but he didn't.
F: Oh, that's sad! How long have they been married?
E: Not very long. Four years, I think.
F: What a shame. They're both such nice people.
E: I know. I hope we can stay friends with both of them.

Conversation 4
G: Did I tell you I have a date on Friday?
H: No. Who with?
G: A guy in my French class.
H: So what's he like?
G: He seems very nice. He's quite quiet, but he's funny.
H: Is he good-looking?
G: Yeah, not bad. He's quite tall and he has lovely eyes.
H: OK. So what are you going to do?
G: We're going to have a drink together and then we're going to meet
 some of his friends for karaoke.

🔊 16.2

1 A: How long have you been together?
 B: Three years.
2 A: How long have you been married?
 B: 15 years now.
3 A: How long have they known each other?
 B: Not very long. A few months, I think.
4 A: How long have you lived in this house?
 B: All my life!
5 A: How long has she worked there?
 B: Ages.
6 A: How long have you had your car?
 B: Two weeks.

16.3

1 My husband and I spent two years looking for the right place to live. We weren't looking seriously to begin with, but then I got pregnant and we had to find somewhere fast. We saw five houses every weekend for four months, but didn't like any of them. One day, we were driving home from another appointment when suddenly we saw it – the house of our dreams! And, incredibly, it was for sale. We knocked at the door and offered the price they were asking for it immediately.

2 When I was growing up, I always loved music and musical instruments. For my twelfth birthday, my uncle gave me a guitar – and it was love at first sight. He was playing in a band at the time, and this had a big influence on me. After that, the guitar became the centre of my world. I played it 24 hours a day, seven days a week. Later, I studied music at university and now I make guitars for a living. All because of that special day!

3 I love Second Life, an online world where you create virtual characters – you design them, choose their names and then create lives for them. Last year, I was spending a lot of time online and one night, I met my future husband. I was working in a Second Life nightclub, he came in and it was love at first sight. His 'character' soon asked my 'character' to marry him and I said yes. We were married online in July. He then asked me in the real world and I accepted. We haven't actually met yet, but he's the one for me.

16.4

1 Sorry. I wasn't listening.
2 She wasn't feeling very well, so she went home.
3 I couldn't hear because you were talking.
4 We weren't getting on so we broke up.
5 I was working in Greece when we met.
6 I lost because I wasn't trying.

REVIEW 08

R8.1

forget machine target protect remove marriage power method

R8.2

1 threaten	2 remain	3 development	4 effective
5 advantage	6 diary	7 document	8 negotiate

R8.3

Conversation 1
A: What's that burning smell?
B: It's the hairdryer. It just has some dust or dirt in it. It sometimes has that smell, but then the smell goes.
A: Really? Are you sure it's safe?
B: Yes, it's fine. I don't need a new one.

Conversation 2
C: Do you know anything about computers?
D: A bit. Why?
C: My laptop is quite slow and it always has a problem when I use this software.
D: I don't know. Maybe you have a virus or you don't have enough memory for the program.
C: Maybe I need a new computer. Can you recommend anything?
D: Not really.

Conversation 3
E: Did I tell you Jack and Gayle are thinking of moving?
F: Really? How long have they been there?
E: Not long. They only got married last year, but they're thinking of having a baby.
F: Right. Do you know where they're going to move to?
E: Not far. They just want something bigger.

Conversation 4
G: Did I tell you Rebecca's pregnant?
H: No. Really? I thought she and Clive were breaking up!
G: No! They're fine. They had a big argument a few months ago, but they're getting on fine now.
H: Obviously! So when is the baby due?
G: Next March.
H: Wow, that's great news.

CREDITS

Although every effort has been made to contact copyright holders before publication, this has not always been possible. If notified, the publisher will undertake to rectify any errors or omissions at the earliest opportunity.

Text

The publishers would like to thank the following sources for permission to reproduce their copyright protected texts:

Page 48: from Newbury Park Primary, http://www.newburypark.redbridge.sch.uk/langofmonth/); page 90: from Positive News, www.positivenews.org.uk.

Photos

The publishers would like to thank the following sources for permission to reproduce their copyright protected images:

Alamy – pp16l (PhotoAlto), 38bm (Allstar Picture Library), 38br (David R. Frazier Photolibrary, Inc.), 41 (Visions of America, LLC), 47 (ICP), 48(5) (Ross Kelly), 49 (David Colbran), 53t (Paul Paris), 61 (Georgella), 69b (William Robinson), 88ml/107br (Pictorial Press Ltd), 88mr (Lebrecht Music and Arts Photo Library), 88br (INTERFOTO), 97br (PeerPoint), 104bl (Genevieve Vallee), 105mr (bhutan view), 105bl (Alistair Laming), 105br (NRT-Travel), 107tr (Imagestate Media Partners Limited - Impact Photos), 107mr (Rolf Richardson), 108tl (magestate Media Partners Limited - Impact Photos), 118tl (Moreleaze Travel London), 118tr (Mike Goldwater), 135br (TVeermae_Tallinn_Estonia); **Cartoonstock** – 143br (Dan Reynolds); **Corbis** – pp38bl (Steve Schapiro), 72l (Gavriel Jecan), 80m (Ulises Ruiz Basurto), 81t (Frans Lemmens), 141ml (Gerhilde Skoberne), 141mr (Peter Frank), 141br (Michelle Pedone), 141bl (Steve Hix/Somos Images), 141bm (Greg Hinsdale); **Getty** – pp39ml (JOSE LUIS ROCA/Stringer), 88bl (Alexander Tamargo), 123 (Desmond Lim/The Straits Times/Contributor), 128bl (Jamie McDonald/Staff), 135bl (Scott Boehm/Contributor), 140b (Taylor S. Kennedy); **Greg Mortenson website** – pp97t (Image courtesy Central Asia Institute (http://news.boisestate.edu/newsrelease/102008/Greg_Mortenson.jpg); **iStockphoto** – pp8t (Dmitry Mordvintsev), 9(1) (Dennis DeSilva), 9(2) (Chris Elwell), 9(3) (Andrey Nekrasov), 9(4) (Gallo Images), 9(5) (Brenda A. Carson), 9(6)/26(7) (DNY59), 9(7) (thumb), 9(8) (Ildar Akhmerov), 9(11) (Robyn Mackenzie), 12t (Ali Mazraie Shadi), 16–17t (Arie J. Jager), 18(1) (Andy Hwang), 18(2) (Bonnie Jacobs), 18(3) (Russell Shively), 18(4) (bncc369), 18(5) (YinYang), 18(6)/78–79t (egdigital), 18(7) (Franky De Meyer), 18(8)/50–51t/136b (Alberto Pomares), 18(9) (Phooey), 18(10)/78br (rest), 19a (Kevin Cook), 19b (Slobo Mitic), 19c (fotoVoyager), 19d (Zhan Tian), 20br (Valentin Triponez), 21a (Daniel Laflor), 21b (Tom Marvin), 21c (Christine Glade), 22–23t (Suzanne Tucker), 22a (claudiobaba), 22b/26(6)/95tr (craftvision), 22c (Olga Mirenska), 25t (druvo), 25mr/104ml (Darren Baker), 25br (Kevin Russ), 26(1) (RainforestAustralia), 26(2) (David Russell), 26(3) (TayaCho), 26(4) (Ingvar Bjork), 26(5) (Yunus Arakon), 26(8) (rusm), 26(9) (Diane Diederich), 26(10) (Rudyanto Wijaya), 26(11) (Kristin Smith), 26(12) (Kenny Sembiring Kembaren), 26bl (Vasko Miokovic), 27bl (Jason Mooy), 30–31t (Ewen Cameron), 30blc (syagci), 30ma (David Cannings-Bushell), 30tr (Dr. Heinz Linke), 30bd (Slobo Mitic), 33tl (Ana Abejon), 33tr (Teodor Todorov), 33ml (Sadık Güleç), 36–37t (Eric Belisle), 36ml (Jovana Cetkovic), 36mr/52t/130d (Sean Locke), 37bl (kzenon), 38mr (rotofrank), 39bl (Ben Blankenburg), 40ml (rognar), 40br (Daemys), 44–45t (Joe_Potato), 44a/48(6) (Tom Hahn), 44b (ranplett), 44c/83 (Matthew Dixon), 44d/85 (naphtalina), 44e (Paul Cowan), 44f (Alena Dvorakova), 46 (Giorgio Fochesata), 48(1) (Hans F. Meier), 48(2&6) (Tom Hahn), 48(3)/135tr (Maciej Noskowski), 48(4) (Tibor Nagy), 52m (Simone van den Berg), 52b (Nancy Louie), 53m (Isabelle Mory), 53b/130c (bobbieo), 58–59t (Ryan Lane), 59a/59b/95br (Catherine Yeulet), 59c (Glenda Powers), 59d/135bm (Neustockimages), 59e (Stephanie Phillips), 60l (Glenn Frank), 60r (Steve Debenport), 62t (Eva Serrabassa), 62a/64–65t (digitalskillet), 62b (MikLav), 62c (leluconcepts), 62d (Joseph C. Justice Jr.), 64b (appleuzr), 68t (Brandon Laufenberg), 68b (Ian Francis), 69m (Devy Masselink), 72–73t (Galyna Andrushko), 72b (Vincenzo Vergelli), 73b (Saqib Hasan), 75 (Jim Kolaczko), 77 (Blackbeck), 78bl (Corstiaan van Elzelingen), 78bm (hfng), 80–81(1) (quavondo), 80–81(2) (Anthony Brown), 80–81(3) (Alessandra Litta Modignani), 80–81 (4) (alandj), 82ml (Marco Maccarini), 82bl (Eliza Snow), 82mr (Konstantin Tavrov), 82br (Chris Gramly), 86–87t (Stephanie Horrocks), 87b (Niko Guido), 92–93t (Amanda Rohde), 94 (Sean_Warren), 95bl (Barbara Reddoch), 95bm (Joshua Hodge Photography), 100–101t (James Thew), 100bl/136a (Denis Jr. Tangney), 100bm (seraficus), 100br (Phil Morley), 102 (Cindy Singleton), 103 (Brigitte Smith), 104r (rusm), 105ml (ErikdeGraaf), 106–107t (Dawn Liljenquist), 108tm (technotr), 108tr (Agnes Csondor), 108b (Grafissimo), 110b (Christopher Futcher), 111tr (Roxana Gonzalez), 111br (Giray Kömürcü), 114–115t (dem10), 115br (Jonas Van Remoortere), 117a (Chris Schmidt), 117b (Eileen Hart), 117c (Ju-Lee), 117d (Nicolas Hansen), 117e (Cliff Parnell), 118bl/120b (Jacob Wackerhausen), 118br (Jeffrey Smith), 120–121t (Peter Zelei), 120b (Jacob Wackerhausen), 121br (TriggerPhoto), 122bm (Robert Kohlhuber), 122br (Eline Spek), 128–129t (Dmitriy Shironosov), 128bmr (MorePixels), 128br (Roberto A Sanchez), 129bml (James Steidl), 129br (Kyu Oh), 130–131t (Carmen Martínez Banús), 130a (Wolfgang Steiner), 130e (Christine Glade), 130bl (Bill Noll), 131 (Sean Randall), 132–133t (Valerie Loiseleux), 132(1) (Elena Kozlova), 132(2) (Marina Zlochin), 132(3) (James Thew), 132(4) (dra_schwartz), 132(6) (Sherry Zaat), 134–135t (Levent Ince), 135ml (Stijn Peeters), 135mm (Anthony Ladd), 135bm (Neustockimages), 136–137t (nullplus), 136c (syagci), 136d (eliottero), 136e (konradlew), 136f (Kevin Tavares), 136g (Richard Melichar), 136h (zbruch), 136i (Jeremy Edwards), 138–139t (CandyBoxPhoto), 138a (KM4), 138b (Laurent Renault), 138c (Hywit Dimyadi), 138d (isa-7777), 138e (Joe Gough), 138f (Elena Zapassky), 139br (Claus Mikosch), 140–141t (Diego Cervo), 140m (Olaf Bender), 142–143t (Neustockimages), 142l (John Krajewski), 142m (Laurent Davoust, jsemeniuk), 168cat (Sondra Paulson), 168dog (Fenne Kustermans), 168cow (Heiko Potthoff), 168horse (Markanja), 168pig (Eric Isselée), 168sheep (Sawayasu Tsuji), 168bear (Suzann Julien), 168lion (Alan Merrigan), 168rabbit (janeff); **Newbury Park School** – pp54 (Newbury Park School); **Photolibrary** – pp 97bl (Walter G Allgöwer), 101bl (Urs Flüeler), 129bl (eVox Productions LLC), 129bmr (Gavin Hellier), 130b (GoGo Images); **Positive News website** – pp97 (Positive News –http://www.positivenews.org.uk/Positive_News_images/pages/golowen 015.jpg); **Shuttershock** – pp9(9) (Dusan Zidar), 9(10) (Sergey Peterman), 9(12) (Mau Horng), 30ba (Patricia Hofmeester), 30bc (Csaba Vanyi), 128bml (Naomi Hasegawa); **SWNS** – pp122bl (South West News Service).

Cover photo: Shutterstock (Viktor Gmyria)

Ilustrations: KJA Artists